"Andrea Lani has crafted a true story on many levels, and her apt depictions of the journey bring the reader along with her, exposing personal peaks and valleys along with actual ups and downs. The geology of the Rockies she and her family trek across is an engaging saga told with close-up precision and sweeping landscapes, and her candid vignettes of family dynamics add humor and realism. *Uphill Both Ways* weaves a complex fabric of time and place—an adventure for anyone who treks through its pages."

—CLOE CHUNN, author of *Fifty Hikes in the Maine Mountains*

"This lovely book manages to be a geological drama, an environmental history, a trail memoir, and a case for the protection of wild places—all while musing brilliantly on what it means to be a wife, a mother, and a person in the world. If you put Terry Tempest Williams and Cheryl Strayed and Kelly Corrigan in a room together, this is the book they would write. I loved it."

—CATHERINE NEWMAN, author of *Catastrophic Happiness*

"Andrea Lani is an insightful guide as she takes readers on a fateful family hiking trip along the legendary Colorado Trail. In language both witty and lush, she vividly portrays this remarkable terrain while also sharing a personal story of self-examination and persistence. *Uphill Both Ways* gripped me from its hopeful start to its jubilant finish."

—AARON HAMBURGER, author of *Nirvana Is Here*

"Andrea Lani seamlessly weaves history, geology, and ecology in *Uphill Both Ways*, a moving memoir about nature, family, and learning to live in the moment. . . . Lani's prose is lovely, even as she is examining the environmental cost of human error, misguided forest management, and ignoring climate change. In the end, Lani accomplishes what she set out to do, and she and her family learn that 'even sucky things can sometimes be awesome.'"

—KATE HOPPER, author of *Ready for Air* and *Use Your Words*

"It was with great anticipation and pleasure that I read Andrea Lani's new book, *Uphill Both Ways*. . . . In my opinion, the trail is where the family belongs, and thanks to Lani's book, more families will become inspired to go to our country's rich plethora of long distance wilderness trails and enjoy their gifts together. Well done, Andrea and the whole Lani family!"

—CINDY ROSS, author of *Scraping Heaven: A Family's Journey along the Continental Divide Trail*

Uphill Both Ways

Hiking toward Happiness on the Colorado Trail

ANDREA LANI

UNIVERSITY OF NEBRASKA PRESS   LINCOLN

Acknowledgments for the use of copyrighted
material appear on page 254, which constitutes
an extension of the copyright page.

Library of Congress Cataloging-in-Publication Data
Names: Lani, Andrea, author.
Title: Uphill both ways: hiking toward happiness
on the Colorado Trail / Andrea Lani.
Description: Lincoln: University of Nebraska Press,
[2022] | Includes bibliographical references.
Identifiers: LCCN 2021035831
ISBN 9781496229007 (paperback)
ISBN 9781496231598 (epub)
ISBN 9781496231604 (pdf)
Subjects: LCSH: Lani, Andrea—
Travel—Colorado—Colorado Trail. |
Hiking—Colorado—Colorado Trail. | Hikers—
Colorado—Colorado Trail—Biography. | Women
hikers—United States—Biography. | Nature
writers—United States—Biography. | Colorado
Trail (Colo.)—Description and travel. | BISAC:
BIOGRAPHY & AUTOBIOGRAPHY / Personal
Memoirs | SPORTS & RECREATION / Hiking
Classification: LCC F782.R6 L36 2022 |
DDC 796.5109788—dc23
LC record available at
https://lccn.loc.gov/2021035831

Set in Whitman by Mikala R. Kolander.
Designed by N. Putens.

Frontispiece: Anglewing butterfly (*Polygonia* sp.)

For my grandmothers:

Elsa Lani

1907–1991

and

Arlene Meyer

1923–2016

MAP 1. The Colorado Trail

Maybe the best journeys are the ones that are worth repeating and are repeated.

—REBECCA SOLNIT

CONTENTS

ILLUSTRATIONS

FIGURES

MAP

PHOTOGRAPHS

UPHILL BOTH WAYS

FIG. 1. Colorado blue columbine (*Aquilegia coerulea*)

PROLOGUE

Be still, and the world is bound to turn herself inside out to entertain you.
Everywhere you look, joyful noise is clanging to drown out quiet desperation.
—BARBARA KINGSOLVER

DAY 11: JULY 20, 2016
Searle Pass

Dark gray-brown clouds roil and churn low over the mountain meadow where I crouch among willow bushes with my husband and three children. Lightning licks at the snow-patched ridges surrounding the three-mile-long basin we were crossing when fluffy white clouds coalesced into thunderheads. Rain pummels our flimsy umbrellas and thin nylon jackets. My son Zephyr huddles next to me. His brothers, Emmet and Milo, crowd together in another gap in the bushes. My husband, Curry, hunkers around the corner.

We are eleven days and not quite 130 miles into a six-week, 489-mile hike from Denver to Durango on the Colorado Trail. We have already covered more miles each day than I ever thought possible for my kids or myself. Each night we scrunch into a single tent and each morning we eat bowls of cold oatmeal. We've seen four moose, a herd of bighorn sheep, and the most stunning scenery. We've hiked through scorching heat, wind, rain, and patches of last winter's snow, but this is the first real thunderstorm we've encountered, and it's a doozy.

I peer out beneath my yellow umbrella at the sodden meadow. The precipitation streaks so hard and fast I can't tell if it's rain or hail. The pounding drops drown out all other sound. Mist shrouds the ridge. I can barely make out two hikers heading toward the saddle as black clouds roll over them and thunder echoes off the rimrock. I will them over the top and to safety on the other side.

As I was planning this journey, friends and relatives regaled us with a litany of dangers they feared we'd face: rattlesnakes, bears, mountain lions, tick fever, rockslides, deranged people, overzealous rangers. They worried we'd get lost, break a bone, fall off a cliff. People asked if we were taking emergency whistles, bear bells, bear spray, bear-proof food canisters, snakebite kits, a gun. They shared helpful news stories with headlines like: HERO MOM PRIES FIVE-YEAR-OLD'S HEAD FROM THE MOUTH OF MOUNTAIN LION. HIKER'S JOURNAL SHOWS SHE SURVIVED FOR CLOSE TO A MONTH AFTER GETTING LOST NEAR APPALACHIAN TRAIL. WHAT HAPPENED WHEN A COLORADO MOM LET HER ELEVEN-YEAR-OLD HIKE AHEAD BY HERSELF.

But I knew that the most dangerous thing we would face out here would be the weather: late- or early-season snow, hypothermia, lightning. Colorado has the highest lightning-strike-related fatality rate of any state because of daytime convective storms that occur at times when people are hiking on high, exposed trails. When Curry and I hiked the Colorado Trail twenty years earlier, the thunderstorms we dodged were scary enough. Now we have our children with us and so much more to lose. I nudge closer to Zephyr, peer around at Milo and Emmet in their clump of willow bushes.

Bringing them out here was a risk, I knew, but one I was sure would be outweighed by the rewards. Over the past few years I had hit a wall—a dead-end job that grew more miserable and soul-sucking with each passing day; family life that had been robbed of joy by the constant need to keep up with the demands of school, sports, and housework; and my own personal ache at living in my husband's home state of Maine, far from the mountains and wide-open sky I grew up with. Returning to hike the Colorado Trail was, I admit, a selfish move. I wanted to hit a reset button on my life, to revisit the last time I made a deliberate decision and followed through on it, rather than being buffeted by circumstances. But I also believed it would be good for my kids, for us as a family, to travel through the mountains and forests of my homeland together, at a moment when the twins hinged on the verge of teenagerhood and Milo on adulthood, a chance for us to grow closer before life takes them on their own paths.

Now here we are, miles from the nearest sheltering tree, more than a day's hike from civilization, crouching in a wide-open meadow, next to a pond, twelve thousand feet above sea level. Icy rain drums down on us and thunder shakes the air. Have I put my whole family at risk because I couldn't find a way to be happy in our comfortable life? How do the kids feel? Cold? Wet? Terrified?

After somewhere between ten minutes and a hundred hours, the pounding on our umbrellas eases to a drip. The sky brightens. The thunder dies down to a distant grumble. I stand up, my knees and hips howling at the indignity of having had to crouch for so long, and shake out my umbrella. The kids peer out from beneath the bright toadstools of their umbrellas, not sure yet if it's safe to emerge. I wonder if this is it. Will they mutiny? Refuse to hike another step?

Zephyr and Milo creep out of the willows, shaking raindrops off like wet puppies. Emmet, last to emerge, leaps to his feet, his orange raincoat bright against the misty green meadow, his matching umbrella swinging in a wide arc.

"Was that fun or what?" he shouts.

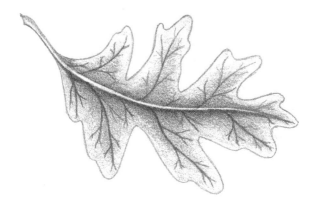

FIG. 2. Gambel oak leaf (*Quercus gambelii*)

1

HEADWATERS

We are not the first family group to laze under these trees and count our riches and our sorrows. In a wilderness, relatively few humans have come before and it is permissible, I think, to imagine an intersection.

—SHARMAN APT RUSSELL

DAY 1: JULY 10, 2016
Roxborough State Park to Bear Creek

We arrive at Roxborough State Park a little after seven—later than we wanted to, but early enough that the air still holds a trace of last night's coolness. Curry and I make last-minute adjustments to buckles and straps on our packs, take last-minute trips to the bathroom. Stalling. Milo, cool in sunglasses, leans back on a low wall. At fifteen, he's perfected the art of the nap and takes advantage of every opportunity to snooze. The twins, Zephyr and Emmet, do handstands on the flagstone courtyard of the visitors' center. They've just finished fifth grade, and they played their last Little League game of the season the day before we left Maine, which means they're in the best shape of any of us, in addition to being naturally full of energy. Over the last few months all three kids have expressed reservations about the journey we're about to embark on, having never hiked farther than seven miles, but now, yards from the trailhead, minutes from takeoff, they're all nonchalance.

My sister Valerie and her boyfriend, Josh, snap pictures and laugh at our antics. Our first trail angels, they let us camp on their living room floor last night and will take our car back to town after accompanying us a few miles up the trail. Curry, Milo, Emmet, Zephyr, and I will keep going, with luck, all the way to Durango, 489 miles away.

The scene is more chaotic and exuberant, but no less fraught with anxiety, than the scene twenty years ago, when Curry and I set out on the same journey, a couple of twenty-two-year-olds with minimal backpacking experience on my side and minimal Rocky Mountain experience on his. My dad drove us to the trailhead in his blue Suburban early on the morning of August 12, 1996. Curry and I clambered out and hoisted our heavy packs, his bright red and borrowed from a friend, mine teal and purple, bought used from another student at college. We wore matching necklaces of seeds and colored beads—his red, mine yellow—that I'd bought in southwestern Colorado earlier that summer. Standing beside the Colorado Trail sign and leaning on our aluminum ski poles, we squinted at the camera, full of hope and trepidation.

Curry and I had met at a small college on the coast of Maine, but we didn't start dating until after graduation. That summer we both stayed in Bar Harbor and spent the next three months hiking, biking, sea kayaking, and falling in love. At the end of September, Curry went home to central Maine and I returned to Colorado, where I spent ten months living on a decommissioned air force base working as an AmeriCorps volunteer, my postcollege plan of last resort after graduating with a degree in human ecology, an eclectic course load, and zero job prospects. On a weekend trip to a bookstore I discovered a small green book called *Hiking the Colorado Trail* by Robert P. Denise. I'd known people who'd hiked the Appalachian Trail, but I had no interest in that. This trail was something different, a chance to do what I'd dreamed of since I was a little girl sitting with my nose pressed to the glass of my dad's pickup truck window, watching Colorado's mountains and forests fly by, imagining what it would be like to walk into those trees and keep going.

I proposed the idea to Curry, and he responded as a smitten boyfriend should—with enthusiasm—and we began planning. He'd grown up hiking and backpacking with an outdoorsy stepmom. I'd grown up car camping all over Colorado, but had only taken a few short backpacking trips, all mildly disastrous—being edged out from under the tarp and waking up in a damp cotton sleeping bag at camp when I was eight, hiking through a snowstorm with bronchitis in college, losing my water bottle down a ravine and sleeping tentless in a cloud of mosquitoes on the only flat spot—the middle of the trail—on a solo overnight. Far from daunted, however, I was anxious to hit the trail and truly see the mountains that had stood on the western horizon of my childhood.

When my AmeriCorps term ended in July, I flew back to Maine and Curry and I drove across the country in his old Volvo, stopping in Vermont to visit my four closest college friends. The next morning my friends and I went out to breakfast. As I looked at those dear faces around the table, each about to embark on an adventure of her own, my confidence broke. I'd been so sure for so many months that I was doing the right thing, hiking five hundred miles into the wilderness. Now I realized I had no idea what I was getting into. Despite long letters and longer calls on the pay phones in the former air force dorm hallway, I barely knew Curry. And although I'd spent my last month in the AmeriCorps building trails high on a mountain, hiking from base camp to the worksite each day, I wasn't at all sure I could manage hiking mile after mile, day after day. All I could do that morning was clutch the journal I'd just bought and cry. I lost my nerve and wouldn't get it back for nearly five hundred miles.

Still, we got into Curry's teal Volvo, drove to Denver, shopped for noodle dinners and GORP ingredients, marked our stack of little green maps with intended campsites and resupply points, and packed the gear we'd amassed all winter and spring, mine a motley and low-budget collection of thrift store finds and discount-catalog purchases. At the trailhead, my dad snapped a photo, gave us both awkward hugs in our bulky packs, and drove away, leaving us alone with each other and miles of wilderness ahead.

A journey of five hundred miles begins with a single step. At some point you've got to stop stalling and take that step. I make one last visit to the bathroom—the last flush toilet I'll see for nearly two weeks—roust Milo from his nap, and round up the twins. We hand our cameras and phones to Valerie and Josh and line up in front of a low pink wall at the edge of the courtyard. In the photos our clothes are bright and unfaded, not a speck of dirt among us. The twins make goofy faces and drape themselves over the wall. Curry smiles and sticks his thumb up for the camera. Milo, hands in pockets, gray bucket hat shading his eyes, looks as casual as if he's waiting for the school bus. I squint into the sun, still not convinced we're actually here, about to embark on the trip of a lifetime.

Behind us rise massive fins and knobs of red sandstone. The stones are remnants of the Ancestral Rocky Mountains, a range that formed about three hundred million years ago. Wind and water ground those ancient mountains to sand and gravel, which washed downstream and across the plains in alluvial fans. Oxidation of iron-containing minerals turned the sand pink, and time and the weight of subsequent layers of sediment from swamps and inland seas compressed it into a layer known as the Fountain Formation. About seventy million years ago another period of mountain-building, the Laramide orogeny, thrust ancient stone from deep within the earth, heaving the layers of sedimentary rock out of the way, standing them nearly on end. Geologists call this the trapdoor—mammoth slabs of stone hinging upward, as if the Precambrian rocks that formed the Laramide Mountains came up from the cellar with a jar of pickles. Millions of years of erosion rounded edges and washed away softer layers, leaving behind the knobbed and fluted red humps that today appear in a narrow band along the Front Range. The famous concert venue, Red Rocks Amphitheater, is part of this formation, as are the Flatirons outside of Boulder, Garden of the Gods in Colorado Springs, and these stones that form the backdrop to the start of our journey.

Curry, dressed in the gray shorts, gray shirt, and electric green gaiters I bought him for Father's Day, gives me the thumbs-up sign. The skin around his brown eyes crinkles when he smiles, gray hairs salt the trail beard that he's given a two-week head start, and the dark curls hidden under his floppy hat are growing thin. Otherwise, he appears unchanged from the boy I hiked the trail with twenty years ago, his body as lean and wiry as it was at twenty-two. He's a hair shorter than I am, and as he turns and heads up the trail his lanky arms and legs bounce as if connected to his body by springs. Milo, dressed in a turquoise shirt, beige shorts, and gray swirled gaiters, follows. At fifteen, he's the same height as his dad, and he has his dad's build—broad shoulders, long arms and torso, skinny legs. But his slender hands and blond hair he got from me, and his sapphire-blue eyes came straight from my mom and my grandmother. His easy gait, as he lopes up the trail, matches his dad's.

Before we left Maine, I gave Curry and the boys their first-ever buzz cuts. Differing hairstyles have always been the quickest way of telling the twins apart. Now the differentiating characteristic is a long, fluffy lock of golden hair, originally meant to be a Padawan braid, that escaped the clippers and dangles over Emmet's right shoulder like a squirrel's tail. As always, Emmet wears his lime-green shirt inside-out and backwards. He's paired it with acid-yellow leopard-spot gaiters and a chartreuse bandana around his neck. Beige shorts and a beige Lawrence of Arabia–style hat tone the outfit down only slightly. Zephyr wears dark gray shorts and a turquoise shirt. His white knee socks stick out above hot pink gaiters, and his tan bucket hat is pulled low over his forehead. A couple of months past their eleventh birthday, the twins are still a full head shorter than me. The contours of their faces are soft and round and their mouths gap-toothed, with several baby teeth still waiting to fall out, but their hair is darkening from the white-blond of babyhood. At eleven they're on the verge of growing into men, but for now, they're still little boys, and their bulging backpacks and the vast blue sky make them seem even littler. They follow Curry and Milo up the red, dusty trail, their skinny arms and legs swinging carefree as they enter the cool shade of the scrub oak forest.

The red rocks and the single-track trail that winds through Gambel oak and ponderosa pine are the primary reasons we're starting our second Colorado Trail hike here, in Roxborough State Park, rather than at the trail's official northern terminus in Waterton Canyon. The Waterton portion of the trail follows six miles of dirt road, originally the railbed of the Denver, South Park and Pacific Railroad. The walk through the canyon is pleasant, but I wanted to begin our journey in a more dramatic setting. I also like the idea of bookending this trip, which will culminate in the red sandstone canyon of Junction Creek outside Durango, with the red sandstone of Roxborough. Most of all, I want to spend as much time in desert-like landscapes as possible.

I have a deep love of the desert. My earliest memories are of trips my family took to deserts and desert-like places—Mesa Verde, Great Sand Dunes, Arches, Taos, Santa Fe. Colorado sits squarely in Major Stephen H. Long's Great American Desert, that area west of the hundredth meridian where rainfall averages less than twenty inches a year, the minimum amount required for agriculture without irrigation. This area was initially considered by white settlers to be uninhabitable, before old-fashioned American optimism, combined with a large dose of snake oil and the allure of gold and silver, overrode the entreaties of soberer minds. While Roxborough does not fall into the category of true desert, its annual precipitation falling surprisingly near the twenty-inch mark, this iconic park has a desert-like atmosphere, with red sandstone reminiscent of southeast Utah and low, scrubby Gambel oak trees, pincushion and prickly pear cacti, and yucca growing among the prairie grasses and wildflowers.

Another reason I didn't want to hike Waterton Canyon lies at the end of the road that makes up the first six miles of the Colorado Trail, Strontia Springs Dam, a 243-foot-high plug of concrete that blocks the upper portion of the canyon, creating a 1.7-mile-long reservoir. My love of deserts is entwined with a love for canyons, for earth exposed to its bones, evidence that wind and water carry away grains of sand and mighty boulders, carving deep into geologic history. I love the colors and shapes of bare rock, the tenacity of trees and flowers that cling to steep walls. That a wilder, more rugged portion of Platte Canyon is drowned beneath 243 feet of water hurts my heart. I can't find a description of the canyon prior to the dam, but Randy Welch, the last kayaker to run it, writes of the river in Kyle McCutchen and Evan Stafford's anthology *Whitewater of the Southern Rockies*: "Think Clear Creek with water that is actually clear, and more of it; more room (no highway); better scenery. . . ." Not being a whitewater kayaker, I would probably never experience Welch's view of the canyon, but I'd be more whole knowing it was there.

"Stay in sight of an adult," I remind the twins as they scurry up the trail ahead of me. There's a mountain lion in heat roaming the park. Our route doesn't take us near the trail that was closed to give her space— and presumably she has other things on her mind than snacking on children—but I'd hate for any of our naysayers to be proved right this early in the hike.

"And don't pick up any snakes."

Emmet and Zephyr think that anything that crawls, hops, or slithers is dying to befriend them, and no amount of garter snake bites, frog pee, or high-speed chipmunks eluding their embrace can shake them of this belief. Though I never saw a rattlesnake in my whole childhood in Colorado, Roxborough is rumored to be rife with them, and a two-year-old was bitten by a rattler here earlier this summer. If there's a snake anywhere around, the twins will find it.

The sun beats down as I head up the trail after them, and I realize there's yet another good reason to hike here in the shade of oak and pine trees instead of on six miles of exposed canyon road—today's forecast calls for record-breaking heat. It's not an auspicious start to a walk in the near desert, but delay is not an option. We have a tight schedule—six weeks to hike the trail and another week to make our way home to Maine before school begins. I'm determined to complete the trail on August twentieth. For more than a year, I've had a note stuck to my desk with "CT by 43" scrawled on it—my notice to the universe that I intended to hike this trail before my forty-third birthday. It took a lot of work to plan and gear up a family of five to make this happen. It took an even more herculean effort to convince Curry that I should quit my job and he should leave his company in his employees' hands so we could do it. Now we have exactly forty-two days to finish the hike on my birthday and fulfill my resolution.

In a few days, the trail will take us up into high mountains, where pink-tinged snowfields cling to ridges and hundred-degree heat will be a memory, but in the meantime the partial shade cast by the scrubby oaks offers blessed relief. Curry, Josh, and the boys disappear around a bend in the trail. I creep along with Valerie. My legs feel weighted and my back aches from the repeated bending and lifting I've done over the last several weeks while packing. As the trail steepens, my steps slow to a trudge. My lungs, lazy from years of living at sea level, suck air. Joining us for only a couple of miles, Valerie hikes sockless in light shoes, her hair pulled back in a jaunty kerchief. She carries only a water bottle. I imagine her reviewing CPR techniques as I gasp alongside her. I pause and, to make it look like I'm not resting, try to take a picture of a golden-orange fritillary butterfly perched on a magenta thistle blossom. But I haven't figured out the functions of my new compact camera and the butterfly flees before I get it in focus. I aim my lens instead at a spotted towhee singing from the top of a dead branch.

We hike on and I try to focus on the details of the world around me—the small, rounded leaves of the Gambel oaks, the feathery fruits of mountain mahogany, the pungent leaves of skunkbush. Tiny red blooms of fairy trumpets, creamy white mariposa lily, and purple star-shaped spiderwort with leggy leaves peek out among the grasses. Birds sing, butterflies flutter. The forest is bright, busy, and alive for all its dry, deserty appearance.

We catch up with Zephyr sitting on a bench. We rest with him for a while, and when we hike on, he drags his feet, letting his pack straps slide to his elbows.

"My arms are falling asleep."

"Remember when we hiked to Russel Pond?" I ask him. We had taken the boys on their first—and only—backpacking trip two summers ago in Maine's Baxter State Park, a seven-mile hike to a remote campground from which we went on day hikes and canoe paddles. "You had the same trouble until we got to the lean-to. After that, you were fine. Once we hit seven miles, you'll be used to your pack." I hope I'm right and that it doesn't take all the way to Durango for him to settle into his pack, or I into mine.

"How far have we gone?" he asks.

"About two miles."

He sighs. Two miles down, 487 to go.

A half mile or so later, Valerie and Josh turn back toward the trailhead and home. We won't see them again until after we finish the trail six weeks from now. We continue on our journey alone, the five of us, the rest of the way to Durango. Zephyr has already gotten used to his pack and zooms ahead with Curry, Milo, and Emmet. I fall behind and make my way up to Carpenter Peak, our first summit.

My feet move as if weighted, as they did every weekday morning for the last five and a half years, as I climbed the slate stairs of an old mental-hospital-turned-state-office-building. Every fiber of my being rebelled against climbing the stairs to my cubicle. But there lay my paycheck, our health insurance, and our stability while Curry wrestled with the vicissitudes of running a small business. I had big plans for life after we hiked the Colorado Trail the first time—Peace Corps in Africa, graduate school in Montana, a lifetime of travel and adventure. But while I day-dreamed about those plans, I made decisions that seemed insignificant at the time yet led incrementally and inexorably in the opposite direction, to marriage with three children, a house in Maine, and a job that was killing me. Expecting our time in Maine to be temporary, I went to work at a state environmental agency, with vague notions of "saving the earth." It didn't take long before I realized that a regulatory agency isn't in the business of saving the earth, but rather controls who is allowed to pollute, where, when, and by how much.

When Milo was born, I took three months off work, which grew to six months and then a year. I wanted to be with my baby, witnessing his daily growth and change, holding him close to me, even as he strained away, eager to sit up, crawl, and run. My first day back at work, I sat listlessly in my cubicle. For the first time, I knew what was important in life, and it wasn't pushing paper around on my desk. But we needed the money, and now that we had a family, we needed the health and dental insurance, a retirement plan, security. I worked part time for the next seven years, with another year off when the twins were born, trying to be everything to everyone—fitting a full-time load of work into three days and a full-time load of stay-at-home mothering into the other four. I tolerated the job because it allowed me this flexibility. Six years ago, I took different position within the department, one that focused on children's environmental health, a passion of mine and an area where I believed I might, for the first time, make a difference.

For a year I loved my job. It was challenging and interesting, and though I was working full time, I came home each evening energized. Then disaster struck. A reactionary governor installed lobbyists of polluting industries to run our agency. Each day I stewed in half-suppressed rage as our policies, inadequate as I thought they were, were rolled back, and coworkers who had dedicated their lives to clean air and water were belittled, stripped of duties, and forced into early retirement. Meanwhile, even though my kids no longer needed the constant care and attention of babies and toddlers, gone too was the simple joy of time spent with small children. My role had shifted from nurturer to drill sergeant. The few hours we had together each day I spent trying to make them do things they didn't want to do—get ready for school, do homework, go to bed—and rushing to get to engagements we were late for. On top of it all, I was sick of living in Maine—the long winters, the snow, the humidity, the closed-in feeling of the trees. I longed for a view of the sky and a lungful of clear, dry air. When the mantra inside my head became "I hate my life, I hate my life," I knew I had to do something drastic. I couldn't uproot and move, but I could hit pause on a life that was grinding my soul to dust and take a six-week sidetrack through my heart's home, not leaving my family behind but bringing them with me on this quest to make myself whole, to seek happiness. But here on the trail, my feet feel as heavy as they did in my office stairwell.

As I trudge uphill, day hikers pass me by on their way up to Carpenter Peak. Early morning ambitious hikers pass me on their way down. A young couple asks where I'm headed.

"Durango." It sounds silly. I expect them not to believe me. *I* don't believe me.

"Wow! That's amazing. Good luck!" They bound up the trail, unencumbered by heavy packs or even heavier expectations.

I want so much from this trip. When I hiked the trail twenty years ago, I hoped to develop a closeness with nature, a growth in my relationship with Curry, and some kind of spiritual awakening. But I struggled—with the weight of my pack, the miles, rain and snow, getting to know a new boyfriend who had a different hiking style and different expectations. This time I want even more. I want to relive that first Colorado Trail hike and, even more, redo it, better this time, with a lighter pack and a lighter outlook. I want an epiphany—a revelation that tells me what life is about and how I should live mine. I want to slow time, to watch the world pass at two miles per hour, and to witness who my children are now, at this moment in their lives. I want our family to grow closer, relying on each other, undistracted by the modern world. Most of all, I want to restore some joy to my life.

At the top of the Carpenter Peak, I find the boys tucked into shady spots, eating snacks and enjoying the view of slabs of red sandstone rising out of the prairie. Curry stands on a rock, his phone affixed to the tip of his hiking pole as he rotates in a slow circle, recording a 360-degree video of the view. He plans to document our trip through daily videos that he'll post online when we go into towns. Milo stretches out on a rock, his hands folded over his stomach, the brim of his hat pulled over his face. I sit beside Emmet, who's working his way through a bag of cheddar crackers. Zephyr crouches on a nearby rock, like a mountain lion wound tight and ready to pounce.

Curry holds up his phone, video camera on, and says, "I've come up with a scale to gauge everyone's mood. Zero being *I'd rather have my head in the mouth of a mountain lion* and ten being *this is the best day of my entire life.*"

He points the camera at Milo, who sits up and squints as he thinks. After a moment he gives a not very encouraging assessment: "Four-point-four."

Zephyr's is only slightly better: "Four-point-seven."

Emmet offers a more enthusiastic, "Eight . . . or seven."

"It's an eight for me," Curry says.

I say eight and a half, because of course this has to be nearly the best day of my life, after so much wanting and planning and preparation. But I'm anxious, uncomfortable. When packing everything the five of us would need for this trip, I forgot my favorite orange hat. I bought a hat yesterday, but I hate it already. It's too hot. The back of the brim bumps my pack, the front flips up and down in the wind, and the chin strap chafes my neck. I pull out my phone, in this brief spot of cell service, and try to order a cap like the one I left behind, to be sent to my parents' house and brought with our resupply at the end of the week. I hit submit, but the screen freezes. I try again and the same thing happens. I'm being ridiculous. I've already spent too much money on a hat I hate and don't need to spend another forty bucks on a new one. Plus I've wasted our first viewpoint on the internet and drained half my phone's battery. I put the phone away and sit with my family, looking out over our last view of the plains.

Before we set out, friends, family, and even Curry doubted that three kids could hike nearly five hundred miles. I reassured them: "They'll fly up the trail while I struggle behind." I'd clutch my chest and gasp for air to demonstrate my relative unfitness. Already I've been proved right. After our brief rest on Carpenter Peak, Curry and the boys galloped down the trail ahead of me. I have no idea how far ahead they are or when I'll see them again.

A passing day hiker asks where I'm heading.

"Durango." I still don't believe it.

"Really? Wow, your pack looks so light."

It doesn't feel light, despite years of research and months of careful selection to lighten our loads as much as possible. I knew I could not hike the trail again with a pack as heavy as the one I had last time, when Curry and I each carried a pack roughly the size and weight of a baby elephant. They were made of heavy-duty nylon and had dozens of pockets, flaps, and internal compartments and enough zippers and buckles to hold a continental rift together. Inside, in addition to a four-season tent, sleeping bags, and mats, cookstove, fuel, and stainless steel cook set, water filter, water bottles, and water bag, cameras and film, long johns, rain jackets, and fleece pullovers, spare socks and underwear, tiny metal flashlights, multi-tool knives, and first aid and repair kits, we carried such essentials as a jar of boot grease and application brush, an extra stainless steel bowl with folding handles for mixing instant hummus, insulated coffee mugs, candle lanterns and spare candles, field guides, books to read at night by candle lantern, the hard-covered journal I bought in Vermont and Curry's spiral notebook, fanny packs for day trips, town clothes, camp sandals, and mini binoculars. My sleeping bag, a green-and-purple nylon mummy bag from the army surplus store that never kept me warm enough, was enormous, and I could only wrestle it into my pack by first cinching it into a compression sack. My only lightweight item was an accordion-folded sleeping mat that offered very little in the way of comfort or insulation. My hip bones bruised, my collar bones chafed, and my back bowed over under the weight of that pack.

In the last twenty years, a lightweight movement has revolutionized backpacking, and I followed the developments with interest and pared our gear down to the bare minimum, buying the lightest items I could afford and making the rest. Our Gossamer Gear packs are thin nylon rucksacks with drawstring closures and simple straps. I made our sleeping quilts from kits designed by the high priest of the church of lightweight backpacking, Ray Jardine. We each carry minimal extra clothing for warmth and rain, a mini headlamp, a tiny journal, and a trekking umbrella. Curry carries our tent, a six-pound, five-person pyramid I bought from a company called Go-Lite right before it went out of business, and I carry our cook set: a stuff sack filled with five lidded plastic food storage containers, five bamboo spoons, a tiny bottle of biodegradable soap, and a scrubby.

Before we left Maine, I weighed each item on our kitchen scale, cut off tags and tabs, and weighed them again. Curry doesn't share my religious fervor for lightening the load, and he optimistically placed his inflatable Therm-a-Rest mat on the scale (three pounds), his hundred-tool Swiss Army knife (nearly a half pound), and his Limmer hiking boots (two and a half pounds each), before he gave in and accepted the RidgeRest foam mat and mini knife I bought him and came home from the shoe store with a pair of light trail runners. Filled with gear, my pack weighs less than fifteen pounds, Curry's weighs eighteen, and each of the kids' weighs around ten. But once I added food and water—the kids each carry their own water and snacks, while Curry and I divvied up the rest of the food—my pack weight doubled to thirty pounds, which doesn't seem so light.

The trail crosses the boundary of the state park and enters Pike National Forest. I take a picture of a worn sign that says "Colorado Trail" with an arrow pointing left, the first official verification of our journey. Outside the park, the trail becomes a knee-deep trench between grassy banks, gouged out by mountain bikes and erosion. I step on a loose rock, turn my ankle, and lose my balance. My pack, top-heavy and unbuckled at the sternum, cants to the right and flings itself to the ground, hauling me with it. The trench is so deep that I don't fall far, landing on the bank with my feet dangling. I roll the ankle to see if it's sprained, but it's okay. My right arm and hip are bruised and there's a scrape on my knee, otherwise no harm done. I struggle to vertical and continue up the trail, slipping and sliding on loose rocks.

I can't get comfortable. My pack bumps against the brim of my stupid hat. The mini carabiner dangling from my umbrella handle thunks me in the head with each step. Every rock and pebble on the trail pokes the bottoms of my feet through the thin soles of my trail runners. I lost my sunglasses miles ago. I'm thirsty, but I can't reach my water bottle without taking off my pack, and whenever I stop for a drink or a snack or to adjust my gear or dig a cat hole—all of which I've done in the last hour—I fall farther behind Curry and the boys.

The trail emerges from scrub oak into a meadow of tall, waving grasses edged in Douglas fir. It's quiet and peaceful here, except for the occasional passing mountain biker, and I pause to enjoy the calm before following switchbacks uphill, passing through sun, shade, sun, shade, sun. I stop beneath a ponderosa pine and breathe in its butterscotch scent. I'm tired. My hips ache. I'm hot. So hot. Temperatures will hit a record 102 degrees at Denver International Airport before the day is through. I take a sip of water, adjust my pack straps, and hike on. I hum the Proclaimers' song "I'm Gonna Be (500 Miles)," which ran through my mind our entire Colorado Trail hike twenty years ago. I rewrite the words in honor of this new adventure and sing to myself as I trudge up the slope: "I did hike five hundred miles and I will hike five hundred more, just to be the gal that walks a thousand miles in Colorado-o."

I'm the one who wanted this trip so badly, who coaxed and cajoled my family into dropping their summers to hike, who quit my job, who did all the planning and shopping and packing and preparing. Yet I'm the one having the hardest time, with the weight, with the heat, with the effort of moving one foot in front of the other. It was the same twenty years ago. I was a plodder then, too, and my pack was so heavy. Every step was a struggle. At the end of the first day, I wrote only one word in my journal: *Ouch.*

A white tiger swallowtail butterfly flutters past me, beckoning me down the trail. I follow. I did this once. I can do it again. I will do it again.

The trail winds down a steep hillside to a dirt road, and I step into suburbia: green lawn, shade trees, a ranch-style brick house, construction vehicles and trucks parked in front of a garage. Curry and the boys sprawl on a patch of grass in the shade of a cottonwood, talking and laughing. We've joined the official Colorado Trail. A right turn would take us down the road through Waterton Canyon to the trailhead. A left will take us uphill, into the mountains, to Durango. This patch of suburbia has to do with the management of Strontia Springs Dam, the concrete plug in the Platte River that lies a short way down the road.

If water is the lifeblood of an arid city, the South Platte is Denver's main artery. Dozens of creeks drain snowmelt from the east side of the Continental Divide and converge to form the river, which flows north through Denver and its suburbs before heading northeast toward Nebraska. Between the 1860s, when the City Ditch was dug, until 1983, when Strontia Springs Dam was completed, a canal, two reservoirs, and six dams were built to store and move the South Platte's water, along with two tunnels that transported water from the Western Slope into the Platte River basin. These dams and diversions, built in the era of big water projects, were welcomed by residents of a growing city. But by the time Strontia Springs Dam was in the works, the world had changed.

When voters approved a bond for construction of the dam in 1973, the regulatory climate had shifted to weighing environmental values against gains promised by an expensive dam. In the preceding years, the U.S. Environmental Protection Agency was established, the Clean Air Act was expanded, and the National Environmental Policy, Clean Water, and Endangered Species Acts went into effect. Public sentiment had changed as well, elevating recreation and the environment over manipulation of nature. The fate of the dam became entangled in litigation that was resolved through a long and complicated mediation process. The resulting agreement allowed the dam to go forward but placed conditions on future water projects, including a system-wide Environmental Impact Statement. This requirement helped sink Two Forks Dam.

Before the last batch of concrete was poured at Strontia Springs, Denver Water was planning Two Forks. The proposed dam would block the channel of the South Platte two miles upstream of Strontia Springs Reservoir. At 615 feet tall, it would be the fifth-tallest dam in the country and would create a two-pronged reservoir more than seventy-three-hundred acres in area, extending into both the north and main forks of the river. The project would also expand West Slope water diversions to transport water across the Continental Divide. The reservoir would submerge a gold-medal trout fishery and habitat for bighorn sheep, peregrine falcons, and an obscure little butterfly called the Pawnee montane skipper. It would also disturb sandbars three hundred miles downstream in Nebraska, where sandhill and whooping cranes gather each spring, en route to summer breeding grounds.

The Environmental Impact Statement process required by the Strontia Springs consent decree took seven years to complete and was followed by heated public hearings, with environmental groups and West Slope residents pitted against Denver Water and a consortium of forty-two suburban entities. In November 1990, the EPA administrator vetoed the project, and a federal judge upheld the veto the following spring.

We could walk a few hundred yards down the road to see Strontia Springs dam, where water sluices through a tunnel to Foothills Treatment Plant outside Roxborough's gates and from there to taps in Denver and the suburbs. But while part of my intention in taking this hike is to confront the toll humans have taken on the environment in my beloved mountains, I'm not ready to look too closely at the damage on day one. Instead, I drop my pack and flop beside my family. Curry and I each pull out a drawstring bag and pass around crackers, cheese, hummus, and nut butter. Emmet makes a sandwich with two crackers and a rectangle of warm, greasy cheese and points toward the buildings behind me.

"Look, deer."

Curry looks up from the cashew butter he's squeezing onto a cracker. "Those aren't deer. They're goats. They must use them for weed control."

I turn and see a herd of about twenty-five dust-colored animals milling around in front of the garage, nibbling at the gravel, babies nuzzling mothers. They do look a bit goat-like, with barrel-shaped bodies, knobby legs, long, bony faces and short, curved horns.

"Those aren't goats. They're bighorn sheep."

Mothers and young, they're smaller, with less magnificent horns, than the iconic males. The only hesitation I'd had about not taking the Waterton Canyon route was that we'd miss the opportunity to see the Rocky Mountain bighorn sheep that live in the canyon. They didn't make an appearance when Curry and I hiked through twenty years ago, but I've come upon them on day hikes in the canyon, six or eight sure-footed sheep high on a cliff. This herd is the biggest I've seen, and the closest. We watch them while we eat, awed by our very first wildlife encounter of the hike. The sheep appear almost domesticated, in their ease near the vehicles and buildings, oblivious to our presence, but when a mountain biker comes up the road they bunch together and scramble down canyon. It's time for us to move on, too. We gather our things and make our way uphill, past the Colorado Trail map etched into a slab of brown wood, and onto the trail proper.

I dream of Bear Creek, the only reliable source of water between the trail's departure from the South Platte in Waterton Canyon and its crossing of the river more than ten miles later. We camped at Bear Creek the first night of our hike twenty years ago and will camp there again tonight. I can't wait to strip off my clothes and soak my body in cold water. But when I reach the creek, I find that a group of six young men have set up camp directly beside both the water and the trail. Most established campsites along the Colorado Trail are wedged between trail and stream, with large fire rings as centerpieces, not exactly leave-no-trace arrangements. Emmet scampers down to the trail and leads me uphill to a bigger, better campsite, well away from the trail, with minimal dirt and soot and our own private creek access.

I scoop water from the stream with my most useful piece of backpacking equipment—a gallon milk jug with the top cut off—and pour the water through a prefilter into a wide-mouthed bottle, stir for a couple of minutes with a SteriPen, a pocket-sized wand that kills microbes with ultraviolet light, and hand the bottle to Curry to pour into lighter sports drink bottles. I fill another bottle, press the button, and stir. The process is so much easier than the laborious pumping of our old water filter that I have a hard time believing it works.

"What if this is really the Placebo Pen?" I say.

Curry studies the water in the bottle he's holding. "I was wondering that myself."

I came down with an intestinal bug on our first Colorado Trail hike, and more than snakes, bears, falls, and lightning, I'm worried about my kids getting sick from the water we'll drink out here—streams that flow through cattle, sheep, and hiker country. I give the water an extra vigorous swirl with the pen.

Emmet, Zephyr, and Milo soak their bandanas in the stream and dribble water over their heads and necks, shrieking with the cold. After one day and eight miles, crouched dusty and sweaty around the trickle of icy water, they already seem a part of the trail.

I scrunch as much of my body as I can into a pool six inches deep and a foot and a half wide. It's frigid. Somewhere uphill snow is still melting in the hundred-degree heat. About 80 percent of Colorado's water supply comes from snowpack, which explains the urge toward dam-building:

humans trying to control the uncontrollable and hang onto a precious, temporary resource before it all flows downstream. In the months leading up to our trip, I obsessively checked snow-depth charts, willing enough snow to fall so we would not have to worry about water and enough to melt so we'd not have to hike on icy trails. This, I imagine, is the prayer people have said since they first set foot in this land that is dry but prone to flash floods, blizzards, and avalanches: *let there be enough water but not too much.* So far, if the flow in Bear Creek and the few seasonal trickles we've stepped over are any indication, our prayers have been answered.

FIG. 3. Paintbrush (*Castilleja* sp.)

2

SUCCESSION

The palpable sense of mystery in the desert air breeds fables, chiefly
of lost treasure. Somewhere within its stark borders, if one believes
report, is a hill strewn with nuggets; one seamed with virgin silver;
an old clayey water-bed where Indians scooped up earth to make
cooking pots and shaped them reeking with grains of pure gold.
—MARY AUSTIN

DAYS 2–3: JULY 11–12, 2016
Bear Creek to Tramway Creek

I wake at 4:58 a.m. Our little hollow near Bear Creek is still dark, so I lie
quietly and look at the puzzle piece of fading sky between the trees. We
pitched our tent without the fly last night because of the heat, nothing
but a pyramid of noseeum netting between us and the world. A hermit
thrush flutes its lonely song nearby and a robin carols. Other birds add
their songs to the chorus.

The sky grows brighter and, beneath my quilt, I squirm into my hiking
outfit—sports bra and underwear of quick-dry fabric, synthetic purple
tank top, stretch nylon skirt, ankle socks. I brush and braid my hair, do
a short yoga sequence, read a walking meditation and a poem from the
pages of a Mary Oliver book I dismantled and distributed among our
resupply boxes, memorize an affirmation, which I will repeat when the

going gets rough, and sit in silence for a moment, visualizing myself hiking strongly through the day. In preparation for our hike twenty years ago, I read every backpacking book the library carried. One author claimed that backpacking is 5 percent physical, 95 percent mental. I didn't know what that meant and had no idea how to prepare mentally, so I didn't. After my confidence broke that morning in Vermont, I had no resources to build it back up. This morning routine, I hope, will help me keep my head focused on the trail so I don't break down with every challenge. Not only do I have to keep it together for myself, I have to stay strong to support my children, help them when they're struggling, and absorb their emotions.

I prod kids out of their quilts, and they wriggle into their clothes. Yesterday's heat forgotten in the cool morning, they zip the legs onto their pants and put on puffy jackets and fleece hats. Emmet adds gloves and a neck warmer pulled up over his nose. Curry, too, is dressed in all his clothes—rain pants, fleece pullover, raincoat, fleece hat. I put on a long-sleeved, UV-blocking shirt to protect my arms from the sun that will beat down later, but otherwise try to soak up as much coolness as possible.

I hand out breakfast: five containers of cold, gooey oats that have been soaking in purified creek water overnight. Early in my planning, I realized we could save a lot of weight by leaving stove, fuel, and cook pot behind and eating cold rehydrated food. To my surprise, Curry agreed. The oatmeal does not taste as good as I envisioned back home, when Milo and I mixed rolled oats with freeze-dried fruit, powdered milk, protein shake mix, chia seeds, and date sugar, and now we have forty-one more mornings of cold, slimy oatmeal to look forward to. I try shoveling it down as fast as I can, but the gelatinous texture created by the chia seeds makes this hard to do without gagging. Emmet crouches on the ground spooning his gruel as slowly as possible, in hopes that the contents of his bowl will disappear, stolen, perhaps, by a hungry but undiscerning ground squirrel.

After we've broken camp and stuffed and loaded everything into packs and purified more water, we hike through the cool shade of morning, past the six guys still asleep in their tents, past another pair of hikers just rolling out of theirs. Curry, Milo, and Emmet rush ahead. Zephyr, his pack hurting again, hikes with me. He and I have similar styles. He stops to notice interesting things, like bowl-shaped spider webs in yucca plants, takes pictures, asks the names of wildflowers, smells the bark of a ponderosa pine to see if it's chocolate, vanilla, or butterscotch. He describes to me the house he'll build after he wins the lottery with the ticket he expects me to buy him when we finish the trail. I love seeing the world through his eyes, and I'm enjoying this opportunity to interact with one kid at a time.

As we wander along a forested switchback on a steep hillside, Zephyr stops and looks into the gully. "Is this Waterloo Canyon?"

He's read my mind. The pain in my shoulders, knees, and feet has me wondering if I'll be able to finish this week, let alone the whole trail. But how does he know about Napoleon's final defeat?

"Waterloo Canyon? Why do you think it's called that?"

"I saw signs for Waterloo Canyon yesterday."

"Oh, you mean Water*ton* Canyon. That's the official start of the Colorado Trail. If we'd turned right at the bighorn sheep, we'd have gone there."

Today will not be my Waterloo. I square my shoulders and march up the trail as it switchbacks uphill from the Bear Creek drainage through the shade of a Douglas fir forest. From the ridgetop we descend back into the almost-desert, through Gambel oak, mountain mahogany, dry-land wildflowers, and prickly pear cacti, down to the Platte River. By the time we reached this spot twenty years ago, also at lunchtime on our second day of hiking, I was in tears. I didn't know if they were tears of exhaustion, pain, relief, or all three. Here we learned that Segment 2 of the trail, from the South Platte to the Buffalo Creek firehouse, was closed due to a fire and subsequent floods that had ravaged the area earlier that summer. We got a ride in the back of a pickup truck to County Road 126, where we picked up Segment 3. Curry was infuriated to miss hiking part of the trail, but I was relieved. By skipping nine miles, we would make up time and be sure to reach our first resupply point at Kenosha Pass on time.

Today we get no reprieve; we'll hike through the burned area and see what we missed last time. But I'm not crying yet. I'm sore and tired and not entirely sure I'll make it forty-two days, but we're making good time and the kids are proving to be every bit as strong of hikers as I thought they'd be. The sky is blue, the sun is shining, and the Platte River runs clear and sparkling. I feel good, despite my aches and pains. We sit on a damp sandbar at the edge of the river and eat lunch. Curry takes video of flowing water. Emmet and Zephyr skip rocks. I scoop cold water with my half-jug and rinse off my hot, dusty body. Milo stretches out on the sand, hat over his eyes. We're about a half mile upstream from the proposed site of Two Forks Dam. Had the dam been built, this stretch of river, the road we crossed, and the deserty hillside we hiked down would be submerged deep beneath the waters of a turgid lake. Instead we have the swift, clear water of the river, the dry, rugged beauty of the valley, and the Colorado Trail, which would have had a hard time finding its way around a seventy-three-hundred-acre reservoir.

"Hey, Milo," Emmet says, "why do you nap so much?"

"Because I'm Batman," Milo says in a deep, gravelly voice from beneath his hat. Energized by lunch, Emmet and Zephyr hop from rock to rock on the edge of the river, growling "because I'm Batman" at each other. Milo pushes his hat back and sits up.

"Hey, Mom, what's the name of that plant with the long, spiky leaves we keep seeing?"

"Yucca."

"Because when you trip and fall on one of them, your guts spill out, and that might make a weak-stomached person say 'yuck'?"

"Exactly."

The kids are, I think, having a good time. A little tired, a little dusty, a little sweaty, but they seem genuinely content, if not happy. I, too, feel content. We shoulder our packs and cross the river on the Gudy Gaskill Bridge. I send out a silent "thank-you" to its namesake. The "mother" of the Colorado Trail, Gaskill was a longtime member of the Colorado Mountain Club, that organization's first woman president, and the chair of the Colorado Mountain Trails Foundation's Colorado Trail Committee. The idea for the trail was born the same year I was, in 1973, but progress lagged until 1986, when Gaskill established the Colorado Trail Foundation, persuaded U.S. Forest Service ranger districts to buy into the Colorado Trail idea, and recruited, trained, and led volunteer trail-building crews.

Through her indefatigable efforts, the Colorado Trail went from dream to reality a year later. At eighty-nine, Gaskill is still the voice of the trail. She wrote the foreword to the latest guidebook and each segment includes "Gudy's Tips." About our next segment, she writes, "When you reach the South Platte River . . . fill up on water because it is a long dry climb to Top of the World ridge." The trail crosses no water for the next thirteen miles and we'll have a dry campsite tonight. We're all carrying full water bottles and Curry and I each have added a full 2.5-liter water bladder to our loads.

Curry, Milo, and Emmet disappear down the trail, and Zephyr and I stick together again as we climb from the river through a sparse ponderosa pine forest. He notices the burn area before I do.

"Some of the trees were killed by the fire." He points to dead snags among living trees with blackened bark. "And some just got singed."

As we hike on, singed trees begin to outnumber those with no sign of past fire, and, farther along, dead snags outnumber both.

On May 18, 1996, three months before Curry and I started our first Colorado Trail hike, temperatures in Denver reached ninety-three degrees, the fourth day in a row of record-breaking heat. Suburbanites flooded the mountains to enjoy the summery weather, including a group from a Lakewood charter school. Sixteen students and two teachers set up camp near the town of Buffalo Creek. That Saturday morning, five of the teenagers poured water on their campfire, stirred the embers, and, believing they'd put the fire out, went rock climbing, only to later see smoke. They returned to the campsite to find that forty-mile-per-hour winds had whipped smoldering coals into a conflagration. The students fled, along with hundreds of other campers and residents, as the flames spread to cover a swath two miles wide and ten miles long. More than 850 firefighters went to work building fire lines and dropping fire retardant from the air, at a cost of nearly $3 million, but it took a change in weather—dropping temperatures, increased humidity, and reduced winds—to contain the fire five days after it began. In total, 11,900 acres of forest burned and the fire destroyed eighteen structures.

Fire, both naturally occurring and human-caused, has been a part of the landscape in the West since the last ice age, at least. Forests depend on it to thin trees, return nutrients to the soil, and, in the case of species such as lodgepole pine, open cones and release the seeds of another generation. When white settlers came west, they brought with them grazing herds that cleared grasses from the understory, increasing the proportion of hot-burning woody vegetation. Beginning in the early twentieth century, forest managers instituted a practice of suppressing all fire. The combination of grazing and fire exclusion over the last century has led to a buildup of fuel and an increase in the potency of fires. Although an understanding of the ecological role of fire has shifted fire management policies from total exclusion to a more nuanced approach that includes allowing some fires to burn and prescribing fires in some areas, fires continue to grow in size, intensity, cost, and destructiveness, fed by the buildup of fuel, a hotter, drier climate, and an influx of people and homes into fire-prone areas.

When fire moves through an area on a regular basis, it tends to stick to the ground, burn less intensely, and clear out the understory, leaving mature trees undamaged. But when fuel builds up to the levels seen now across the western United States, fires can grow so hot they burn living needles. These crown fires move faster than ground fires and often destroy everything in their path, including live, mature trees and the soil itself. About three-quarters of the Buffalo Creek fire was a high-intensity crown fire. The extreme heat burned away organic material and topsoil from the forest floor and fused the surface of the remaining mineral soil with a waxy substance melted from the burned vegetation, resulting in a water-repellent coating over much of the burned area. Not long afterward, a torrential thunderstorm ripped through the area, washing ash and soil into Strontia Springs Reservoir.

In an attempt to stave off further erosion, the U.S. Forest Service dumped eighty thousand pounds of oats over a third of the burned area, hoping the fast-growing seeds would take root and help retain what soils remained after the fire and thunderstorm. But less than a month later another massive storm dumped two and a half inches of rain in two hours. With no vegetation to hold the water back and the ground turned into a water-repellant patina, the rain rushed down hillsides, raising the north fork of the South Platte fifteen feet over its banks and washing away trees, cars, utility poles, and propane tanks. The flood killed two people, washed out County Road 126, lifted the community center and fire station off their foundations, and put the town of Buffalo Creek's water supply and phone service out of commission. Again, mud and debris washed into Strontia Springs Reservoir, an influx of sediment almost as great as what had entered the reservoir over its first fourteen years of existence.

Having been ferried around the burn zone, Curry and I didn't experience the magnitude of the effects of the fire and floods, but now, twenty years later, we'll see the scars left on the landscape. Zephyr and I soon leave behind the standing singed and burned trees and enter the burn proper, a ghost forest of downed logs with only a few standing skeletal trees. With the trees gone, we can see the contours of the landscape: rounded hills puckered with washes and ravines, exposed slabs of granite bedrock. The hillside is surfaced in bare, pink gravel eroded from the Pikes Peak Batholith, a massive granite intrusion formed about 1.1 billion years ago, when an upwelling of magma solidified deep in the earth's crust. This twelve-hundred-square-mile chunk of pink granite is the youngest of Colorado's "basement" rocks that formed in the Precambrian era. In the ensuing eons, continents drifted apart and collided. Inland seas and swamps formed and receded, laying down sediment. Periods of volcanism added formations of volcanic rock at the surface and intrusions of magma below. Mountain ranges rose up and washed away. Finally, in the last five million years or so, the Pikes Peak Batholith heaved above the surface, forming the mountains in the southern part of the Front Range. Over time, surface granite weathered to grüs, the porous pink gravel that covers these hillsides.

Here and there grow patches of grass, wildflowers, yucca, and prickly pear. Around each plant a hula skirt of dried leaves and stems lies dead but not decayed against the bare ground. The slow work of soil-building begins here. Small shrubs of mountain mahogany and cinquefoil dot the hillside, but I see no sign of trees returning twenty years after disaster swept through this area. Still, I'm fascinated by the incremental restoration of the landscape, one blade of grass at a time.

We come upon an old quartz mine, a hole in the pink ground with white crystals spilling over the rim. Around a bend in the trail, we take a short detour to check out another, larger quartz quarry with an old-timey car smashed in the middle of it. It looks like the kind of car bootleggers would have driven in the 1920s, and Zephyr invents a story about a gang of robbers who had their windows shot out as they drove out here. Both the good guys and bad guys, he tells me, were killed in the chase. I don't often get a window into my kids' imaginations anymore, and I love hearing Zephyr's story, picturing the wild chase along with him.

Colorado Trail hikers complain about this segment—so hot, so dry, so exposed. Today is more than ten degrees cooler than yesterday, a steady breeze blows, and white puffy clouds block the sun now and then. Yet the heat is intense. The sun's rays soak into the bare ground and radiate back at us, especially when our winding trail takes us along the west face of the hill's contours. I put up my umbrella, and though it diffuses some of the sun's light, it traps the heat beneath its dome, like I'm walking in an oven. Despite the heat, I am enthralled with the spare beauty—the stark outlines of the few standing dead trees, the diversity in color, shape, and texture of the wildflowers. In the Douglas fir forest we hiked through yesterday afternoon and this morning, many fewer plants grew in the understory—a little grass, a few purple lupine and harebells—its dense canopy allowing little sunlight through and limiting the growth of other plants. I like seeing the bones of the earth, the exposed pink soil, the contours of the land: rock, gully, hill. I love having the vast sky spread out above me. Living in Maine's thick forests, I miss this wide-open view of sky and stone.

Curry, Milo, and Emmet wait for us where the trail reenters the trees at the edge of the burn. Emmet points to a dead tree downhill from us. A solitary bird hops among the withered branches. A western tanager, its tropical plumage—a bright yellow body with a red head and black wings—contrasts with the dry and brittle landscape we've been hiking through, and I see it as a good omen, for today, for the hike. The tanager doesn't seem to mind our presence, and I point my camera at it, only for the screen to go black. I forgot to charge the battery before we hit the trail.

As we hike on, I feel for a fleeting moment that the trail is real. We are really here, hiking the Colorado Tail, heading to Durango. Perhaps it was the glimpse of the tanager, a bird I've seen only in Colorado. Perhaps my body feels more settled into my pack, my shoes, the act of walking all day. Perhaps it's because my kids have adapted so quickly. Perhaps it was the raw beauty of the burn area, the hopeful resettlement by wildflowers. Whatever brought it on, I try to hold onto the feeling, but it wisps away like a puff of smoke as I sweat through the afternoon, hiking up and up and up to our day's destination, my body aching more with each step.

In late afternoon we find a good campsite, a broad, flat shoulder of land with scattered ponderosa pine trees and a view of hazy mountains in the distance. In our food containers, I add water to a mixture of instant refried beans, brown minute rice, freeze-dried corn, and a leathery strip of dehydrated salsa and leave it to rehydrate. Each evening we'll rotate our dinners among beans and rice, whole wheat couscous with instant Alfredo or pesto sauce, and brown-rice ramen noodles with freeze-dried peas. I tested the meals at home, and they all took between thirty minutes and an hour to rehydrate with warm tap water. We'll soon find out how long it takes with cold stream water. I roll out a sleeping mat and lie with my legs up against a tree to wait it out. My minimalist trail runners don't offer enough support or protection from either the rocks underfoot or the ones I routinely stub my toes on, and my feet ache.

Curry works on his video. The boys alternately explore the area and sprawl on their mats. Milo and Emmet pull out books and read. Zephyr lines up chunks of wood on a log and throws pinecones at them, pretending they're the robbers from the burned-out car. When we crawl into the tent, the sun still glows golden on the western horizon. We've hiked about twelve miles, two miles farther than we planned, five miles farther than the kids have ever hiked in one day, farther than I've hiked in years. Despite my optimistic route planning to get us to Durango in forty-two days, I was worried we wouldn't make it. Now, after twelve miles on day two, those worries diminish. We can do this.

I wake up aching all over and can barely hobble around camp. Yoga helps some, but the first several miles hurt like hell. I hike alone all morning—Zephyr found his trail legs and zoomed ahead with his dad and brothers. I try different tricks to help myself stay positive and keep moving forward. I repeat today's affirmation: *I am vibrant and full of life. I am vibrant and full of life.* In reality I am dull and near death. I pretend a fast-walking friend hikes beside me and try to match her pace. I name all the trees and wildflowers I pass. I come close to crying, I am in so much pain. My feet hurt. My ankles hurt. My calves hurt. My knees, thighs, hips, back, and shoulders hurt. What was I thinking, dropping everything to come out here and torture myself this way? Why did I think trading one form of misery for another would be an improvement? A sane person would have looked for a different job or taken up a satisfying hobby or gone on a normal vacation. The first time we hiked the Colorado Trail, I found the third day of hiking easier than the first two. This time, it's the worst so far. I realize this hike is going to be different from the last hike in every way, except being all uphill.

I'm trudging through a haze of pain when a mule deer bounds down the hillside a few dozen yards ahead of me. It turns to look at me with dark, liquid eyes. Two more deer stand nearby. They prick up their big ears and watch me watching them. After a while they move quietly on, and I resolve to pay more attention to my surroundings and less to the complaints inside my body and head.

The trail winds around a bend and I come upon a hillside of dead trees. I stop short, heartsick at the sight of gray, brittle branches. I knew we would see many such "ghost forests" on this hike—an outbreak of pine beetles that spanned much of the time since we last hiked the trail has decimated pine forests across the West—but I didn't expect to run into one so soon, and not in a Douglas fir forest. These trees have likely fallen prey to the Douglas-fir tussock moth. The caterpillar of this moth hatches in late spring, drifts on a silken thread to a nearby tree, and feasts on tender new needles. Over the summer, it grows into an inch-long bottle brush with gray-blue fuzz and reddish-brown tufts. At this stage, the caterpillar eats older needles, and a crowd of them can defoliate upper and outer branches, stunting growth and killing the tree. Once moths weaken a stand of trees, Douglas-fir bark beetles often move in and attack larger trees.

The sight of the brown hillside makes my heart ache, but it's not necessarily a bad thing. Both the Douglas-fir tussock moth and Douglas-fir bark beetle are native species and have long been an integral part of forest and tree life cycles. An insect infestation thins a tree stand and feeds nutrients back into the soil, aiding the growth of surviving trees. Ponderosa pine may take over as the dominant tree species in defoliated areas, diversifying the forest and enhancing wildlife habitat. Prior to the last century, fire and periodic insect outbreaks led to varied and diverse forests across the landscape. Fire suppression resulted in dense, single-aged stands of shade-tolerant species, like the Douglas fir forests we've been hiking through—conditions ripe for insect infestations and catastrophic fires.

While many people who see dead trees think fire danger, research in the Pacific Northwest indicates that insect outbreaks may have no effect on the likelihood of fire on a regional scale. When needles fall from trees, with them go the terpenes and volatile oils that feed crown fires. Locally, an area that was defoliated in the 1993–96 tussock moth outbreak served as a fire break during the 2002 Hayman Fire, the largest fire in Colorado's history. Nevertheless, the U.S. Forest Service and the city of Colorado Springs conducted aerial spraying operations earlier this summer on a Douglas-fir tussock moth outbreak near that city, following the same misguided instincts that led officials to treat small-scale outbreaks with DDT in 1947 and 1949.

A recent change in the Farm Bill allows the Forest Service to carry out "emergency" operations, such as spraying for moths, without conducting an environmental assessment. An article in the *Denver Post*, sensationally titled TREE-KILLING MOTH CATERPILLARS ARE INVADING THOUSANDS OF ACRES ACROSS COLORADO FORESTS, quoted a Forest Service spokesperson who said the agency has a "commitment to diverse forests and wildfire concern," to justify the spraying. Neither the spokesperson nor the author of the article acknowledged that insect outbreaks diversify forests and may possibly reduce fire intensity. Further statements about the "aesthetics" and "beauty" of a living forest point toward a more likely motivation for spraying: people don't want to see dead trees, and perceptions of what a healthy forest should *look* like drive management decisions, without regard for the insects' ecological role. Historically, as American attitudes evolved from seeing wild areas as wastelands to be feared and conquered to valuing them as landscapes worth preserving, preservationists' rhetoric often traveled along aesthetic pathways. It will take further evolution to see beauty in dead trees, or to recognize that beauty is beside the point.

Later in the morning, the trail winds into another portion of the Buffalo Creek burn. Revegetation seems to have advanced more here than in the area we hiked through yesterday. Grass fills in the spaces between clumps of wildflowers and mountain mahogany, leaving little of the pink, gravelly soil visible. More standing dead trees dot the hillsides, along with a few small stands of surviving ponderosa pines and some young, dense aspen groves. We've been hiking uphill all morning, rising higher in elevation. The few trees here reflect what scientists have discovered when studying regeneration of ponderosa pine forests after fires: trees come back sooner in cooler areas, such as at higher elevation and on north-facing slopes, as well as in areas closer to seed trees. Tree ring studies demonstrate that, historically, trees tended to reestablish within thirty years of a fire. Increasing temperatures from climate change may reduce the likelihood of trees coming back to lower elevations at all. The area we hiked through yesterday may persist as a grassland well into the future.

A cool breeze blows. A few birds sing and twitter in both burned snags and the few live trees. It's calm and peaceful here. The austere beauty of this slowly regenerating land speaks to my heart.

As I approach the junction with County Road 126, another hiker approaches from behind and pauses to chat. Her name is Aiden, and she tells me she started this morning at the South Platte, where we ate lunch yesterday, meaning she's hiked five miles more than we have already today.

She glares at the sun from beneath her hat brim. "How are you handling the heat?"

"Not too bad. We spread the burn out over two days, hiking it in the morning today."

She looks dubious, but we wish each other luck, and she heads down the trail at a fast clip while I mosey behind, finding my family resting on a log near the road. I join Emmet and Zephyr on the log, while Curry and Milo go to get water at the firehouse down the road.

"How are you guys doing?"

"Fine," Emmet says. "You know why? Because I'm Batman."

I tuck my shirt into my pack and take a long drink of water.

"It's getting hot."

"I'm not hot," Zephyr says. "Because I'm Batman,"

"I wonder what's taking your dad and brother so long," I say.

"Because I'm Batman," they say together.

When Curry and Milo return, we cross the road and wind our way through the maze of Little Scraggy Trailhead, busy with horse trailers and mountain bikers. We see Aiden having lunch near the trail and wave as we pass. We stop for lunch a while later and wave again as she passes us. It's the last time we'll see her, her fast legs sweeping her along the trail ahead of us. While we eat, Emmet and Zephyr continue to reply "I'm Batman," to every question and comment.

"Mom, make them stop," Milo says.

"You started it."

"Yeah, but it was funny when I said it."

I'm just glad they're finding ways to entertain themselves out here with no screens.

In the afternoon, I round a bend in the hillside and the dry, Douglas fir forest gives way to aspen and spruce trees, with a steep hillside towering in the background and lush green plants covering the ground. The scent of sun-warmed aspen leaves fills the air and I'm transported to childhood, the wonder and adventure of a hundred camping trips sweeping over me. I want my children to forge the same kind of deep connection to this land, so when they smell an aspen leaf or see a red paintbrush flower it stirs a deep-seated memory for them, of being warm and safe inside a tent with their family, sharing the adventure of a lifetime.

FIG. 4. Elephant's-head lousewort (*Pedicularis groenlandica*)

3

BACKCOUNTRY

There may be people who feel no need for nature. They are
fortunate, perhaps. But for those of us who feel otherwise, who
feel something is missing unless we can hike across land disturbed
only by our own footsteps or see creatures roaming freely as they
have always done, we are sure there should be wilderness.

—MARGARET E. MURIE

DAYS 4–6: JULY 13–15, 2016
Tramway Creek to Kenosha Pass

Emmet, Zephyr, and I set out together from our campsite at Tramway
Creek, trailing behind Curry and Milo as we hike in the deep shade of
the valley. Before long, we meet a hiker at a stream crossing, and he
introduces himself by his trail name, Davy Crockett. The twins, who
have been chattering about movies and video games, grow shy and quiet
in the presence of a stranger. Davy Crockett wears a bandana and wide-
brimmed hat over his cropped blond hair. His face is as ingenuous as a
baby's, with wide blue eyes and a button nose. He tells me he lost the
small bottle he uses for scooping up water to pour into the gallon jug
hanging from his pack, so I lend him my half-jug. He dips water from the
creek, pours it into his jug, then digs through a large ziplock. The bag
holds full-sized bottles of sunblock, bug repellent, medications, lotion,

and soap—enough personal care products to stock a family medicine cabinet. More containers poke out of the side pockets of his enormous pack. From underneath the top flap dangle the arms of a black cotton sweatshirt.

He finds a jar of iodine tablets and drops two into the jug. "I should have gotten a filter. All this clear mountain stream water and it tastes like iodine."

"I've heard you can neutralize the taste with vitamin C," I say.

"You mean like Emergen-C?" He fishes through the bag again and comes up with a handful of shiny packets.

"Yeah, that would probably work. Just wait until the iodine has finished its job. What does it take, twenty minutes?"

"Thirty." He pours orange powder from two packets into his jug and gives it a vigorous shake, the undissolved iodine tablets swirling in the milky orange liquid. "Do you want some?"

He hands me three Emergen-C packets and the boys and I add the contents to our water bottles. Zephyr and Emmet each take a swig and make a face. I take a sip of mine. It tastes slightly sweet, slightly sour, and very vitamin-y.

Davy Crockett hoists his pack. "The altitude is getting to me."

"Did you get a chance to acclimate before you started hiking?"

"No. I took a bus straight from Wisconsin to Denver and stayed in a hotel one night."

"You'll get used to it eventually."

When friends regaled us with the terrors we'd face on the trail, they forgot to mention altitude sickness. The northern terminus of the Colorado Trail sits at 5,522 feet above sea level, the lowest point on the trail. The average elevation of the trail is more than 10,300 feet, with a high point of 13,271 feet. Rapid ascent to elevations above 8,000 feet can induce a variety of illnesses ranging from the mild headache and nausea of acute mountain sickness to the more serious conditions of high altitude pulmonary edema and cerebral edema, both of which can be deadly and require immediate removal to a lower elevation. Altitude sickness demonstrates a democratic spirit uncommon among disease, affecting healthy and fit hikers as readily as those who are out of shape. Slow adjustment to higher elevations can help. We arrived in Colorado a week prior to our start date, spending time in Denver and at my parents' house at over 8,000 feet, in hopes of easing in. After a day spent above tree line in Rocky Mountain National Park, Curry, Milo, and I each developed headaches and nausea—symptoms of acute mountain sickness—while Emmet and Zephyr suffered no ill effects. I hope that this early exposure to high elevations before our gradual climb into the mountains was enough to stave off serious illness.

We hike on, Davy at my heels, the boys trooping ahead. I tell him that Curry and I hiked the Colorado Trail twenty years ago and have come back to relive it with our kids.

"Can I ask you something?" Davy says. "Did you have an easier time hiking then than you do now?"

"Oh, it's much easier now."

"Really? Even though . . ."

"Even though I'm old now?"

"Well, not old, exactly."

I laugh. "Back then we had really heavy packs. Like yours. And we started later in the season, so we ran into a lot of bad weather, and the days were shorter, so we had less time to hike."

I don't mention the mental resilience I've gained over the ensuing twenty years. Trudging miles a day over rough terrain through heat and hail is a piece of cake compared to pregnancy, childbirth, and taking care of small children. And, unlike this trail, which crosses a road every ten to twenty miles, there's no opportunity to bail from parenting. At twenty-two, ten weeks was a lifetime. At forty-two, with my first baby fifteen years old, I know how fast time moves. This six-week hike will go by in the whisper of an eyelash. I also appreciate the opportunity to be out here more than I did twenty years ago. I gave up stability but also escaped years of misery for the chance to fulfill this dream. I have a much clearer sense of why I'm here and what a gift it is.

Davy Crockett falls behind, and I take comfort in knowing I'm not the slowest hiker on the trail. Throughout the day we leapfrog with Davy and two other hikers he's joined up with, a scrawny blond guy with a little dog and a tall redhead carrying a pack even bigger than Davy's. Curry dubs them the Bros. They pass us during our lunch break; later we pass them sprawled on the edge of the trail, smoking.

"That's not going to help you with the altitude," I scold as we hike past.

Davy looks at his boots. "I know, I know."

I've taken a motherly interest in him and worry about the influence of the two older hikers on this wide-eyed kid.

Besides the Bros, several day hikers and backpackers pass us by going in both directions.

"I liked the Colorado Trail better when we had it all to ourselves," I say to Curry.

By the end of this season, more than 350 hikers will have registered as "completers" on the Colorado Trail Foundation's website, while fewer than 30 completers are registered for 1996. The information is self-reported—no organization or agency keeps official track of Colorado Trail hikers—and the ease of online registration likely means a higher rate of reporting now than twenty years ago. Yet we didn't meet a single other Colorado Trail thru-hiker that summer. Other than a handful of day hikers and mountain bikers, a few hunters and ranchers, a few too many dirt bikers, and a trio of Continental Divide Trail thru-hikers, we saw few people, often going days without meeting another soul. Solitude was as much a part of the wilderness experience as the mountains and trees. Now the trail feels more like a busy sidewalk than a remote path in the wilds.

Curry has a more generous view of the hordes. "More people hiking means more people to stand up for the protection of wild places," he says.

This is also the view of Gudy Gaskill, and it's the motivation behind the creation of the trail in the first place: get more people into the mountains so that they, too, will love and protect them. I'm skeptical. Studies have found little correlation between outdoor recreation and conservation values. Even backpackers don't always take care of the areas they enjoy; last year two hikers cleaned more than a thousand pounds of trash off the Appalachian Trail. The Colorado Trail, more remote and less used than the AT isn't that trashy, but even without garbage on the ground, an important quality of wilderness is lost as more people flock to the wilds.

Though I'm not unwilling to share the trail, I don't want to share it with so many people, and I'm not alone in wanting a quiet spot in nature to myself. Solitude has always been considered an inherent characteristic of wilderness, and the Wilderness Act of 1964 includes "outstanding opportunities for solitude" in its definition of wilderness. Wilderness historian Roderick Nash succinctly sums up the challenge of preserving wilderness in the face of its growing popularity in his classic book *Wilderness and the American Mind*: "Solitude is not easily shared."

Not only is the trail exponentially busier than it was twenty years ago, I have brought my own noisy entourage with me. The boys tell stories, laugh, and chatter constantly. I hear a steady stream of: "Hey Mom, what's for dinner?" "Hey Mom, how far are we hiking today?" "Hey Mom, when will we stop for lunch?" When I hike with either Emmet or Zephyr, they describe in long, elaborate detail their dreams, their plans for when we get home, their ideas about the future. Perpetually short of breath, I talk little, grunting in reply to their questions. But leaving them behind in order to hike the trail on my own would have been like leaving my arms or legs behind. I love hiking with them and listening to their stories and imaginings, but sometimes I need to be alone with the silence of the trees. I get a bit of a break this morning; the twins have charged ahead to catch up with Curry and Milo, leaving me with my thoughts and small doses of solitude between passing hikers.

When I reach the road to the Meadows Group Camping area, I take a short detour to avail myself of the outhouse. Inside it's so clean, with a glossy gray-painted floor and a gleaming white throne, that I want to curl up and stay for the next six weeks. But I wrest myself out and back onto the trail. A short while later, Emmet comes running toward me, a worried expression on his face.

"What's up, bud?"

"I thought you'd missed the turn!" He doesn't wait for a response, but turns and runs back up the trail, his neon gaiters flashing.

I expect to find the others around the next bend, but I hike and hike and hike and don't come across them. I pass several forks and trail crossings, none well marked, and I worry they took a wrong turn. Finally I catch up with Curry and Emmet, eating snacks by the side of the trail.

"Why did you let him run back?"

"I didn't. He just ran off without telling me." We're not doing a good job of keeping the kids in sight of an adult.

I look at Emmet, sitting on a log, peeling the wrapper off fruit leather.

"Don't do that, okay?" I say to him. "What if you'd come by while I was in the outhouse? You might've run all the way back to Maine."

Emmet nods as he folds a strip of fruit leather into his mouth, but he doesn't appear too concerned. His anxiety about me being lost has evaporated. Transferred to me. I love the independence my kids are developing. I love giving them their freedom. But I don't want to lose them either.

Curry hikes ahead and Emmet sticks with me for a while. I point out a patch of red paintbrush and blue columbine, and he asks me the names of other flowers we see. But I can't relax and enjoy this time with him. My flesh is buzzing as if bees have entered my bloodstream, and my airways seem to have shrunk to half their usual capacity. How far ahead have Zephyr and Milo gotten? What if they accidentally went down one of the side trails? They've done a great job so far staying on the correct trail, but the trail has also been marked at regular intervals with either confidence markers or hatchet marks in the trees, and, up to this point, there haven't been a lot of trail crossings. If they accidentally went down a side trail, how long would it take them to realize they were on the wrong route? How long would it take us to realize they were lost? Curry and I have phones, but the kids don't, and the reception here is spotty and my battery nearly dead. Curry carries the maps and I have the data book; the kids have no navigation aids at all. When I envisioned this hike, I pictured Curry hiking up front and me bringing up the rear, with the kids distributed between us, within a half mile or less. But it's not working out that way. Our hiking styles and speeds are too wildly different.

One advantage of the trail's popularity is that it's safer for us to travel as a family. The trail is better marked now than it was twenty years ago, the path more trodden. Most of the creek crossings, which Curry and I had negotiated on wobbly logs or by taking off our boots and wading through icy water, have been spanned with sturdy log bridges. The steady stream of hikers increases the likelihood that if one of us runs into trouble another hiker will pass by before long.

After a long while Emmet and I find the others resting on rocks near the trail, digging into the lunch bag. No one is lost. The bees exit my veins, my lungs expand, and I'm able to relax my clenched forehead and release my lips, which I now realize have been clamped between my teeth. All is well.

Later in the afternoon, we enter Lost Creek Wilderness, a 119,790-acre parcel of protected land, the first of six wilderness areas the Colorado Trail passes through. President Lyndon B. Johnson signed the Wilderness Act into law on September 3, 1964, after seven years of negotiations, nine hearings, and decades of advocacy. Previously, the Forest Service had set aside some areas for wilderness protection, but without Congressional designation these areas were vulnerable to reduction in size or protections through the same administrative processes that had created them. The Wilderness Act established the National Wilderness Preservation System and set aside 9.1 million acres of National Forest land in fifty-four designated areas in thirteen states. The act also gave Congress the authority to designate additional wilderness areas. Today, the system encompasses 765 wilderness areas, covering more than 109 million acres, about 5 percent of the country's land area.

The tragic irony of wilderness preservation is that Americans did not begin to see the value in untrammeled wild places until those places hovered on the brink of disappearing altogether. "Like winds and sunsets, wild things were taken for granted until progress began to do away with them," Aldo Leopold writes in the foreword to *A Sand County Almanac*. In *Wilderness and the American Mind*, Roderick Nash traces the evolution of the idea of wilderness, which, to the Western mind, was synonymous with "wasteland" from at least biblical times well into European colonization of North America. Early settlers sought to tame the wilderness, turn it into a garden, free of beasts, "savages," and demons, but over time the American attitude toward wilderness evolved. As pioneers pushed west, Romantic notions of the "sublime"—a sense of awe, mingling perceptions of horror and beauty, when regarding a wild vista—crept into the culture, transforming wilderness from a godless place to a place where one finds God. Around the same time, the idea emerged that our nation's character was forged on the frontier and wilderness was an essential component of what it meant to be American. Later, Transcendentalists viewed the natural world as a reflection of the divine. Of course all these Western notions of wilderness divided the human and natural worlds into separate realms and either ignored the fact that Indigenous peoples lived in the so-called wilderness of the Americas for millennia prior to Europeans' arrival or relegated those people to the status of savages and beasts.

As Americans' appreciation of wild places awoke, the vast untamed frontier was on the verge of disappearing; forests had been cleared, prairies broken under the plow, mountain ranges penetrated by railroads. Early calls for protection of wilderness often centered on those areas' utility (watershed protection in the Adirondacks), unique features (Yellowstone's geysers and hot springs), or aesthetics (Yosemite's dramatic peaks and wildflower meadows). Over time, wilderness preservationists moved away from Romantic and Transcendentalist ideas of God-in-nature, and sought to articulate ecological, psychological, and philosophical reasons for wilderness protection—wilderness as a storehouse of biological diversity, a testing ground where humans can face the kinds of dangers built into our DNA, a treasured place protected from the depredations of man.

The Wilderness Act was the first legislation of its kind in the world, and at the time of its adoption not everyone's perception of wilderness had progressed. Even today the idea continues to have its detractors, from politicians who propose bills to scale back wilderness protections to academics who argue that leaving wild places strictly alone is a misguided approach when human activities are affecting the climate to such an extent that tinkering in wilderness might be the only way to save it. The former seek to profit from the nation's resources, the latter fail to acknowledge that tinkering put us in the position of scrambling to save species and parcels of land in the first place. Still others oppose the idea of wilderness on principle.

When we hiked the trail twenty years ago, a clerk in a small bookstore we visited on one of our town stops asked me, "Are you like a strong Sierra Club or something?" when I told her I'd majored in human ecology. "I don't like that Sierra Club," she said. "They want to close everything off, and what about the handicapped people? Most of the roads around here were built by miners and it's our history. I like to hike and all, but I can only tell my handicapped friends about what I see while those Sierra Clubs go sticking things in trees. Bunch of rich Californians."

I'd been too taken aback by her onslaught to point out the hundreds of thousands of miles of roads already in Colorado that provide access by car, jeep, and off-road vehicle to vast amounts of scenery for those unable to seek out wild places on foot. But there's more to wilderness than scenery. Journalist Elizabeth Kolbert, in a *National Geographic* article commemorating the fiftieth anniversary of the Wilderness Act, articulates a reason to hold strong in protecting wilderness against its detractors: "In the age of man the Wilderness Act may seem futile—but it has arguably become more important. Designating land as wilderness represents an act of humility. It acknowledges that the world still transcends our comprehension, and its value, the use we can make of it."

Our path into Lost Creek Wilderness is, ironically, an old logging road, the Old Hooper Road, named after a lumberman who built it in 1885 for access to his sawmill. The sun reflects off the bare dirt of the wide grade, hot and bright. Hooper and his business partners must have been successful in cutting trees. Short, dense stands of second- or third-growth lodgepole pines crowd both sides of the road but cast no shade at midday. This hot road and the dull forest are not much like my ideal vision of a wilderness, or even wilderness as defined in the act: "An area where the earth and its community of life are untrammeled by man, where man himself is a visitor who does not remain." But of course, more than a century and a half after the discovery of gold in Colorado's creeks and drainages, "untrammeled" must be a relative term. Explorers, trappers, prospectors, miners, pioneers, and other outsiders likely trammeled every inch of the state. Inclusion of places like the Old Hooper Road in designated wilderness provides an opportunity for the land to quietly untrammel itself, at its own pace.

So far, the Colorado Trail has been a stranger to me. This made sense for the first three days, since we started in Roxborough State Park instead of at Waterton Canyon and hiked through the Buffalo Creek burn area, which had been closed twenty years ago, but now we should be treading familiar ground. Yet I don't recognize any of it. My memories of the first hike are like an album of specific scenes. One of them, a mental snapshot of Lost Creek Wilderness, is of a long, grassy creek-side meadow, clearly not where we're hiking now. I remember, too, the pain, the blisters, the weight of my pack, my struggle to keep up with Curry, the endless rain that yielded to snow that eventually drove us out of the mountains. As I planned this hike, I thought of it in part as a redo, a chance for me to hike this trail with more grace, less struggle. But now I picture that young woman staggering under her huge pack and see she doesn't need a redo. She finished the hike, even though every step of the way hurt and every day she questioned her reasons for being out here. This thought brings me a measure of peace, a sense of closure on a part of my life that I had for so long thought I'd done poorly. I wish I could take that young woman's hand and tell her she's doing beautifully, that she has no cause for regret.

I find Curry and the boys setting up camp on slanty ground among sparse trees near Craig Creek. Three other groups have settled in the same grove, including a couple in their sixties, Randy and Georgia. I try to imagine coming back and hiking the trail again in another twenty years. My knees hurt so badly now, I doubt I'll be able to walk when I'm sixty-two, let alone hike. Curry pitches the tent on the flattest spot he can find on the sloping hillside, yet we all slide to one end during the night, piling on top of Zephyr. In the morning, we set out early, shortly after the older couple. We cross Craig Creek, round a bend in the trail, and come upon Randy laughing and pointing at an expanse of flat ground and few trees, a perfect campground.

Curry and the boys charge ahead while I hike as hard as I can to at least not be passed by senior citizens. After about a mile, the trail takes a left turn, leaving the road and rising uphill through a dense spruce and fir forest. Hooper must not have made it this far up the hillside to cut these trees. They grow tall and thick in the trunk, a few so large it would take two people to reach around and hug them. As if in deference to the massive trees, tiny flowers cling to the ground—pink double-blossoms of twinflower, pale waxy green stalks of pyrola, four-petaled rosettes of bunchberry. A leafy ground cover fills the spaces between. For the first time since we entered Lost Creek Wilderness, I feel like I'm in true Wilderness. Stately trees. Delicate flowers. Deep, abiding stillness. Beyond the narrow brown scrape of trail it looks as if no human has ever set foot in these woods. The forest "appears to have been affected primarily by the forces of nature, with the imprint of man's work substantially unnoticeable," as the Wilderness Act defines such places. I pause to rest and hear only the sound of my own breathing and a few birds high in the trees. I see one flutter to a landing and hop from branch to branch, a dark-eyed junco, with a near-black head and rusty-red shoulders and back. It clutches nesting material or a leggy bug in its bill and makes a *tsp* noise around its cargo. As I watch the bird, I hear, far off in the distance, the haunting, ethereal fluting of a veery, a melody of deep woods and ancient trees.

What is the proper speed at which to travel through the world? Seventy-five miles per hour? Thirty-five? One? I am the slowest hiker in our group of five—the slowest hiker in most groups. This was a good pace when my kids were small and interested in every pebble and beetle they came across. But now even they leave me in the dust. I would like to stand here all day—all summer—and listen to the birds. Zero miles per hour. But my family outpaces me every moment I dawdle, and I move on.

The trail winds up the hillside, reaches its high point, and drops back down. I pick up my pace on the downhill, tree trunks flying by in my peripheral vision as I race past, no longer noticing every leaf and flower. Curry and the boys wait where the trail rejoins the Old Hooper Road. We hike on together in the cool shade of morning, the road surface softened by a layer of spruce needles. A short while later, we pass the Bros, sprawled by the trail, tending a few sticks of smoldering wood. A small campfire can so easily grow to a conflagration here, as evidenced by the Buffalo Creek fire. I should say something, but I'm reluctant to confront Davy Crockett and his two surly friends. Four women hiking in the opposite direction have no such compunctions.

"You know there's a fire restriction on the entire forest?" one of the women says.

"Yeah, and there's a swamp right over there." The blond Bro points to a cluster of willows on the other side of the trail.

The women hike on and so do we, leaving the Bros to their campfire. For many people "camping" is synonymous with "fire." While I have fond memories of my dad getting up early to split wood and fry bacon on the griddle on childhood camping trips, I don't *need* a fire. The hassle of starting, tending, and putting out a fire is more than I want to deal with while hiking, which is good, since fire restrictions in effect across the Pike and San Isabel National Forests limit recreational fires to permanent fire grates at campgrounds or picnic areas. Three wildfires were burning in Colorado on the day we started hiking, one far to the north, near the Wyoming border, one well south of us, near Salida, and a third, smaller one near Boulder. No fires threaten the Colorado Trail corridor yet, and I hope the Bros don't change that.

At the bottom of the hill, the forest opens into a huge meadow—a six-mile-long valley along the North Fork of Lost Creek—and the trail leaves the wilderness area. Across the creek, dozens of dirt roads thread their way through the woods and over the ridge that separates the north and south forks of the creek. One criticism of wilderness protection is that it has mainly set aside "rock and ice"—lands of grand scenic wonder but not the most valuable in terms of habitat nor the range of landscape types needed to protect a variety of species. These less remote, lower elevation lands are often more economically valuable—for timber, grazing, housing, or other human development. Is it a coincidence that these headwaters valleys lie outside of the wilderness area, or were they developed to such an extent at the time of designation that they didn't meet the criteria?

The trail contours along a gentle hillside, parallel to the creek. This is the Lost Creek I remember, but the valley of my memory was carpeted in thick, green grass, dotted with willows. The wide meadow, stretching to a horizon of blue mountains, looked to me how I imagined Alaska to be. Perhaps it's the heat, but I don't get an Alaska vibe today. The gentle slopes look dry, and in place of the green carpet of my memory, cinquefoil shrubs and clumps of brittle grasses dot the hillside. But still the creek runs fast in a winding channel dense with willows. A rainbow of wildflowers blooms along the trail. I come upon two of my favorites growing together: elephant's-heads, whose pink blossoms are shaped like the trunk and ears of an elephant, and shooting stars, whose magenta petals angle backward from a sharply pointed tube of pistil and stamen. It's the first time I've seen either on this hike, and the sight of the two growing together makes me smile.

As the corners of my lips strain upward, my cheeks ache. Has it really been so long since I smiled? For more than five years, I've been too unhappy at work to enjoy my home life, too unhappy to find humor in my days. I got up each morning, took care of my children, went to my terrible job, did what I had to do to get through each day, but meanwhile my face was creasing into a mask of stoic misery. My dad warned me this would happen. "You keep making that sour face, you'll look like your grandmother," he used to say when I was in a bad mood as a kid. He referred to his mother, Grandma Lani, a tiny woman with curly gray hair, an Austrian accent, and thin, wrinkled lips pursed in permanent disapproval. I don't recall seeing her smile. But she'd had a hard life, living through both world wars in Europe, raising seven children, often on her own as my grandfather traveled for work. After enduring six years of postwar economic and political chaos in Austria, the family emigrated to Leadville, a place of harsh winters and short summers. Less than ten years later, my grandfather died in an accident and Grandma was left on her own to finish raising the teenagers still at home and endure in that high, cold town. She had plenty of reasons to not smile. But she grew red poppies in front of her house, and my dad tells me she was fond of wildflowers. Perhaps she too favored elephant's-heads and shooting stars. Perhaps they made her smile.

As I proceed down the valley, I come upon a small herd of cows, some tan, some pink, others black, all with calves the color of butterscotch. I agree with Edward Abbey's assessment of cows as "ugly, clumsy, stupid, bawling, stinking, fly-covered, shit-smeared, disease-spreading brutes," but the sight of my favorite wildflowers has made me generous, and I smile upon the brutes. They mill around the hillside, close by the trail, and I tighten my grip on my trekking poles as I approach. Magnanimous though I feel, I don't trust them to not trample me to death. An image comes into my mind of my other grandmother, Grandma Meyer, picking up a stout stick as we prepared to cross a meadow dotted with black Angus. We were on a camping trip, one of many in which my parents set up our big, green canvas wall tent, my grandparents parked their fifth-wheel trailer, and various aunts, uncles, and cousins, joined in their tents and campers. I don't remember who was with us in the meadow that day, perhaps my older sister and my two youngest aunts, when Grandma hefted the stick, ready to fend off any bovines that threatened her daughters or granddaughters. Grandma was a prim, fussy woman, with never a hair on her head nor a knickknack in her living room out of place. But she grew up on a farm in Nebraska, riding the draft horses bareback for fun. When she was a teenager, she moved to Denver to work at Gates Rubber Factory, returning home in the summers to help her dad run the farm. I don't doubt she would have wielded the stick and driven back every cow in that field if she had to. But the cows stood and watched us pass, chewing their cuds dumbly, until we approached too close for comfort, at which point they lumbered away.

Right now, Grandma Meyer is probably in the same position she was in when we visited her last week—asleep in a wheelchair in her rose-pink living room, folded almost in half from a lifetime of poor posture, osteoporosis, and, I imagine, the deflation that ensues when the spirit leaves the body. Last summer, when she was still communicative, if not exactly lucid, I asked her if she remembered riding the horses on her dad's farm. She grew angry and agitated. "I never did that! That's stupid. Why would I do anything stupid like that?" She hasn't recognized me for years. She never knew who the twins were. When we came to Colorado for Christmas five years ago, she asked when she saw them, "Who are these little girls?" while I sat beside her, tears streaming down my face. I missed my grandmother already then, and now all of the parts that made her her—caretaker, cake baker, gardener, obsessive cleaner, oil painter, church goer, mother, grandmother, stick-wielding cow chaser— have slipped away, leaving behind a husk of a woman kept alive by a pacemaker. But she's with me now, if only as a memory of the woman she once was, the way Grandma Lani was a few moments ago, as I grip my poles and stare down the cows, who regard me placidly as I pass by.

When I encounter another cluster of variously colored cows and calves, I modify my favorable attitude. They gaze at me as I approach and galumph downhill to the creek when I get close, buttering the trail with fresh cow pies and trampling and muddying the streambanks. I'm glad we don't need to collect water from this creek.

I find Curry and the boys sitting in the shade of trees at the far end of the meadow. I join them on their log. Curry has his phone out, editing video. Emmet is reading. Milo's eating an energy bar and tapping out a silent tune on the side of his leg. Zephyr digs through the pockets of his pack.

"I can't find my iPod." He bounces on his heels, frantic, near tears.

He's been using it to photograph confidence markers—the little white- and-green two-peaked emblems of the Colorado Trail nailed to trees and fence posts. The iPod could be anywhere along the last six miles of trail since we last passed a tree. I look at Curry, lounging on a log, headphones in, eyes on his screen.

"Do you want me to help you find it?" I'm hot and tired and I really do not want to backtrack over ground I've already covered, looking in vain for the lost iPod, which I'm sure I would have noticed when I hiked through if it were anywhere visible. Nevertheless, I hoist myself off the log.

Emmet hops up. "I'll help, too." They run ahead, and I walk slowly along, scanning the ground. Before we've gone half a mile Emmet shouts, "I found it!" and hurries ahead to find Zephyr while I trudge back to the trees to resume my rest break.

Beyond the meadow we weave in and out of sparse stands of bristlecone pines. The branches of these trees curve out and upward, and five or six fresh twigs sprout from the tips of each branch. The short, spiky needles on these new twigs, not yet unfurled, are tightly compacted to the thickness of a finger, and the center twig stretches several inches longer than the others. The overall effect is of the tree holding its branches aloft like arms, middle "finger" aimed at the sky, flipping off the world. I admire this impertinence on the trees' part. I also admire their persistence. Rocky Mountain bristlecone pines live as long as two thousand years, with the oldest known tree estimated to be around twenty-five-hundred years old. That tree has been around since the time of the Persian Empire and the Greek city-state. It was born about the same time as the philosopher Heraclitus of Ephesus, who's most well-known for his philosophy on flux as the nature of the universe: "Upon those who step into the same rivers different and again different waters flow," or, as most people say, "You can never step into the same river twice." Change is constant.

Does a tree that has lived two and a half millennia disprove Heraclitus's statement? Or, having lived through the rise and fall of distant empires, would the twenty-five-hundred-year-old bristlecone agree? The slender trees we hike among stand ten to twenty feet tall, possibly in the neighborhood of forty to a hundred years old, mere babies. But, true to Heraclitus's philosophy, the future of these trees is uncertain. Because they mature slowly, have limited genetic diversity, and live at the upper reaches of elevation, bristlecone pines are vulnerable to the effects of climate change as well as to pests and diseases like mountain pine beetle and white pine blister rust. The trees along our trail look healthy, bushy with vibrant green needles, and I wish them a long life as I pass between their insolent branches.

In the afternoon, the trail reenters Lost Creek Wilderness and continues to wind through groves of bristlecone and aspen. Signs of fire appear among the young aspen—dead standing trees and sparse ground cover similar to Buffalo Creek—but large living bristlecones and spruce trees also inhabit the area. Aspen is a pioneer species, colonizing areas cleared by fire, avalanche, or other disturbance, and I'm fascinated to see this process in action, slightly more advanced than at Buffalo Creek, perhaps because we're in a wetter area, or perhaps the fire that cleared this area was less severe.

After lunch, Curry and I confer over the map and data book to figure out where to stop for the night. The book and the map don't always agree, and neither do we. Curry usually wants to hike farther; I want to stop sooner or at a more scenic location. With our big tent, our quantity of gear, which inevitably gets spread out, and our greater number of people trampling around, it makes sense to use established sites. But bare ground and fire rings make for dirty, sooty campsites. They're also located uncomfortably close to the trail, affording little privacy, and uncomfortably close to the water source, so cold air settling in the valley settles onto us as well. This evening, however, we find a nice site carved out of an aspen grove. The ground isn't too trampled or sooty and, though it's right on the trail, it's set well back from the creek. A handful of hikers, including the Bros, pass by after we've settled in, then we have the area to ourselves, sharing it only with a melodious thrush and a Wilson's warbler, a tiny yellow bird with a black cap who darts among the willows along the creek.

The boys and I crouch by the stream, scooping and treating water. Curry sets up the tent. I pour cold water over couscous and Alfredo. After dinner, I clean the dishes and mix oats for tomorrow's breakfast while Curry hoists a cord over a tree branch to hang our food bags. Twenty years ago, he and I worked together to set up our tent, filter water, cook dinner, hang bear bags. "Nice shootin', Tex," he always said when I sent a well-aimed rock with our bear line tied around it over a tree branch. Now we each have our own tasks that we work on separately. Our pyramid tent takes only moments to stake out the corners, extend the center pole, and sheath with the fly. Most days Milo and Curry have it pitched before I arrive in camp. With no stove to tend, it's easy for one person to stir water into dried food, and I have a particular way of washing bowls to ensure none of us gets sick from food, soap residue, or untreated water. Water treatment with the UV wand is so simple that, even though it's nice to have a second or third person to help scoop and pour, any of us can do it alone. Still, I miss the camaraderie of working together toward shared goals, and it's not lost on me that our camp chores have divided along gender lines: house-building and protection from bears the man's job; cooking, cleaning up, and nurturing children the woman's.

Chores done, we crawl into the tent, arrange our sleeping quilts, and wriggle out of our hiking clothes and into long johns. Milo and Emmet sling their dirty socks and underwear around the tent a few times before draping them over the piece of line strung near the peak of the tent, to "air out." Each day I wash a pair of socks and underwear in my half-jug and hang them from my pack to dry, so that every morning I have a clean pair to put on fresh. I can't convince anyone else to take up this habit, so their socks smell foul. Curry puts in earbuds and edits video. I coax the kids into writing a page in their journals and postcards to friends and family, then read them a chapter from *Treasure Island*. Emmet and Zephyr try to squeeze between me and Milo, the three of them tussling over space before they settle down.

Months before we came on this trip, months before I convinced Curry we needed to come on this trip, I would lie in bed at night listening to the boys bicker in their shared bedroom across the hall. We suffered from too much togetherness, yet I longed to bring us closer together, the five of us squished in a ninety-square-foot tent, as we are now. I love this part of the day, piled together, reading out loud to boys far too old for story time. Milo falls asleep and Emmet and Zephyr retire to their places to read their own books while I write in my journal before turning off my headlamp and trying to sleep.

I never sleep well in a tent. Even though I'm exhausted, I'm too uncomfortable to relax. My scalp itches. The backs of my calves are tender with sunburn and itchy with a rash caused by the sunburn. I wish I'd brought a pillow. My air mattress is so narrow that my arms slide off onto the tent floor when I lie on my back. When I lie on my stomach, my lower back aches. When I lie on my side, my hip hurts. I roll from position to position, trying to get comfortable. Every time I move, the fabric of the mattress crackles like dried leaves. Curry and Milo, positioned on either side of me, are both snoring. I angle my head to take in the fresh air flowing in under the fly, to escape their breath and the smells of a tent full of five unwashed bodies and five sets of sweaty clothes, and wait for Benadryl and ibuprofen to kick in and allow me a few hours' repose before we must rise and hike again.

In the morning the trail heads downhill. I repeat the day's mantra: *I have arrived*. It comes from my walking meditation book, *How to Walk*, by Buddhist monk Thich Nhat Hanh. Hanh writes, "When we return to our breathing, we return to the present moment, our true home. There's no need for us to struggle to arrive somewhere else." The point of this hike is not to get to Durango but to be here on the trail, experiencing every step, every moment. So often I desire to *have done* something while the actual doing seems like too much trouble. I've already hiked the Colorado Trail. Hiking it again adds nothing to my list of accomplishments. But being here and experiencing the hard work of walking step after step and the beauty of each tree, rock, and flower, while offering this experience to my children, that is the point.

After a morning break, Milo, Zephyr, and Emmet hike off together. I hear snippets of their conversation before they disappear around a bend—talk of superheroes, food they want to buy when they get to town (beef jerky, potato chips, peanut butter), movies they want to watch when they get home. So far, the three of them are getting along better than they ever do at home, as if the four-year age difference between Milo and the twins has compressed. Out here, they've had to mature in some ways, taking on responsibilities not expected of them in daily life, while at the same time Milo is freed from age-appropriate aloofness to be silly and have fun. If that camaraderie among brothers is the only gift the trail bestows this summer, it will be enough.

The trail winds in and out of forests, wet meadows, dry, grassy hillsides, and waist-high aspen trees that couldn't have been here twenty years ago. I love moving through the varied landscapes, noticing how tree and flower species change with altitude, direction of slope, proximity to water. Now I'm walking among bristlecone pines with an understory of pink geranium, deep purple dusky beardtongue, yellow stonecrop. Now

I'm in an aspen grove with red paintbrush, white mariposa lilies, yellow sunflowers, blue-and-white columbines. Now I'm passing a streambank, cool and moist and pink with elephant's-heads and shooting stars.

The first time we hiked the Colorado Trail I knew the names of quaking aspen, ponderosa pine, a few flowers, a couple of birds. Over the last twenty years, I slowly learned to identify elements of the natural world in Maine, eventually training to become a Maine Master Naturalist. On trips to Colorado, I take along stacks of field guides and try to soak up as much natural history as I can in one-week windows. I used to worry that naming the natural world was akin to colonizing it, that knowing the human-constructed identity of trees, plants, and animals would strip them of their wonder. Perhaps a young child seeing the world for the first time should approach wild things as a mystery to be discovered, but over time the world loses its novelty and the wild riot of growing things becomes a dense green curtain, a barrier to connection. By learning their names, I've learned to more clearly see the difference between one green thing and another, as well as what connects them. Because I know so much more about nature now, I *see* much more than I did then. I greet the wildflowers, trees, birds, mammals, and insects like old friends, while before they were a sea of unfamiliar and indistinguishable strangers.

A white admiral butterfly alights on a spruce branch, fanning velvety black wings striped with a bold white line. I try to take its picture, but it flies off and lands farther down the trail. I put the camera away and walk on, leapfrogging with the butterfly, appreciating its beauty without trying to capture it. Throughout the day, more butterflies appear, rising from and landing on flowers, their bright colors—yellow, pale green, orange, brown, amber—and gentle flutterings guiding me down the trail.

After another break, Curry and Milo power hike ahead, while Zephyr, Emmet, and I follow more slowly. The trail mounts a long, gently sloping hillside of pale green grass and colorful wildflowers. A mountain biker coming down the slope stops to chat.

"Where you headed?"

"Durango." I believe it a little more now that we've almost finished our first week.

"Wow. I wish my parents had been so cool." He turns to Emmet and Zephyr. "You'll remember this trip for the rest of your lives."

"Why does everyone say that?" Zephyr asks after the biker has ridden off.

I laugh. "Because it's true. You *will* remember this trip for the rest of your life."

The boys give me a skeptical look and troop ahead uphill. They have no idea what a rare experience it is for a couple of eleven-year-olds to spend a whole summer hiking through the mountains. If we were normal parents, we would have taken them to Disney World, but we're just crazy enough to think a five-hundred-mile walk through the wilderness is the perfect family vacation.

Beyond a ponderosa grove, mountains come into view, distant and hazy-blue. *The* mountains. We have been, technically, hiking in mountains all week—the Platte River and Kenosha Mountains of the Front Range. But our route has taken us through an area of forested uplands north of Pikes Peak and south of the cluster of high peaks that includes Mount Evans. There, on the horizon, the real mountains start, our first crossing of the Continental Divide at Georgia Pass the day after tomorrow, beyond that the Tenmile Range, and then the Sawatch Range, where the highest mountains in the state rise. While the entire Front Range stood resplendent before us as we drove across the plains toward Denver, we've caught only brief glimpses of mountain skylines since we entered the Gambel oak forest back in Roxborough. Now the mountains appear snow-dotted and real, just a few days' hike away.

Some people like to point out that the Rocky Mountains are so tall and jagged because they're so young. At around 25 million years old, the Colorado Rockies are mere infants compared to the 480-million-year-old Appalachians. But the rocks that make up these mountains formed through a long history of mountain building, volcanic activity, and sedimentation. Most of the rock that forms today's mountains, the "basement rock," dates from the Precambrian era—the oldest about 2.75 billion years old. Prior to the formation of the Modern Rockies, at least three mountain ranges rose and fell here, beginning with the Colorado orogeny around 1.7 to 1.8 billion years ago, followed by the Ancestral Rocky Mountains

300 to 320 million years ago and the Laramide orogeny 40 to 80 million years ago. Between each mountain-building event, erosion, deposition, and layers of volcanic debris smoothed the landscape to a flat plane, like an Etch-a-Sketch shaken clean. Meanwhile, the continental plate on which the rectangle we call Colorado sits scudded around the surface of the planet, bumping into and ripping apart from other plates, lolling around the equator, and submerging under shallow seas and swamps. After the formation of the Modern Rockies, Ice Age glaciers sharpened peaks, carved cirques, and deposited moraines, giving the mountains their rugged appearance. We're hiking through just a moment in a long history of geological drama, stretching far back into the past and far into the future.

The boys have gotten ahead of me again, and I hike alone for a while, until I come around a bend in the trail to find Emmet crouching over something on the ground.

"What do you see?"

"A dead chipmunk."

He points to a rodent, curled as if in sleep in the middle of the trail. It's a golden-mantled ground squirrel, a regal name for what is essentially a big chipmunk, and it appears to have had a fatal run-in with a boot or bike tire. Emmet takes its picture and we hike on. When we reach a grove of pine trees, he pauses and looks back over the hill we just climbed, and sweeps his arm to take in the green, red, orange, yellow, and purple of the hillside.

"Isn't it so beautiful, with all the wildflowers?" he says.

I stand beside him and look at the flowers and drifting butterflies, the aspen groves and bristlecone pine forests beyond, the foothills in the distance and, out of sight, the plains stretching across the Midwest, the farms and forests we traveled through on our way from Maine. It is so beautiful.

I take Emmet's hand and we hike on, into the trees.

4

DISTURBANCE

Maybe something ancient in my mind
seeks meaning in the lay of the land,
the way a newborn rejoices in the
landscape of a familiar face. Maybe I
go to the wilderness, again and again,
frantically, desperately, because wild
places bring me closer to home.

—KATHLEEN DEAN MOORE

DAYS 6–10: JULY 15–19, 2016
Kenosha Pass to Guller Creek

We reach the highway at Kenosha Pass before lunchtime. On its way from
Denver to Santa Fe and points south, U.S. Highway 285 roars through
this rift in the Kenosha Batholith, a spine of granite that borders the east
side of South Park. The highway is the latest in a long line of routes to
make use of this break in the mountain barrier of the Front Range. Bands
of Ute traveled this way to access hunting grounds, a toll road and stage
line crossed the pass en route to mining camps during the gold and silver
boom, and in 1879 the Denver, South Park and Pacific Railroad laid rail

FIG. 5. Lodgepole pine cone (*Pinus contorta*)

across the pass in a losing gambit to beat the Denver and Rio Grande Railroad to the mining towns. Later on the trail, when we enter the high mountains, each day will be defined by a pass, the geographic high point, the goal of a strenuous climb, and an opportunity to pause and drink in the scenery. But today we approach Kenosha Pass from above and reach it at the bottom of a gentle descent. The pass itself, below tree line and defined by the roaring highway, is a bit anticlimactic. Still, it is our destination and therefore the pinnacle of our day and of this first week of hiking. Across the treacherous highway, our campsite—and a day of rest—awaits.

Tomorrow's day off is the only "zero" day we have planned. With a six-week hiking window, we don't have time for breaks. To hike 489 miles in forty-two days, we have to average almost twelve miles per day. Twenty years ago, Curry and I averaged less than eight. It took us sixty days to complete the trail; a dozen of those were zero and near-zero days, and two we spent climbing peaks. With lighter packs, far fewer days off, and more hours of daylight since we're starting a month earlier, I hope to cover more ground in less time. Most hikers whose online journals I've read over the past few years average twenty or thirty miles per day. I've imagined an invisible barrier has been breached, so that what was a strenuous twelve miles in 1996 is an easy twenty today. It turns out this wasn't entirely magical thinking. We've arrived at Kenosha Pass at the same point we reached it twenty years ago—lunchtime on the sixth day—despite hiking nine more miles and having three kids in tow. For the first time since I dreamed up this crazy idea, I believe we have a shot at finishing the trail this summer.

Our campsite in the Forest Service campground is pure luxury: a flat tent area, a picnic table, an outhouse, potable water. When we arrived at Kenosha last time, we went through our packs, looking for items to jettison to lighten our loads. Our small pile weighed perhaps a pound or two, including Curry's camera, which had broken that morning. Not enough to make our packs comfortable for the next eight weeks, but a small step in our progression toward lightweight hiking. The only extra weight we'll send home this time is the long underwear top I bought for

Milo, which he discovered on the first night doesn't fit over his head, and his ukulele. I thought six weeks would be too long for him to go without playing guitar, so I encouraged him to pack the ukulele. But after hiking all day, we're all too tired to do much more than eat dinner and crawl into bed. From now on, his only musical instrument will be air guitar, and I'll see his fingers dancing over imaginary frets whenever we stop to rest.

As we did twenty years ago, we've arrived twenty-four hours ahead of my parents, who will bring our resupply box tomorrow. We go to bed early, the thrum of traffic on the highway serenading us through the night. I sleep in late—6:30 a.m.—and mix a special treat of granola and powdered milk for breakfast. The boys and I are thrilled to take a break from cold, slimy oatmeal, but the ration of granola is small, and Curry, who is always hungry, prowls the campsite like an underfed lion all morning, exactly like he did twenty years ago. Back then we drank cups of hot chocolate and tea while we waited for food to arrive. We don't have that luxury this time, and all we have left to eat is a bag of couscous with powdered pesto. No one is hungry enough to eat that.

Curry pauses his prowling and sits with me at the picnic table, where I watch vehicles circle the drive, powdering everything with fine dust. Three families arrive at the site across from us and unload their gear. One of the dads unfurls acres of nylon, fumbles with tree-length poles, unspools miles of guy line, stakes, cinches, and restakes. Pole by vestibule by rainfly, a mansion appears, a Tent Mahal, with multiple rooms and a porch.

"I'm having tent envy," I say, thinking of our crowded nine-by-nine-foot home.

"Have you noticed how long it's taking him to set that thing up?"

True, our little pyramid takes moments to pitch, but it's a tight squeeze. Milo, Curry, and I lie side-by-side in the three full-length sleeping spots, with Milo along one wall and Curry and me in the middle, the center pole between us. Zephyr sleeps on the other side of Curry, his spot shortened by a third where the corner is cut off to form a vestibule. Emmet sleeps perpendicular, along our feet, his spot also shortened by the corner. It's cramped, but it's home, and we don't spend much time inside.

Today, however, Emmet, Zephyr, and Milo stay in the tent until ten, playing cards, reading, and strewing their belongings around. When they start bickering, I evict them and put them to work washing their clothes in the cut-off jug and hanging them to dry on the bear bag line strung between trees. Zephyr, who should be resting a strained groin muscle, chases ground squirrels around the campground. I give myself a bucket bath, then wash the boys' hair with the last of the biodegradable soap. Everyone's filthy after a week on the trail, especially Emmet, who attracts dirt even in civilization, but they balk at having ice-cold pump water poured over their heads. Showers and laundry complete, Curry and the boys settle at the picnic table to play poker, using pinecones as chips, and I take multiple trips to the outhouse, just for the luxury of using toilet paper. On one of these trips, I spot a young woman leaning against a railing near the campground entrance. Her backpack, the fabric patterned like graph paper, matches the one I saw on a young man I directed to the water pump a few minutes earlier.

"Are you thru-hiking?" I ask.

"Yeah," she says in a soft Southern accent. She's the first female thru-hiker I've met since Aiden. She tells me her name is Kelsey and she and her husband are hiking the trail for their honeymoon.

"He's hiked the AT and part of the PCT," she tells me. "But this is my first hike like this. I think I'm doing really well."

Her husband joins us and I tell them we've returned after twenty years to hike with our kids.

"That's so cool," Kelsey says. She turns to him. "We'll have to do that, too, come back and hike the trail again with our kids."

"Our kids?" His eyes widen and he takes a small step backward, as if parenthood were contagious. I laugh. Kids were the furthest thing from my mind the first time I hiked the trail, too.

I offer them the use of our picnic table—the only thing we have to share—but Kelsey hoists her pack. "We have to hike fifteen miles a day to finish in time. I start school back in Indiana on August twenty-second." I wish the newlyweds luck as they head up the trail.

My parents arrive at lunchtime, bearing a feast, and we descend on the food like bears emerging from hibernation. The box of fried chicken is reduced to a pile of bones, the casserole dish licked clean of chile rellenos. The pasta salad vanishes by the plateful. Curry sips hot coffee, and my dad heats cocoa over a camping stove for the kids. Replete, we lean back with our hands resting on our domed stomachs, making occasional return forays to the picnic table for potato chips, yogurt, cheese, and homemade cookies. In addition to the food, my parents have brought news that Gudy Gaskill died two days ago. We'll have to carry on our trek without the spirit behind the trail in the world with us.

My dad takes Curry and Zephyr to the nearby town of Fairplay to charge devices and search for Wi-Fi. Milo and Emmet stretch out in the sun on their camping mats, and my mom and I walk to the trailhead and check out the register. The wooden box holds a stack of notebooks, each filled with paragraph-long messages. I can't tell how many entries are for thru-hikers or how many are from this year. Dozens, perhaps. Maybe hundreds? We walk up the trail a short distance. It's well worn and wide, lined with aspen trees scarred with graffiti. Crowds of people pass in both directions—day hikers, joggers, families with small children. Mountain bikers whiz by, skidding to a stop when they meet us, or cutting corners through the trees to avoid us.

Late in the afternoon, my parents pack up and head home. Twenty years ago, when they left Kenosha, I was relieved to sink into the quiet left behind by their absence. The noise and energy of my four younger siblings and niece—ranging in age from five to fourteen—had been jarring after a week of near-silence on the trail. But I also felt bereft, as if my lifeline to civilization had been cut. This time the noisy children are mine, and they stay. I feel bereft again, not because I'm cut off from civilization, but because civilization has found its way to the trail—the notebooks full of backpackers, the dozens of hikers and bikers, the busy campground and noisy highway. I can't wait to get back on the trail. I hope we'll be spaced far enough behind or ahead of other hikers to attain solitude.

We slip out of the campground early, our fellow campers still asleep in their palatial tents and trailers. A couple of young guys with the look of thru-hikers—scruffy beards, dingy clothes, funny hats—mill around the trailhead, flipping through the register books. They step aside so we can sign in and tell us they're taking a day off to rest and heal blisters. Curry opens a notebook to a blank page and we each sign it. Zephyr writes *Wolverine*, his chosen trail name. None of the rest of us have trail names yet, and we toss around ideas as we start up the trail.

Milo scratches his scalp, dandruffy from a week without a shower. "I think I'll go with *Flaky*."

I look at Emmet, his hands and face already grimy after yesterday's bucket bath. "How about we call Emmet *Pigpen*? Or *Dirt Magnet*?"

He shoots a dirty look over his shoulder at me, and Milo waves his arm at the cloud of loose dirt raised by Emmet's shuffling feet. "Nah, let's call him *Dusty*."

"Yeah." Emmet smiles and kicks up another rooster tail. "Dusty."

To me he says, "We should call you *Slug*, because you're so slow."

I return his dirty look with interest. "How about *Hey Mom*, since that's all I hear all day?" I'm totally missing the point of a trail name as an opportunity to reinvent one's identity.

"What's your trail name, Papa?" Milo asks.

"How about *Warg*?" Curry throws out.

"What is that? Some *Lord of the Rings* thing?" I say.

"Never mind. Trail names are stupid." He's not entering into the spirit of things.

"How about *Ken Burns*?" I offer, thinking of the creator of endless public television documentaries. This brings a twitch of a smile to Curry's face. Weeks later, after we've finished the hike, I'll come up with the perfect trail name for him: *Paparazzi*, because the boys call him Papa and he's always chasing us with his video camera.

I thought we'd avoid mountain bikers by getting an early start, but we've only walked a few feet when the first bikes pass us. All day long we step off the trail as they come by, singly, in pairs, and in packs, heading toward Georgia Pass in the morning and back down again in the afternoon. Trail etiquette requires that the downhill traveler step aside for those moving uphill and that bikes yield to hikers, but in reality it's safer and more expedient for a hiker to step out of the way of the bigger, faster bikes. But it's exhausting to break momentum, step off the trail and back on, fifty or sixty times, over the course of a long morning's climb. When I express frustration with the mountain bikers during a break, Milo shrugs.

"It's not that big a deal," he says. "I think you just don't like mountain bikes."

It's not that I don't like mountain *bikers*. When I first knew Curry in college, he and his friends were known affectionately as the "Biker Boys," a half-dozen handsome, ponytailed young men who rode their brightly colored fat-tire bikes around campus, zipping up and down stone staircases and hopping on and off rocks. Mountain bikes were a relative novelty back then, and the Biker Boys were cute and sexy. But now that I have to haul myself off the trail every few minutes to avoid getting run over, I'm less impressed, and the dudes conquering the trail on their two-wheelers (the great majority we see are men) don't strike me as cute or sexy, only annoying.

The trail emerges from the aspen trees, revealing a view of the mountains we'll traverse over the coming days, and the trail winds down a sunflower-studded hillside and skirts the north edge of South Park, a thousand-square-mile grassy plain between the Front and Mosquito Ranges. One of four vast intermountain prairies in the state, South Park was once home to bison and was a prized hunting ground for the Ute. Today it's made up of ranches, small towns, and mining-themed tourist attractions, with trout-fishing streams and the occasional pronghorn antelope as relics of past abundance. Beyond the park the trail heads uphill again, and as we near Georgia Pass, it enters a gloomy subalpine forest. If an ember of the old Puritanical terror of wild places still smolders in the heart of Americans, these woods would ignite it. It's not an open, breezy ponderosa woodland or a sun-dappled aspen grove, but a deep, dark, spooky forest. The trees stand tall and dense. No breeze stirs their branches and no bird song breaks the silence. The woods are still and full of a watchful, brooding presence. I walk quietly, aware of the looming trees, trying to figure out why this forest has a creepy atmosphere while the high forest in Lost Creek Wilderness felt majestic. The gloom may, perhaps, be the nature of subalpine forests in general. Naturalist Ann Zwinger writes in *Land Above the Trees*, "Subalpine forests are thick and dark and somber. . . . After being enveloped in shadow, intimidated by invasions of one's own three-dimensional space, the tundra seems such an open vacuum that one is physically drawn to it."

Indeed, it feels like a release when the trail emerges from the forest onto a wide-open, sloping expanse of grass, pink paintbrush, and the short-stalked, big-headed alpine sunflowers known as old-man-of-the-mountain. We wind our way up the gently sloping meadow and stop to rest on the Continental Divide. The divide runs from western Alaska to Tierra del Fuego, along the spines of the Rockies and the Andes, separating the North and South American continents into two major watersheds. Precipitation that falls on the west side of the Continental Divide is destined for the Pacific Ocean, while waters that fall on the east head for the Atlantic, except in the far north, where the divide separates the Pacific and Arctic Ocean watersheds.

Twenty years ago, I'd been disappointed by this first crossing of the divide, expecting a spiny ridge with water droplets labeled "Atlantic" and "Pacific" trickling down either side of it. Here the actual divide is a mere smoothing out of the alpine meadow, an almost imperceptible shift from walking uphill to walking downhill. On that first hike, the trail had been so different from my expectations—the noise of airplanes and highways intruding on the wildness, the difficulty of hiking under a freighted pack. Wilderness travel pioneer Colin Fletcher writes in his book *River*, about following the Colorado River source to sea, "I saw that what kept my journey alive was the daily tension between expectation and realization. That's what any traveler learns. What makes his journey run is not events but events' refusal of his expectations." At the time of our first hike, I did not appreciate this tension. Instead I resisted reality, growing more frustrated with each day that did not live up to my image of primeval wilderness bliss. Now, after fifteen years of parenting, which is a constant process of compromise between ideals and reality, I'm better equipped to deal with events' refusal to meet my expectations.

Anyway, the divide here is not so bad. Beautiful, even. Mountains tower on both sides of us, stony gray peaks dappled with snow fields and cornices. Ahead, in the distance, more mountains rise in jagged ranges. The trail will take us into and beyond those ranges. We planned to camp not far from here tonight, down a side trail where a spring emerges below a pink snowfield, the same place we camped last time. The view from that campsite had been magnificent. A month later in the season, many of the wildflowers had gone by, but fields of alpine grasses rolled in gentle hills all around our site, trimmed at the lower borders by krummholz, those gnarled and stunted trees that grow at the edge of the alpine zone. To the south, the mountains parted in a V, offering a vista of South Park and the Kenosha Mountains; to the west, the great rock cone of Mount Guyot stretched its southern flank in a jagged knife-edge, wrapping around a talus-filled cirque. Today, however, the crowds of bikers make camping here less appealing, and it's still early, so we forge on.

At Glacier Ridge Road the Colorado Trail joins the Continental Divide National Scenic Trail, a 3,100-mile footpath that takes hikers from Mexico to Canada, sticking as close to the divide as possible. The two trails share tread for the next 314 miles.

As we cross the road, we meet a couple walking up the road, their off-road vehicle parked a short distance away. They ask where we're heading.

"Durango." It still seems like an absurd thing to say.

"You're kidding," the woman says. "How far is that? We just hiked five miles yesterday and our feet are killing us."

"Our feet hurt, too."

"How far do you hike every day?"

"About twelve miles."

"Man, my feet are killing me from five." She looks down and rolls her ankle in its hiking boot. She has long, bleach-blond hair and long, acrylic nails. He wears a leather jacket and motorcycle boots. They're as different from us as they could be, but they're genuinely interested in our hike.

"Where do you sleep? What do you do for food?"

We tell them about cold oatmeal and our cramped pyramid tent.

"We could never do anything like that." The woman elbows the man and laughs. "We're too dysfunctional. What do you do about thunder and lightning?"

"Get below tree line."

"We could never do that," she says again. "What about bees? Do you have an EpiPen?"

"We're not allergic to bees."

"How do you know?"

"We've all been stung before."

"I've never been stung and I carry an EpiPen. What about water? Do you carry all you need?"

"We collect water from streams and treat it with UV light."

I shift my feet and shrug my shoulders. Standing still hurts more than hiking. "In fact, we're on our way to find water now," I say. "We're almost out."

"Oh, we have water." She gestures toward the ORV. "Let me get you some."

Curry starts to decline, but I'm not about to pass up our first trail magic. "We'd love water. Thank you."

She hands us two liters of Evian and we thank her profusely.

"From the French Alps to the Colorado Alps," Curry says, holding up the bottle like he's in a television commercial.

"Well, good luck," the woman says and jabs her partner again. "We could never do that. Too dysfunctional."

We wave goodbye and head downhill, back into trees. Curry and the boys trot ahead, and I smile to myself, thinking of the couple. The woman was my exact opposite—loud, talkative, outwardly enthusiastic, generous. She was not only willing to admit to strangers that she was not cut out to hike long distances, she found it hilarious. I prefer to delude myself that I can do anything to put my mind to, and when I know I can't do something, I keep that knowledge to myself.

Late in the afternoon, I find Emmet sitting beside the trail, reading. He jumps to his feet and leads me past a solo camper with a small orange tent, farther into the woods, to our campsite in a clearing. There I find our tent set up and Curry, Milo, and Zephyr sitting on logs around a plywood board across a box. A four-wheeler trail runs nearby, accounting for the outsized accommodations. At the stream I chat with another hiker with whom we've leapfrogged throughout the day. He tells me he started at Kenosha this morning and plans to reach Durango in four weeks. All day I've been eyeing his pack, which is the size of a daypack.

"Dare I ask how much your pack weighs?" I ask.

"Fifteen pounds, without food and water."

"Awesome!" I refrain from mentioning that his tiny pack weighs the same as mine—before I add water and food for five people—but I don't refrain from feeling a tiny bit smug.

Back at our site, I mix beans and rice at the plywood table, and we rest on the logs to wait for it to "cook."

"I have a proposal for you guys," Curry says. "If we keep up the pace we went today for the next two days, we can get to Leadville a day early. That will give me time to upload videos."

We hiked seventeen miles today, a new record. I feel good, but I don't really want to hike two more seventeen-mile days, especially not for the purpose of spending more time in town, on the internet. Half of the appeal of backpacking, for me, is to escape the constant connectedness of computers and smartphones. I want to unplug, but Curry wants to connect the videos he's been making every evening to his viewers, and the kids are game to try, so I too agree to two more long days.

In the morning the trail rises from our campsite through lodgepole pine forests where half of the trees have been felled, and, of those still standing, half are dead. Many of the living trees have pencil-sized holes in the bark, plugged with clumps of sap and sawdust, evidence of beetle infestation. Over the two decades since we first hiked the Colorado Trail, the pine forests of western North America, from Baja and Southern Arizona to British Columbia and Alberta, have experienced an unprecedented epidemic of bark beetles. In Colorado, mountain pine beetle outbreaks spread over 3.4 million acres of lodgepole, ponderosa, and limber pine forests between 1996 and 2013.

Like the Douglas-fir tussock moth and beetle, pine beetles have always been an integral part of the forest ecosystems of the West. The mountain pine beetle is a tiny insect, the size of an apple seed, but it combines forces with others of its kind to bring down massive trees and whole forests. Pine beetles attack a tree en masse, burrowing into sapwood for food and to create brood chambers for their larvae. The beetles bring with them the spores of blue-staining fungus, which spreads in the tree's sapwood, providing additional food for the beetles and further cutting off the flow of nutrients within the tree's vascular tissue, aiding in the tree's strangulation and eventual death. The trees, for their part, fight back against the beetles by generating resin that can drown or "pitch out" invading beetles. But sufficient numbers of beetles can overcome a tree's defenses.

Under normal conditions, mountain pine beetles attack mature trees, making way for new growth and increasing diversity. Lodgepole pine, one of the beetle's primary targets in Colorado, is an early successional species dependent on fire for propagation. Dead needles and trees from periodic beetle outbreaks provide fuel for fires, but, unlike the hot, fast crown fires that burn living forests and destroy pine seeds and the soil they need to sprout in, downed logs in beetle-killed forests smolder slowly. A century of fire suppression led to a mature pine forest from the Pacific Ocean to the Great Plains. Forests already vulnerable from their uniform age and lack of diversity were weakened by years of drought, while warmer winters gave the beetles an edge, increasing their annual survival rate, sometimes doubling or tripling the generations spawned each year, and expanding their range farther north and higher in altitude, turning an outbreak into an epidemic. Responses to beetle infestation—including selective cutting, clear-cutting, prescribed burning, and pesticide spraying—don't appear to have had much impact on the spread of pine beetles and may in some cases have worsened the problem by killing beetle-eating woodpeckers or leaving behind larvae in stumps.

Returning to Colorado every couple of years over the last two decades has been like watching the mountain pine beetle outbreak on timelapse. My parents live in an area hit particularly hard. Each visit, patches of the rusty red of dead needles spread over larger and larger areas of the mountains. Eventually the needles fell from trees, leaving behind hillsides covered in bare, gray branches that look more like Maine in winter than the Rockies in summer. The beetle outbreak in Colorado has subsided in the last few years, but what will happen now remains an open question. Some scientists predict pine forests will regenerate, that in the standing dead wood are conditions ripe for fires to prepare soil, drive out competing species, and release the lodgepole pine's flake-thin seeds from their cones. Others suspect climatic conditions are too altered for trees to thrive and that grass or scrublands will replace forests in some areas. Still others contend that the beetles did the forest a service, weeding out trees most susceptible to heat and drought and leaving behind individuals with the vigor to withstand the stresses of a changing climate. Depending on which experts are correct, we're standing at the edge of either an apocalypse or a large-scale forest renewal.

After lunch, the boys set off three abreast along a wide stretch of trail between stands of low, brushy pine trees, Milo telling his brothers a story. "The tide was rising, and the water inside the cave where El Loco was hiding was getting higher. . . ." It's one of many tales that carry the three of them through part of their hiking days. In addition to the saga of El Loco, they all contribute to the ongoing story of "Tom Lighthouse's World," a land ruled by Emmet's old imaginary friend, Tom Lighthouse. When Zephyr hikes with Curry, he tells him long, detailed stories about Knight, a superhero with a variety of powers, weapons, and armor. In the tent at night, Emmet tells us "Camper Bob and Camper Joe" stories, in which catastrophe follows two hapless and not very bright campers, who usually end up committing murder, dying grisly deaths, or both.

"When they woke up . . ." Emmet intones in a breathy, ghost-story voice. Then his eyes widen and he snaps, "Camper Joe was gone!"

Despite their silly, and sometimes gruesome, details, the stories the boys tell are one of the most magical parts of the hike.

The boys disappear around a bend in the tail, and I lose the thread of El Loco's tale. When we're not hiking through stands of beetle-killed lodgepole pine today, we're passing through areas of young trees not much taller than ourselves. We traveled through a considerable number of clear-cuts and recently replanted tree plantations in this area twenty years ago. Could this shrubby forest be one of those, growing ever so slowly, or is it the result of a more recent cut? I'd been surprised by the clear-cuts then. Though I was familiar with the issue from going to college in Maine at a time when the privately owned forests were being liquidated by the paper companies, I naively believed the Rocky Mountains too sacred to be razed of trees. But to an industry that clear-cut the ancient forests of the Pacific Northwest, and the Forest Service that enabled them, nothing is sacred.

The National Forests have always been the rope in a tug-of-war of competing ideas about public land use. The Forest Reserve Act of 1891 grew out of concern for the rate at which Americans had cleared forests on the East Coast and in the Great Lakes region and the free-for-all of forest consumption taking place on western lands where homesteaders, speculators, and the railroads were gobbling up timber. In addition to seeking to moderate the wholesale clearing of trees and ensure an enduring supply of lumber, the creators of the act were concerned with preventing devastating floods that resulted when heavy rains fell on watersheds devoid of trees. The act gave the president the authority to remove forested lands from homesteading claims, ensuring they remained in the public trust and establishing the precursor to the National Forest system. The White River Plateau Reserve, encompassing the headwaters of three major river systems in Colorado, was among the first forest reserves set aside. The Organic Act of 1897 clarified that forest reserves were to be established "to improve and protect the forest within the reservation, or for the purpose of securing favorable conditions of water flows, and to furnish a continuous supply of timber for the use and necessities of citizens of the United States."

Although timber sales made up only a small portion of the Forest Service's activities in its first decades, even then conservationists debated the role of public forests, with preservationists like John Muir arguing for protection of trees and foresters like Gifford Pinchot, the service's first chief, promoting the concept of multiple use. This idea of the harmonious blending of many uses was codified in the Multiple Use and Sustained Yield Act of 1960, in which Congress decreed that national forests exist "for outdoor recreation, range, timber, watershed, and wildlife and fish purposes." The act, however, put greater emphasis on timber, with a goal of "sustained yield," which means "the achievement and maintenance in perpetuity of a high-level annual or regular periodic output of the various renewable resources of the national forests." In other words: a constant flow of tree cutting.

National Forests were already achieving a "high level output" of timber, with the annual harvest having risen from 68.5 million board feet in 1905 to more than 8 billion board feet by 1960. This increase was due in part to the post–World War II economic boom and in part to the depletion of timber on private forest lands. According to *The USDA Forest Service—The First Century* by Gerald W. Williams, prior to the postwar era, "the timber industry viewed the national forests as huge timber sources that needed to be kept off the market so that the timber industry could keep private timber prices high. The timber industry now sought cheap national forest timber to supplement or replace heavily cutover private forest lands."

Harvests continued to grow, averaging between nine and nearly thirteen billion board feet through most of the next three decades, with much of the timber being cut in "even-age management" stands, or clear-cuts. In a clear-cut, every marketable tree is removed, the remaining brush, slash, and other biomass burned, and the area managed for a single, preferred species, often treated with herbicides to prevent competing species from growing. Clear-cuts can damage the land in a number of ways. Roads, machinery, and falling trees compact soil. Snowpack melts 30 percent faster in a clear-cut, and bared soil washes away with rainstorms and spring runoff, taking away nutrients and organic matter and silting streams. Carbon stored in the soil is released by faster decomposition that results from exposure to sunlight, and carbon stored in the trees is released when the wood is burned for fuel or decomposes. Clear-cuts open the way for invasive species, fragment wildlife habitat, and disproportionately benefit plants and animals that prefer edge habitats. Even if a site is successfully replanted, the resulting tree plantation lacks the diversity and complexity of a virgin forest.

Lawsuits over clear-cuts on National Forests spurred the passage of the National Forest Management Act of 1976. This law established planning requirements and standards intended to protect National Forests from more egregious logging practices. But clear-cuts continued, and controversy swirled around clear-cutting and below-cost timber sales. The Forest Service has always sold timber far below market values while at the same time investing vast resources in road building, timber cruising, site preparation, and replanting. While overall timber revenue has generally exceeded cost, most of the profit came from old growth forests in the Pacific Northwest, while almost all timber sales in the Rocky Mountain Region have been conducted at a loss. Critics contend that below-cost timber operations are corporate welfare, while the Forest Service argues that these sales serve purposes other than revenue, such as providing jobs to local communities, thinning or managing forests for different purposes, and clearing forests of undesirable tree species or downed wood. They also suggest that if timber is required to pay for itself, so should other forest uses, such as recreation.

Over the last two decades, logging operations have largely transitioned from western public lands to private lands in the Southeast. At the same time, plastic and other materials have replaced some wood products. Annual timber harvests declined to around 2 to 2.5 billion board feet per year. However, while the Forest Service emphasizes restoration, climate change, and sustainability in its outreach materials, clear-cuts still comprise 40 percent of the annual timber harvest in the West, and the Forest Service has not ceased clear-cutting old-growth forests in parts of the country, such as Alaska's Tongass National Forest.

Lodgepole pine, which populates the area we're hiking through, is by nature a species that colonizes disturbed ground and grows in dense, single-aged stands. While this forest may not be as complex as a redwood forest, it's characterized by interactions among species, some of which we can see, like kinnikinnick and paintbrush growing in the understory, woodpeckers and squirrels foraging in the canopy, and young spruce and fir rising in the shade. Other interactions are hidden from view, like snowbrush roots fixing nitrogen and mycorrhizal fungi helping the trees uptake nutrients. Can these relationships be replicated among trees planted after a clear-cut? If we come back to hike the trail again in twenty years, we might get a sense of whether this expanse of dense, brushy pine will mature into a functioning forest or if it will always be a diminished tree plantation.

Leaving behind the tree plantations, we enter more areas of beetle kill. The slopes across the valley are ghostly gray, covered in dead, bleached trees. Lodgepole pines grow in such densely packed stands that their lower limbs die from lack of sunlight and it's not as obvious that the trees we walk among also make up a ghost forest. I crane my neck, looking for live green needles in the canopy, and see more dead, gray limbs.

It was my twenty-third birthday when we hiked through this area last time, and this portion of trail had been rerouted to move it off a road. The reroute was longer than the road, neither our guidebook nor map reflected the new portion of trail, and we hadn't planned for extra miles. The trail twisted and turned up and down hillsides, with long switch-backs that seemed to take us on long detours. The ugliness of the recent clear-cuts and replanted monocultures did nothing to improve my state of mind, nor did Curry hiking on my heels, trying to rush me down the trail, singing, "Christmas in Durango, baby why don't we go?" I cried much of the day as I struggled to find the reasons I'd had for hiking the trail. I could remember the words but I couldn't access the feelings. We reached camp after sunset, setting up the tent and cooking in the dark, and I went to bed exhausted and defeated.

After that miserable day, Curry and I changed our hiking system. Rather than him dogging my heels, he'd hike ahead at his pace to a pre-determined spot and I would follow at my pace. This arrangement has continued to this day and is why I spend most of each day hiking alone, or with a tired or out-of-sorts child, at the back of the pack while the others gallop ahead. I enjoy the time by myself and with my kids, but I don't like the way being last cuts me out of decisions about where to stop for rest breaks, lunch, or camping, or how everyone else is ready to get up and hike on when I catch up with them, so that I never get a break. I also know that this isn't the safest hiking arrangement, but I can't stand the idea of speed hikers herding me down the trail, and they would resent slowing down.

Later in the day we pass through an area of forest that burned five years ago. Patches of magenta fireweed grow between charred logs stacked in pyramids. Already small pine and spruce trees poke out of the soil, in stark contrast to Buffalo Creek's tufts of grass dotting the gravel. This sixteen-acre fire was not nearly as intense as that much larger one, and the higher altitude and greater moisture levels of the Western Slope have aided in regeneration. Beyond the burn, the trail skirts a large wet meadow, dense with willows and false hellebore, or corn lily, a tall plant with greenish-white flowers and crepe-paper leaves. I find Curry and the boys standing on the trail, looking out over the meadow. Curry puts his fingers to his lips and points to where four moose with small, spatulate antlers browse.

Moose are the largest members of the deer family, standing around six feet tall at the shoulder and weighing between seven hundred and fourteen hundred pounds. Unlikely looking creatures, they appear to be made up of spare parts: long legs, knobby legs, bulbous nose, bulging eyes, feathery eyelashes, humped back, stub tail, mulish ears, and a dangling neck protuberance known as a bell or dewlap. Usually solitary critters, male moose may gather in small groups during the summer at feeding sites, like this meadow, to eat and practice sparring in advance of the fall's rut. Moose are relative newcomers to Colorado; while historically individuals wandered in from Wyoming from time to time, they didn't stick around to mate and have little moose until wildlife officials began introducing them to the state in the late 1970s, resulting in a breeding population of around twenty-three hundred today. These four ignore us, but when it's time to move on, we pass uncomfortably close, and the moose trot farther down the meadow, equal measures graceful and ungainly, jutting their big, peanut-shaped heads forward, their thick bodies gliding smoothly while each leg appears to operate independent of the others, swinging about like marionette limbs.

After an afternoon of climbing, we reach the top of a ridge, the other side sloping down a steep, barren hillside. At the foot of the slope, where twenty years ago there had been a little village of perhaps a few dozen RVs and travel trailers, now several hundred mobile homes line up in compact rows, each with a patch of green lawn. Every trailer is sheathed in brown log siding and roofed in green metal, as if a giant came by with a can of Lincoln Logs. McMansions climb the surrounding hillsides. The rampant development that has encroached on my mountains since I left Colorado for college depresses me. The population of Summit County, where this neighborhood, situated between Breckenridge and Frisco, sits, grew from just under thirteen thousand in 1990 to nearly twenty-eight thousand in 2010 and is projected to surpass thirty-six thousand by the end of the decade.

The trail skirts the perimeter of the park, passing a stagnant green pond where a boy and an older man fish. Across the highway, we collect water from the Blue River. Scooping water near houses, a highway, and a paved bike path, I feel less like a hiker than a vagrant. We follow the bike path a short distance then turn uphill, passing through an area cleared of trees, with not a twig left standing and nothing to block the roar of the highway. I want to get far away from the houses and highway, but dusk is falling, and we've hiked nearly seventeen miles, so we set up camp in a flattish area in the middle of this open, clear-cut hillside. Today's hike was not as hard, physically or mentally, as when we covered the same ground twenty years ago. Though I'm annoyed with camping near the highway and the houses, my head is still in the hike, and many of my hopes are already being met—seeing wildlife and wildflowers, witnessing my children's wonder and their silliness, hiking stronger and faster than I thought I could.

It rains during the night, but we wake to sun and clear skies. Curry, as usual, is the first one out of the tent, digging into breakfast. I do my morning routine, change into my hiking clothes, and pack my gear before I leave the tent and face my bowl of cold oatmeal. The boys snuggle in their sleeping bags and pretend they don't have to get up. Curry's dressed and packed and is antsy and impatient for us to vacate the tent so he can roll it up and strap it to his pack. Once Milo's up, he packs quickly then gulps down his oatmeal and chases it with an energy bar. Emmet and Zephyr dawdle over their packing and pick at their oatmeal. I can't finish packing until I've cleaned their bowls and spoons, so I, as always, am the last one ready to go, the one holding everyone else up.

From camp, we hike through more clear-cut and selectively cut areas, more stands of both live and dead trees, more logs piled like pick-up sticks. A grouse and her chicks pecking beside the trail offer a moment of respite from the depressing landscape, before we reach a stream and begin to climb through wilder areas. As we near tree line, bright wildflowers carpet the meadows—pink paintbrush, blue chiming bells, lavender asters, sunflowers of various sizes and shades of yellow. I continue to be amazed by how little I recognize. The landscape has been familiar, in a general sense—dense lodgepole forests, airy ponderosa stands, leafy aspen groves—but the imprints of these types of landscapes date back much further than our first Colorado Trail hike, to childhood summers spent camping and picnicking in the mountains. The entire trail might be one continuous reroute from the trail of twenty years ago, for its lack of familiarity. Today's hike will take us through one of the photo-album memories I've held onto from twenty years ago, and I wonder if the landscape will resonate. We had camped farther along the trail, above tree line, in a glorious alpine meadow below a sheer, toothed ridge. At the time, in late August, the vegetation was already turning autumn shades, the last purple asters, fuchsia paintbrush, and yellow daisies bright against a soft background of fading green, red, and russet. Behind a lichen-encrusted rock, we discovered a clump of late-blooming Colorado columbines. Low, gnarly spruce trees, bent and twisted, clung to the lower reaches of the slope, and a marshy stream bordered our camp.

That morning, Curry and I climbed from our alpine garden, gently at first then more steeply, through krummholz and tundra, over a saddle, toward the ridge of the Ten-Mile Range. We walked along gold and red alpine slopes rising to knife-edge crests and jagged peaks, with pink snowfields clinging to the ridges and blue mountain ranges unfurling in the distance. When we topped out on the ridge, icy winds and wooly gray clouds moved in. As I paused to watch a soaring hawk, a golden eagle drifted up from the valley below. Hail pelted us as we descended, and I half ran down the slope, balls of ice stinging my shoulders through my flimsy anorak, thunder and lightning crackling all around. When the hail passed and we stopped to catch our breath, the golden eagle glided by again, close over our heads, like a benediction. We jogged downhill, eager for the delights awaiting us in Copper Mountain, where we collected our resupply package at the post office and spent a few hours in a restaurant, sorting our dried food and gorging on pizza, sandwiches, and cookies, before climbing a gentle ascent to our campsite along Guller Creek.

The day had been one of the most difficult to that point but also one of the best. Between the dramatic views, the delicious food, and the terrifying but invigorating run through the hailstorm, this stretch of trail stamped itself in my memory as a highlight of the hike.

But today I don't recognize our alpine garden campsite when we emerge from the trees and approach the steep climb to the saddle. Perhaps it doesn't look familiar in the bright midday light, or perhaps it doesn't stand out among the meadows teeming with wildflowers we've hiked through already.

Below the saddle, we stop to rest beside a snowmelt creek, and a young couple passes us, heading downhill. Zephyr looks back the way we came, his eyes widening with horror.

"What the heck?"

My gaze follows his, to where the young man has stripped naked and is stepping into the stream. I laugh. "What? You don't want to go skinny dipping in melted snow?"

"I wouldn't want to skinny dip anywhere. Would you?"

I laugh again. "Yeah, sure."

As we near the saddle, the trail angles to near vertical, a steep, eroded wall of bare dirt and rocks. Zephyr studies the ascent with a critical eye.

"What kind of monster would make a trail like that?"

We haul ourselves up and emerge on the saddle, a tumble of broken, lichen-encrusted rocks leading to a meadow of low alpine grass and flowers patched with snow. Distant peaks to the north loom over a pool of blue water nestled in the valley bottom. Too big and blue to be real, it's a manmade lake, Dillon Reservoir, built in the 1960s, over local objections, to collect and transport water to Denver and the suburbs through the twenty-three-mile Roberts Tunnel, one of the longest in the world. The town of Dillon, located at the confluence of Tenmile Creek and the Blue and Snake Rivers, was relocated to make way for the reservoir.

Curry, Milo, and Emmet wait for us a ways down the trail. I'd convinced myself the saddle was the ridge of the Ten Mile Range, that we just had a downhill jog to Copper Mountain. But the trail unspools along the ridge for miles before cresting. The sun shines from a cerulean sky. Hikers and bikers dot the trail as far as I can see. I'm unreasonably furious that we have much farther to go than I expected. I'm annoyed by the throngs of people and by the absence of golden eagles. I'm even disappointed by the beautiful weather. I'd unconsciously expected today's hike to unfold exactly as it did twenty years ago, to recreate that postcard-perfect image.

This is our first time hiking above tree line, except the brief crossing of the Continental Divide at Georgia Pass. The tundra along the ridge is in peak summer bloom, and I try to shelve my grievances and revel in the vast skies, immense views, and tiny wildflowers. There comes a point at which conditions are too extreme for trees to grow—too much wind, too cold, too short a growing season. Heading north, that point is the Arctic Circle; heading upward in elevation here in Colorado, it's around 11,000 to 11,500 feet. Above tree line, the alpine tundra builds and holds soil in place, slows and filters the runoff of snowmelt, and feeds and shelters high-altitude wildlife, like ptarmigan, pikas, and pocket gophers. I love the intricate beauty of alpine flowers and the way these delicate-looking plants thrive in the most extreme of environments.

In the alpine zone, wind, rain, and ice crumble mountain to boulder, boulder to talus, talus to scree. Lichens, mosses, and plants so small you could fit them in your pocket turn rock into soil, each yielding to subsequent forms in a successional march decades or centuries long. Only very special organisms can survive the short summers, intense sunlight, and powerful winds of mountaintops. A variety of physical adaptations allow alpine plants to minimize heat loss, desiccation, and wind damage and maximize photosynthesis. Among these are deep tap roots, cushion, mat, or rosette forms, hairy or wooly coatings on leaves and buds, and succulence. Many alpine plants also have built-in furnaces in the form of red pigments, called anthocyanins, which convert light into heat. Most are perennial and many flower early, in some cases spreading bud and flower development over several years.

Though from a distance the tundra might appear as smooth and unvarying as a lawn, it is a complex landscape made up of different communities—boulder fields, fellfields, scree and talus slopes, meadows and turfs, snow beds, marshes—each forming in response to slope, snow cover, microclimate, and other factors and each hosting a different array of plant life. This varying landscape results in amazing diversity, with more than three hundred species of alpine plants in Colorado alone. Some of the flowers, like dwarf paintbrush and old-man-of-the-mountain, have full-sized blossoms on top of petite stems, others, such as moss campion and alpine forget-me-nots, are miniature in every aspect, with diminutive petals, leaves, and stems growing in a pincushion-sized mass. On this stretch of trail we are undulating through a turf of sedges and grasses dotted with ankle-high wildflowers—king's crown, buttercups, chiming bells—below the bare, rocky ridge of the Tenmile Range.

We crest the ridge and descend toward Copper Mountain in the late afternoon. The trail skirts the town along the tops of the ski slopes, but we drop off the trail and aim for the highway, crossing at traffic lights and traversing a deserted shuttle stop and satellite parking area. From there we follow the edge of a golf course into town. Copper Mountain had an artificial atmosphere two decades ago and now appears even larger and faker. It's meant to mimic a Swiss village, with chalet-style condos and shops in shades of olive green and rusty red. But without mounds of snow, twinkly Christmas lights, and hordes of people dressed in brightly colored ski clothes, it has the eerie emptiness of an abandoned amusement park. Except for some golfers and a modest stream of vehicles, the place is nearly deserted. We wander the quiet streets until we stumble upon a pizza restaurant. We have the place to ourselves, except for the three young guys at the counter, and we spread out our gear and ourselves, taking up most of the dining area.

After placing an order for quite possibly the most expensive pizza-and-french-fry lunch in the history of the world, I find the bathroom a couple of blocks away and buy a handful of postcards in a gift shop, then return to the restaurant and sit on a high stool next to Milo. Our table looks out a window onto a manmade pond where families float placidly in inner tubes on dark water. I watch the strange tableau as I pour blue cheese dressing over my salad and take a luxurious bite of cold, crisp iceberg lettuce.

"Rich people are weird," Milo says, tucking into an enormous slice of pepperoni and echoing my thoughts.

I probably should say something about not assuming people are rich, just because they're floating in a fake pond in a resort, that different people enjoy different activities. But there's something so bizarrely manufactured about the experience they're having in the dark, glistening water, wedged between the base of the ski mountain and rows of condos and shops, with a fountain spraying up in the middle, that I can't help but agree.

"Yeah, they are."

Milo helps himself to another slab of pizza. After a few bites he groans and leans back. "I think my stomach's shrunk from the malnutrition."

I finish my salad and start in on a slice of cheese pizza, happy to be eating anything other than cold oatmeal or couscous.

Milo pushes the remains of his pizza around on his plate. "It feels weird," he says, "not being in the middle of nowhere."

"Good weird, or bad weird?"

"Bad weird. I don't want to be in the middle of nowhere, but I don't want to be here, either."

Milo did not want to come on this trip. "I'm going to miss the whole summer," he'd moaned. He just finished his freshman year of high school, and he wanted to spend the summer hanging out with his friends, taking driver's ed, sleeping in, and playing guitar. Though he hasn't complained since we left Maine, I'm not surprised that he doesn't want to be "in the middle of nowhere." But I'm also glad that the canned entertainment of the resort doesn't appeal to him. Even if he doesn't become a lifelong backpacker after this trip, I want for him to recognize the difference between authentic experience and vapid amusement. This fake pond, fake village, fake world does feel weird, and I want us to get back on the trail as fast as we can and camp as far away as we can get, but dark clouds amassed while we ate, and we'll have to set up the tent before it rains. I stuff the last pieces of pizza in a plastic bag, and we walk toward the chair lifts, where we find a small Colorado Trail sign as the first drops sprinkle down.

The rain holds off and we make it the few miles to Guller Creek without getting wet. Though our campsite is in a small grove of trees bordering a lovely meadow, it's not far enough from civilization. At least five tents are set up within yards of our own. We camped here after our Copper Mountain resupply twenty years ago, and then we had also shared our site, across a meadow from three other tents, whose occupants laughed and shouted and whooped late into the night. Although our neighbors aren't as noisy as those long-ago campers, their presence reinforces all that has changed in twenty years—more people on the trail, more houses sprawling from the towns and up the mountain slopes, more cars roaring down the highways. More of everything except wildness, peace, and solitude. These are in short supply and, who knows, in another twenty years may not exist at all.

FIG. 6. Blue pleasing fungus beetle (*Cypherotylus californicus*)

5

BEDROCK

Even a wounded world is feeding us. Even a wounded world holds us, giving us moments of wonder and joy. I choose joy over despair.
—ROBIN WALL KIMMERER

DAYS 11–13: JULY 20–22, 2016
Guller Creek to Tennessee Pass

Sunlight filters through gold nylon, bathing the tent in a warm glow. I loll in my quilt. We don't have far to go today, and I'm exhausted after three seventeen-mile days. I want to stay in bed all morning, but cigarette smoke wafting in from a neighboring campsite drives me out of the tent, leaving behind bickering kids. For the most part, the boys have been getting along great, but last night Zephyr took Emmet's sleeping spot at the foot of the tent and they woke up spoiling for a fight. At home, they mostly argue about personal property and territory, but out here we have only the clothes on our backs, our sleeping gear, and a few small trinkets. We're surrounded by millions of acres of wilderness. Anyone who desires elbow room need only hike a little faster or more slowly than the others. But in the tent space is at a premium. Every piece of real estate is cramped and uncomfortable and the twins' spots are extra-cramped. Still they wage war over them today. I'm hyperaware of the people in the tents around us, all within earshot of the boys' arguments and my snappish responses. I hustle them out of the tent and hand out slices of leftover pizza. Curry has already eaten his oatmeal and grumbles about the late start. We're all a little off after the break from routine, the junk food, the culture shock of two hours in town. Nevertheless, I'm eagerly anticipating the next town, Leadville, where we'll eat a hot meal, wash our clothes, and take showers for the first time in nearly two weeks.

We finally get ourselves sorted and on the trail at 8:35 and head up, up, up. The first hour of hiking is always the hardest. My head is still groggy from the Benadryl I took to sleep, my muscles, bones, and joints are stiff from lying on the ground, and the ibuprofen I took on waking hasn't kicked in. Bulges from items in my pack jab into my back. I didn't adjust my water bottles correctly in the side pockets, and they bang my elbows with each step. I poke and prod at my pack's contents, tug on straps, rearrange my clothes, eat a snack, drink water, and fidget and fuss my way up the trail. Today's steep climb doesn't help. My legs feel heavy and my lungs gasp for air. Why doesn't the uphill get any easier? Shouldn't I be getting stronger after ten days of hiking? Twenty years ago I had this same problem, wheezing up the trail like an asthmatic goat, infuriated that Curry, a smoker at the time, trotted ahead without the slightest quickening of breath.

Naturalist Ann Zwinger writes of backpacking in her book *Wind in Rock*, "For most of the time, one disciplines oneself to ignore the discomfort of being hot or tired or having sore hip bones or swollen hands or being hungry, thirsty, or all together all at once . . . and it is probably this ignoring of basic misery that makes a backpacker." Perhaps I'm not a backpacker; my basic misery occupies my mind. I'm certainly not made for the thirty-mile days dashed off by *real* long-distance hikers. I'd much rather spend time watching birds, identifying flowers, drawing, and writing. I want to engage with the land the way another naturalist, Edwin Way Teale, describes in *Journey into Summer:* "For a naturalist, the most productive pace is a snail's pace. A large part of his walk is often spent standing still. A mile an hour may well be fast enough."

I love hiking to remote places and experiencing the beauty and silence that can be had only through the labor of a long hike. But once I get there, I want to be still and appreciate the wildness I worked so hard to reach. I resent Curry for hustling us over long days so he can get to town to use the internet. Twenty years ago, by this stage in the hike, we had fallen into "leader" and "follower" roles, him as leader because of his greater strength, speed, and stamina on the trail and his industriousness in camp. He's restless and can't sit still, so once we stopped hiking for the day, instead of taking time to relax, we went to work pumping water, cooking dinner, setting up the tent, hanging the bear bag. I could not take a few minutes to just be. On the trail each day, he tried to hurry me along, reaching Durango his primary objective, while mine was to take in all the sights, sounds, and sensations. Now, once again, he's calling the shots and trying to rush us, while I resist passively, sleeping in and dragging my feet.

The steep trail levels off in a lush meadow spangled in purple larkspur, red paintbrush, and pink elephant's-heads. I barely notice; even the elephant's-heads fail to make me smile. I turn over and over my physical discomfort, my resentment of Curry, my frustration that this hike isn't going the way I'd envisioned. Happiness feels as elusive now, in this spectacular place, as it did when I was dragging myself to a miserable job in the midst of a miserable Maine winter. A butterfly flutters past, across the trail and into the meadow, a simple cabbage white, one we would consider a pest back home on our broccoli plants. As it dances over the flowers in a random, drunken fashion, I remember the tiger swallowtail beckoning me the first day of our hike and the white admiral that led me toward Kenosha. Both butterflies derailed my negative thought train, took me out of myself and into the world around me.

Before leaving Maine, I read an essay in *Orion* magazine by John Landretti called "Nameless Season," about the liminal phase, which he describes as "that strange moment after one has given up a familiar way of being but has not yet come into a new identity." The essay resonated with me, as I prepared to leave a job where I'd worked most my adult life, eager for but uncertain about what would come next. I shared the essay with friends and wrote, "That's exactly where I am now. A snake that has just shed its skin and is fresh and glistening—and vulnerable." A friend commented that I was less a snake, more a butterfly. At the time, I found the butterfly metaphor to be cliché, but now that butterflies appear when I'm struggling, I think she was right. Of course, it's July—flowers are in full bloom and butterflies abound. But even if they weren't sent for me, I can be receptive to their meaning, or my interpretation of it, that I'm in a pupal stage, a time of becoming. Inside a chrysalis, the old, no-longer-necessary parts of the caterpillar break down to feed the growth of the butterfly. That's got to be uncomfortable, if not painful. Like this hike.

The cabbage white flits away and more butterflies appear as I hike along. Two with dark, velvety brown-and-orange wings settle near each other on the trail in front of me. In tandem, they rise and settle, rise and settle again. A bright yellow sulphur flits from blossom to blossom. Tiny blue azures hover over the grass at the edge of the trail. Butterflies drift into sight each time my thoughts drift toward the negative and bring me back to a place of calm receptivity and appreciation.

The trail tops out at Searle Pass. I join Curry and the boys on a pile of rocks at the base of a talus field and we settle in for lunch. Sharp pika calls sing out from the between rocks. The American pika, a fuzzy little handful of a creature, is related to rabbits and hares, though it doesn't look much like a rabbit, with a roly-poly body, rounded ears, and no discernable tail. Pikas don't hop like rabbits either, but they are always in a hurry. When they're not perched outside their dens, sniffing the air for trouble, they dash from one rock hole to another. They farm hay, or at least gather it, spending the summers collecting grass to dry in the sun and store for winter dining. Pikas don't hibernate, so they need food to fuel them through the long, cold months in their dens. Miniature haystacks fill the spaces between rocks. Deposits of a white, chalky substance surrounded by sunbursts of bright orange lichen mark spots where pikas urinate. With each squeak, I look for the caller, but their buffy-gray coats blend perfectly with the rocks and I only catch glimpses as they scurry into crevices.

After lunch, we descend from the pass into an undulating basin with the unlovely name of Searle Gulch. The trail winds along a grass and sedge meadow peppered with white bistort and yellow paintbrush. Willows cluster in the lower, wetter areas, and steep slopes dotted with patches of snow climb up from the meadow edges to meet knife-edge ridges and tumbled talus slopes. White-crowned sparrows dart from bush to bush. The billowy white clouds that drifted around the sky all morning have joined together, massing in gray-bottomed merengues that portend rain. We need to cross this three-mile meadow, crest a saddle on Elk Ridge, traverse Kokomo Gulch, climb over Kokomo Pass, and descend again to the safety of tree line before the rainstorm hits.

I come upon Curry and the boys lounging beside a stream of clear snowmelt washing over bare rock. Curry has eight water bottles lined up before him.

"Think we should collect water here?"

"No. I think we should get out of the open before this thunderstorm hits."

Curry glances at the sky. "I don't think the storm is that close."

Blue patches appear between dollops of cloud overhead, but a dark gray-brown mass hovers over Elk Ridge.

"Fine. Why don't you and Milo collect water while Emmet, Zephyr, and I hike ahead?"

At their rapid pace, they could easily fill a few quarts and catch up. But Curry sighs and gathers up the bottles.

"If it's dangerous for you to be out here, then it's dangerous for us, too."

Curry, Milo, and Emmet quickly disappear down the trail, leaving Zephyr and me trudging behind. The clouds thicken, the sky darkens. Thunder rumbles on the other side of the ridge. We won't get over Elk Ridge, let alone Kokomo Pass, before the storm hits. Another rumble of thunder and large raindrops splash down. We put up our umbrellas and slip on our pack covers. Raindrops come down faster and closer together until we're in a downpour. We pass clump after clump of willow, places to hunker out of the storm, but I see no sign of the others. Finally I catch sight of their bright umbrellas among the bushes near a small pond.

We wade through wet, ankle-high grass toward them.

"Is it a good idea to be near a pond in a thunderstorm?" I shout over the drumming of the rain.

"Why not?" Curry says.

"Because lightning is attracted to water."

"It is?"

I'm pretty sure *lightning is attracted to water* is not top-secret lifeguard intelligence, but it's too late to argue. Rain gushes from the clouds, lightning dances along the ridge, and thunder rolls down the valley, echoing off the rimrock. Zephyr and I scrunch among the bushes beneath our umbrellas, and I soon forget about the pond as our first above-tree-line storm overwhelms my senses. Amid the cracking and booming of thunder and pounding of rain, I watch a pair of hikers make their way over the ridge. Their decision to ascend the ridge in the storm was dangerous, but so was mine to bring my kids here in the first place, where over the course of forty-two days there would be almost no way to avoid exposure to thunderstorms. I'm on edge, nervous not only for my children's safety, but also their mental wellbeing. How will they react to this first real thunderstorm? When the rain finally passes, we emerge from the willows. The kids, undaunted and exhilarated by their first above-tree-line thunderstorm, practically dance as they shake out their pack covers and umbrellas. As we move up the soggy meadow, Curry, Milo, and Emmet trot ahead, leaving Zephyr and me behind again.

The valley to our left, down below our high, pristine meadow, is deeply scarred. The opposite hillside is crisscrossed with roads. A barren, treeless slope weeps ochre and black. At the headwaters of Tenmile Creek, a feeder stream of the Blue River, a stagnant green pool floods the valley bottom. A side stream entering from the other direction fans out in a delta of chalky white that turns sulfurous yellow where it blends with the green water in the pool. At the top of the valley, a sloped earthen dam holds back more green water. Beyond the ponds, a mountain and ridge have been sliced away in terraces of bare, reddish-blond earth. Though I've been bracing for this sight, my heart clenches in dismay at the scene of flayed, oozing earth spread before me.

Since around Breckenridge, we've been traveling along the Colorado Mineral Belt, a roughly 250-mile-long zone of ore deposits that cuts diagonally across the state, from north of Boulder to west of Durango. On a map, Colorado's mining districts roughly follow this ribbon of ore, with a few outliers. Gold, silver, lead, and other metals were deposited here around forty-five to seventy-five million years ago. As basement rocks uplifted during the Laramide orogeny, magma and hot water containing dissolved metals, carbon dioxide, silica, and sulfur compounds welled from deep within the earth's crust into faults along this band. The magma solidified into masses of igneous rock known as plutons, while the metals in the hydrothermal fluids became concentrated, forming the ore deposits that would drive the state's fortunes. Erosion had already reduced the Laramide Mountains to rolling hills when, around twenty-six to thirty-five million years ago, volcanoes spewed lava and breccia, creating new rock, damming streams, and freezing fossils in time. Igneous intrusions from this era formed huge deposits of molybdenum in three areas of the state, one of which we see before us.

During the gold and silver booms of the late 1800s, miners found no use for the slippery gray-blue ore they found on Bartlett Mountain, a 13,555-foot peak thirteen miles north of Leadville. In 1917, as the United States entered World War I, assays found the ore to be molybdenum sulfite, a rare metal useful for hardening and strengthening steel. The price of the ore went up, and the Climax Company opened a mine on Bartlett in 1918. The mine went into a brief postwar slump until car manufacturers began using molybdenum to strengthen steel components of automobiles. Climax operated for much of the twentieth century as the largest molybdenum mine in the world, employing half the residents of Leadville and Lake County, providing economic stability in a region that had been rocked since settlement by the boom-and-bust nature of the mining industry. As a result of reduced demand for vehicles during the recession of the late 1970s and competition from other sources, the mine reduced its workforce in 1982 and shut down in 1992. Over the next two decades, remaining mine workers focused on diverting and treating water, building soil, replanting land, and reclaiming tailings ponds. The mine resumed operations a few years ago amid rising molybdenum prices, but today it employs a fraction of the workers it did in the 1970s.

Initial mining operations at Climax took place in tunnels. A 1935

Popular Mechanics article declared, "When the millions of tons of ore have been removed from this underground mine on a mountaintop with the aid of hundreds of tons of powder its sides will be caved and scarred but the summit of old Bartlett will still remain the same to all outward appearances—as big and as imposing as ever." But Bartlett Mountain is not nearly as big and imposing as it was. The mountain's summit has dropped 150 feet and its south face is gone. The honeycomb of mining tunnels collapsed into a "glory hole" a half-mile across, and underground mining was replaced with open-pit methods, in which mountain and ridge have been shaved into the naked benches we see across the valley.

Over eighty years, Climax produced four hundred million tons of molybdenite ore, which generated about two million tons of molybdenum. The waste rock was dumped in the tailings ponds in the valley below. Fremont Pass, where Highway 91 crosses the Continental Divide west of the glory hole, receives close to thirty feet of snow each year, resulting in around forty thousand acre-feet of water running through the property. Three-quarters of the water is diverted, leaving ten thousand acre-feet to filter through the tailings ponds. If molybdenum mining must happen, it's better here than at an undeveloped site, but the mine sits at the headwaters of four river systems, and its owners have asked the Colorado Department of Health and the Environment to raise the standard for molybdenum in drinking water from 210 parts per billion to 9,000 parts per billion.

Zephyr and I turn away from the scarred mountain and head toward Elk Ridge. As we near the saddle, we pause to take pictures of pikas poking their noses out from the talus. In this spot twenty years ago, a strange creature walked over a hummock, turned onto the trail, and headed toward Curry and me. It was the size and shape of a small footstool, with a pointed face and stumpy tail, and was covered in brown-gray fur with white patches on each cheek and a white stripe traveling from its nose up over his head. We stood transfixed, mentally eliminating all of the animals it was not—marmot, skunk, wolverine—before recognizing it as a badger, the first I'd seen in real life. Like a short-sighted old man who'd lost his glasses, it focused on the trail before its nose as it plodded toward us. When it came within a dozen yards, it stopped, raised its head as if to sniff the air, then turned off the trail and climbed uphill, pausing to look back at us over its shoulder.

No strange animals greet us on the trail today, but dark clouds nose their way over the slope above us. I give Zephyr a nudge.

"Hike as fast as you can over the ridge. Don't wait for me."

I put my head down and will my legs to cover ground, watching tiny alpine flowers zoom by. I want to drop my pack and sit and draw flowers, become deeply acquainted with the world on high. But I need to catch up with my family and get to lower ground before the next round of thunder.

Curry and Zephyr wait for me on the saddle. A powerful manure odor fills the air, but we are too high in the mountains for cows and I haven't seen any sign of sheep.

"What's that smell?"

Curry points to a pile of rocks up slope. Zephyr is taking pictures of the culprit, a marmot who has amassed an enormous poop pile outside his burrow. Marmots look a lot like their cousin, the woodchuck, but are tawnier, fatter, and more endearing, possibly because they're not ravaging our garden. Or maybe it's the sharp, piercing whistle they emit. I tell Zephyr that Grandma Meyer called them "whistle pigs." He likes the name and applies it to all the marmots we see for the rest of the day.

From Elk Ridge, the trail crosses another stretch of alpine meadow and pops over the gentle rise of Kokomo Pass, where Milo and Emmet wait for us. The storm has backed off, for now, the clouds breaking apart in cottony clumps that expose patches of blue. We stop to collect water at a crystal clear seep, then head toward camp. The valley carved by Cataract Creek is carpeted in wildflowers of every color—tall yellow sunflowers and purple larkspur, red and magenta paintbrush, creamy death camas lilies, pale pink wild geraniums. They remind me of Grandma and Grandpa Meyer. No specific moment comes to me, but this valley feels like the kind of place they would have liked. They both grew up on farms and they grew extensive vegetable and flower gardens in their yard in the suburbs of Denver. Grandma painted scenes similar to the one before me—steep gray-blue rock mountains in the background, pointed firs in the midground, bright wildflowers up close. What would my grandparents have thought of this trip? They camped in a trailer, never a tent. Despite, or maybe because of, her childhood on a farm, my fastidious grandmother would have been horrified by the filth that has accumulated on our bodies and belongings, and she would not have tolerated the relentless flies. She wouldn't have cared much for the bathroom facilities, either. Grandpa died when I was twelve and my memories of him are less clear. I remember his smile, close-mouthed and thin lipped, but genuine and bright. Before he died, he and Grandma made several trips around the West in their trailer. Though they might not have appreciated certain aspects of this trip, I think they would have loved this meadow of wildflowers, and I sense them close by as I walk among the paintbrush, sunflowers, and larkspur.

We come to a beautiful campsite just below tree line—a flat area near the creek, ringed by spruce trees. The clouds are gathering again, and I want to stop here and set up camp before it rains. But Curry wants to hike through the rain to keep the tent dry. I suspect he really wants to get to Leadville early tomorrow. So we hike on, and Zephyr and I trail behind as we make our way down the valley. He stops to pick wild strawberries growing along the trail and shares half of his harvest with me, and I savor the sweet, tart, burst-of-sunshine flavor of each tiny red berry. When the rain starts, we put up our umbrellas, and he points to a hole beneath the roots of a tree.

"I wish I was a little chipmunk," he says, "so I could crawl in that hole and stay dry."

I don't want to curl up in a hole in the ground, but I wish I were back at that lovely campsite, snug inside the tent. As we hike, the creek drops into a deep gully, the steep hillsides leaving few camping options. The trail rounds a bend and pops out of the spruce and pine forest onto a sagebrush-covered slope that transports me to childhood visits to my aunt and uncle who live among sage-covered hills outside of Leadville. I pick a sprig of sage and rub the leaves, releasing the warm, spicy smell that, along with sun-warmed ponderosa pine needles, is the essence of home to me. Beyond the sage, we enter a dense aspen forest. The creek runs deep in a channel far below the trail. There's nowhere to set up a tent and we're approaching the boundary of permissible camping. Finally our gold tent comes into view, set up at the edge of a large area of bare, sooty ground with a massive stone fire ring in the center, surrounded by tall trees. It's a dark and gloomy spot deep in the valley Cataract Creek has carved, overhung by dense spruce. Zephyr and I skid down a steep embankment and drop our packs. The rain has stopped, for now, and I mix our cold dinner next to the cold fire ring.

Emmet, Milo, and Zephyr disappear into the woods near the creek and come back a few minutes later. "Want to see the cabin?"

They lead me downstream to where a lean-to perches on the edge of a waterfall. White, foaming water plunges over a sheer wall of pinkish stone as if drilling deep into the center of the earth. I peer into the shelter, the falls roaring in my ears. The open side of the lean-to looks out over the abyss.

"You wouldn't want to stay here if you were a sleepwalker," I shout over the din. My vision swims with images of my kids plummeting over the waterfall, and my insides quiver as I feel myself pulled to the edge of the cliff. I tell them dinner is ready and herd them back to camp.

The rain returns as we crawl into the tent. I'm drifting off to sleep when I'm startled awake by a loud stumbling, breaking of branches, and crash followed by a cry of "ouch!" I'm certain it's a bear, a talking bear. I stick my head out of the tent. The bear is wearing a white rain skirt and has a headlamp strapped to his tattered straw hat.

"Hi," I say.

"Hi," the bear says. "Mind if I share your campsite?"

"Go right ahead."

I crawl back under my sleeping quilt and begin to doze again when I hear more bears.

"Hey, can we share your campsite?"

"Sure," I call out and listen for a while to the sounds of tents being set up, low voices, coughing, until, finally, the bears all settle to sleep and I, too, drift off.

In the morning, we find our campsite shared not by bears but by three young men. They stand around the empty fire ring, chatting with Curry. Milo, spooning cold oatmeal, gazes wistfully as one of them dollops chocolate-hazelnut spread on a tortilla. After breakfast, we pack our gear and wave goodbye to our neighbors. A young woman sitting outside her tent at a campsite a short distance down the trail jumps up and run over to us.

"Here!" She hands us each a square broken off a chocolate bar. "Your reward."

"For finishing our oatmeal," I say.

We gratefully take the chocolate gift and hike on in good spirits. Throughout the morning we leapfrog with the young woman, Abby, and two of the men who had camped by us, Tortilla and Adrian. The bear who first fell into our site never materializes. At a rest break, Curry asks everyone his usual question: "On a scale of one to ten, how do you feel today?" Abby, a teacher, offers a different version—a rose, a thorn, and a bud—the rose being a highlight, the thorn a low point, and the bud something you are looking forward to. While everyone's rose varies, from chocolate to waterfalls, we all agree that the dark, wet morning is the thorn and a night in town the bud.

The trail takes us downhill, through aspen forests and hills of sage-brush, rabbitbrush, and shrubby cinquefoil, to the base of the waterfall that plunged from the lean-to. From there the trail leads us out of the woods into open meadows staked out in a grid of white string. A line of people stands at the edge of the forest, each holding a metal detector. A short, burly man in a Marine Corps cap and mirrored sunglasses tells us they're looking for unexploded ordnance.

For three years during World War II, thousands of soldiers lived and trained here at Camp Hale, the original base of the army's celebrated Tenth Mountain Division. World-class ski champions, New England college skiers, mountaineers, and outdoorsmen from all walks of life were recruited to join the army's first company of mountain soldiers. In the surrounding mountains, the men trained in downhill and Nordic skiing, rock and ice climbing, and combat, while also testing cold-weather gear and equipment and, of course, weapons—leaving behind the unexploded ordnance this crew is looking for.

Marine Cap warns us to stay on the trail and be careful.

"If the bombs haven't exploded in the last eighty years, I'm not too worried," I say cheerfully.

He doesn't crack a smile. "They're every bit as dangerous now as they were eighty years ago."

We hike on, heading into the toe of a long, boot-shaped valley. In late 1944 and early 1945, nineteen thousand of the mountain troops shipped out to Italy. They made their way up the Italian peninsula to Verona and Lake Garda, facing a hundred thousand German soldiers and helping force Germany into its first voluntary surrender of the war. The division suffered heavy casualties: nearly four thousand were wounded and almost one thousand killed. During their four-month campaign, the troops used little of their mountain training, except during a daring nighttime assault on Riva Ridge. On that night, February 18, 1945, members of the division climbed the steep face of the ridge in the dark and fog, taking the Germans by surprise and breaking the Nazi stronghold on the Apennine Mountains. After the war, returning Tenth Mountain Division soldiers went on to create a legacy of outdoor recreation and mountaineering, including the founding of at least seventeen ski areas. Among the Tenth's veterans were Paul Petzoldt, who established the National Outdoor Leadership School, and David Brower, long-time Sierra Club president and wilderness champion.

Prior to its conversion to a military camp of more than a thousand buildings, this valley, then known as Eagle Park or Pando Valley, was a hummocky swamp through which the Eagle River and a number of feeder streams wound. The military drained the wetlands, straightened the river and streams into a network of ditches, and filled and flattened the valley floor with tons of dirt excavated from nearby mountains. Months before leaving for Italy, the mountain troops were sent to Texas to train for swamp maneuvers, and the army made plans to scupper Camp Hale. After a brief stint as a secret CIA training ground for Tibetan soldiers, Camp Hale was deactivated in 1965 and returned to the Forest Service in 1966. Fifty years later, the valley is still flat and dry and the river still runs straight, but not much is left of Camp Hale itself.

We stop to rest near one of the remaining artifacts, a long, crumbling concrete wall built into an earthen berm, the ammo depot of the rifle range. Swallows flutter in and out of the open doorways and graffiti covers the wall. From there, the trail heads uphill into beetle-killed and thinned lodgepole forest, climbs higher into dense, healthy forests, and winds back downhill, through more sagebrush and along a wet meadow and old railbed, part of the original route of a branch line of the Denver and Rio Grande, one of the rail lines caught up in the frenzy to reach the mining camps. The track laid here in 1881 was abandoned in 1890, when the Rio Grande converted to standard gauge and realigned the route. Supply trains serviced Camp Hale over the newer route, and belching coal smoke from the three locomotives required to hoist trains up the steep grades, combined with the soot from the soft coal used to heat buildings, enveloped the valley in a haze that gave the troops persistent sore throats and coughs.

Prior to the arrival of the railroad, which brought this cheap and plentiful coal, the homes and businesses of Leadville used charcoal for heat and cooking, and smelters used it to render oar into silver. Entrepreneurs set up charcoal kilns in wooded valleys all around the mining areas, slowly burning wood under restricted air supply in beehive-shaped ovens to distill it into a purer carbon form that burns hotter and cleaner than wood. In the process they denuded the neighboring hillsides of trees. The trail passes by the crumbling remains of three of these kilns as it nears Tennessee Pass. We pause to inspect the ruins. While twenty years ago, part of all three kilns still stood and one of them maintained its domed shape, only one crumbling wall now stands among rings of rubble. The ruins of the kilns and the forests cloaking slopes that had once been cleared are a reminder of how temporary humans and their activities are compared to the timelessness of mountains and forests.

At the trailhead, we eat lunch and discuss our hitchhiking strategy. We decide to split up, reasoning that few cars will have room for five. Assuming that two cute eleven-year-olds will cancel out the creepiness of a grubby, bearded man, Curry takes the twins and beelines for an older couple in a white Prius preparing to leave the parking lot. They cheerfully rearrange their car to fit Curry, the boys, and their packs while Milo and I head to the road and stick out our thumbs. Car after truck after suv zooms by. Eventually, a big, white delivery van slows and pulls onto the gravely shoulder a few dozen yards past us. A petite blond woman in the driver's seat tells us to hop in.

"I only have one jump seat." She indicates the fold-down black plastic passenger seat next to the open doorway.

"That's okay." I climb in over the seat and into the back of the box truck where I settle myself on a pile of rolled-up black rugs. Milo hands me his pack, perches on the jump seat, and slides the rickety door firmly closed. From my vantage, looking out the windshield from the floor, I can see only the cloudy sky and the tops of mountains zooming by as the truck speeds down the winding road, too fast after having moved two miles per hour for the last twelve days. I'm a terrified we'll fly off the road as the van rounds a curve. But we make it to town, and the driver drops us off in front of the post office.

Milo and I collect the resupply box, find Curry and the twins on a bench out front, and walk a few blocks to a cheap motel. While Curry checks us in, the twins tug at my arm and point to a basket filled with travel-sized tubes of toothpaste. Before we left Maine, I'd attempted to dehydrate toothpaste into what one of my lightweight backpacking books referred to as "toothpaste dots"—pearls of hardened toothpaste you chew into a lather before brushing. But the toothpaste never dried, instead congealing into gummy blobs, which I dusted with baking soda to keep them from sticking together. At some point in the process, the gummies took on a fishy taste, and the boys hate brushing with them.

"Are these free?" I ask the clerk.

"Help yourself."

Emmet and Zephyr each take a tube, but I do not. Even though I'm not a fan of brushing with fishy toothpaste globs, I cringe at the thought of wasting the two full tubes of toothpaste I'd processed.

A short run of outdoor stairs leads to the "family suite," a dim room with two king-sized beds and a couch that smells as if someone died on it and wasn't discovered for a few months. But there's room to spread out our gear. Curry takes our dirty clothes to the laundry facility, located in an alley around the corner from the motel, on his way to the library. The boys and I dump out the resupply box on the grungy coverlet on one of the beds and sort meals and snacks into food bags. I take a long, luxurious shower and, while the boys take turns showering, wash bowls, spoons, and water bottles in the sink. Clean and refreshed, the twins settle down to watch television, while Milo and I, dressed in rain gear, head out to find him a long-sleeved top to replace the too-small one we sent home. Curry has also commissioned us to look for a pair of synthetic underwear for him, an item I'd neglected to pick up when I bought his trail clothes, because he wears mesh-lined shorts, not realizing he'd want underwear to sleep in.

Milo and I walk down Harrison Avenue, Leadville's main drag, and I note the changes since I was last here. When I was a kid visiting my dad's hometown, Leadville was firmly in "bust" mode. Most of the mines had closed, Climax was limping toward shutdown, and even to a child from the not terribly prepossessing suburb of Englewood, it appeared dirty, dismal, and one step removed from a ghost town. We'd visit the five-and-dime store, buy t-shirts at one of the few tourist establishments, and watch the dispiriting Boom Days parade and burro races, where men dressed in buckskins coaxed, dragged, and all but carried recalcitrant steeds across the finish line. But, in a state whose history has been defined by booms followed by busts, Leadville has a special knack for riding the comet's tail of fortune as it rises and crashing to earth when it falls.

Leadville's first boom began in April 1860, when gold was discovered in nearby California Gulch. Within a few weeks, more than ten thousand miners had poured into the settlement of Oro City and extracted some two million dollars in gold by the end of summer. The first bust came a little over a year later, when the gulch's placer gold was spent and Oro City nearly deserted. A mini-boom came in 1868 with the discovery of a promising new vein, but Leadville's real boom days wouldn't begin until 1875, after a pair of miners analyzed the heavy black sand that clogged their sluice boxes and found they were sitting on lead-silver carbonates.

Shipping ore by ox cart and railroad to smelters in St. Louis cost more than it was worth, but once the first smelter came to town in 1877, Slabtown, named for the wood shanties built up around the smelters, took off.

Among California Gulch's first inhabitants were Horace Tabor and his wife Augusta, named for her hometown, the capital of Maine. Prim and practical, Augusta ran the store and post office, cooked and did laundry for miners, took in boarders, and weighed gold dust, which she kept safe in her blouse. Dreamy, generous, and ready to take a chance, Horace, or HAW, prospected his own claims, grubstaked anyone who came through the door, and invested in or bought mines. Augusta's good sense kept the couple afloat in the early days, and HAW's chance-taking made them rich. In 1878, Horace was chosen mayor of the town, rechristened Leadville, and, later that year, elected lieutenant governor of Colorado. As Tabor's fortunes rose, so did Leadville's. By 1879, the town was rife with hotels, saloons, theaters, and brothels.

After the Tabors moved to Denver, HAW built a hotel and an elaborate opera house in the new state's capital and embarked on a series of affairs. In 1880, he met famed beauty Baby Doe. HAW filed fraudulent divorce papers and entered a bigamous marriage with his young bride before obtaining an official divorce from Augusta and legally marrying Baby Doe in Washington DC during his one-month U.S. Senate term. The Tabor fortune, which may have reached as much as $10 million at its peak, and the fortunes of Leadville began to fall after the panic of 1893, with the repeal of the Sherman Silver Act of 1890, which had artificially inflated the price of silver. Tabor's star fell as fast as it had risen, and HAW and Baby Doe lost their homes, their money, and their investments. After Horace's death, Baby Doe returned to the Matchless Mine in Leadville, never doubting in her husband's certainty that one day it would again yield a fortune, and died alone in her cabin in the winter of 1935.

With the devaluation of silver, many mines and smelters in Leadville closed down, while others turned to lower-grade ores, which had been tossed aside during the boom years. The town boomed again during World War II, when the government offered price incentives for copper and zinc, and again briefly during the Korean War. In the 1940s, more efficient milling techniques spurred an effort to reprocess old mine waste, but most mines had closed by the late 1950s and the last smelter shut down in 1961. It would have been bust times for Leadville if not for Climax, still stripping molybdenum out of Bartlett Mountain and employing half the county. The town managed to stay a mining town in more than name, which was more than could be said for the many mining-districts-turned-ski-resorts around the state, and in the early 1970s a lead and zinc mine started up.

But by the late 1970s, concerns began to arise around the technicolor water seeping into the Arkansas River from Leadville's mining district. Some days, the river ran red from dissolved iron. Less visible, but more harmful to fish and wildlife, were other dissolved metals, like cadmium and zinc, and the acidity of the water itself. In 1983, the U.S. Environmental Protection Agency designated California Gulch a Superfund site. Eventually, the entire town would be swept up in the designation, as well as the Arkansas River below its confluence with California Gulch, for a total area of eighteen square miles.

The designation was meant to fast-track cleanup of the sources of polluted runoff to the river and, eventually, the riverbed and floodplain, but it didn't work out that way. The site was complicated by the extent of the pollution sources. The mining district, which covers eight square miles, harbored hundreds of miles of underground tunnels, more than a thousand shafts, half again as many prospect holes, and close to two thousand additional manmade cavities. Among these was the Yak Tunnel, which extended four miles, from high in the Mosquito Range to California Gulch, dewatering mines along the way and dumping the water into the gulch, where it headed straight for the Arkansas. Then there were the tailings piles and slag heaps distributed around town, the smelting waste that had been used as road pavement, and the fine-grained fluvial tailings from the mills, which had been poured directly into the river and nearby streams. An even greater complication was that the people of Leadville did not welcome government interference.

Miners are, by nature, optimistic. In Leadville, that optimism was justified: When gold was depleted, silver became queen. After silver crashed, there came zinc, copper, and lead, and there will be molybdenum for a long while to come. Cleaning up mining's legacy would relegate mining to history. It threatened not only the town's livelihood—the companies that operated the few working mines would be identified as responsible parties—but also its identity, its past, and its future. Initial missteps by EPA and state agencies when trying to implement the new law turned wary townspeople into fierce opponents of the agency, Superfund designation, and any efforts to clean up the mining district.

What followed was more than two decades of a contentious two-step as state and federal agencies grappled with the town, with each other, and with outside parties that popped into the picture each time the main combatants reached detente. Meanwhile, the Reagan and Bush administrations worked to undermine the law, and in 1995 Congress allowed the Superfund tax to expire, leaving the expensive program chronically underfunded. Despite the obstacles, EPA and its ever-shifting dance partners managed to remove some tailings piles, cap others, and divert water around those deemed of historical significance. They instituted a voluntary lead testing and abatement program, installed water treatment systems for the most intractable mine drainage, and created impoundment areas for drainage from active mines. EPA also worked with local organizations to create the Mineral Belt bike trail and to preserve or restore mining structures that had deteriorated over a century of neglect and vandalism. Nine of twelve cleanup units have been partially removed from the National Priorities List, meaning the risks in those areas have been managed to the agency's satisfaction. The work is ongoing and some elements of the remediation, such as water treatment, will have to be maintained in perpetuity.

Today, Leadville appears to be brushing off the dust of the mining and Superfund busts and getting ready to take off with the next boom. While parts of the main street, like our motel, are entrenched in "bust" mode, several brick buildings along Harrison Avenue have been spruced up, with freshly painted signs advertising coffee shops, bars, restaurants, boutiques, even an acupuncture clinic. The people wandering the sidewalks look like they're about to hit the Leadville Trail 100, an ultramarathon that undulates over nearby mountains—women in capri leggings and fleece jackets, long, blond ponytails pulled through the openings in their Colorado-flag-adorned trucker hats; men in running shorts, shiny down vests, and technical sneakers. The town's latest boom, as a mecca for those seeking a cheaper vacation alternative to Aspen or Vail, is taking off.

The town's new identity gives Milo and me plenty of options for places to look for a shirt. After checking three overpriced gear shops, we find him a ten-dollar shirt in an outdoor-themed consignment store, but no underwear for Curry. On our way back to the hotel, we pass the Tabor Opera House, where my dad used to work as an usher in high school. Built by Horace Tabor in 1879 in a record one hundred days from stone, brick, steel, and cement brought from Denver by wagon, it's seen better days. Fading gray paint mars part of the brick facade. The arched lintels are chipped and peeling. Dingy curtains hang in a few second story windows and yellowing newspaper covers others. The opera house, having weathered the bust times and outlived its audacious creator, his pretty young wife, and its more opulent Denver cousin, the Tabor Grand Opera House, which was torn down in 1964, is poised for a facelift and ready to join Leadville in its next boom.

We detour down an alley lined with cast-off furniture and garbage, a symbol of the uneven distribution of fortune even in boom times. In a low building we find the dank laundry room. The wash cycle has finished, but dirty water fills the machine, backwash from a utility sink filled with murky water. I set the washer to spin and Milo and I try to pull the clothes out and into the dryer faster than the nasty water can flood back in. After three spin cycles we get the clothes transferred and return to the hotel, where Emmet and Zephyr are jumping on the beds and bickering over the TV. The room is cramped, the air stale with the stench of past guests and that vile couch.

"Come on guys. Let's go get ice cream."

It's nearly dinner time, but I don't care. I'm exhausted from the last three days of hiking, frazzled from a few hours in town, grossed out by our hotel room, and annoyed with Curry for rushing us here then leaving the resupply chores and the kids' entertainment to me. I deserve ice cream. We all do.

We find an ice cream shop a couple blocks from the motel and sit outside licking our cones. Dark clouds have gathered in the sky and the wind has picked up, blowing chilly air down Harrison Avenue. Leadville, I remember from childhood visits, is always cold. Sitting at just under 10,200 feet above sea level, it has the distinction of being the highest city in the United States. With altitude comes cold. The average annual temperature is thirty-five degrees, and winters get so cold that when my dad was a kid he once broke a frozen sheet in half when taking it off the clothesline.

We pick up our laundry on the way back, change out of rain gear into cleanish clothes, and pack the rest into our backpacks, along with the sorted food and snacks and other gear. When Curry returns, we go out for Mexican food. After we place our orders, Curry tells us about an article he read while he uploaded videos.

"This woman hikes into the Grand Canyon almost every day and packs out the remains of campfires, because coals never break down."

It's a story I would normally be interested in, but I can only stare at him wide-eyed. I can't believe he's calmly telling me about magazine articles he read all afternoon in the quiet library while I spent the last five hours trapped in a smelly hotel room with hyper and overstimulated kids, doing all of the resupply chores, and searching town for underwear for him. If I weren't so exhausted, I'd be furious. Instead I shovel cheese enchiladas into my mouth, stewing in silence.

I can't sleep. The bed is hard and lumpy. The sheets are badly pilled, which makes them feel gritty, and they don't fit the bed properly, sliding around on the mattress. Emmet and Zephyr pull out their sleeping mats and quilts and retire to the floor. The room is hot. The couch exudes its foul odor. Traffic noise roars through the one tiny window. There's apparently a law against mufflers in this town. And I'm still annoyed with Curry.

I must fall asleep at some point, because I'm woken up at six by a diesel truck idling outside our window. Curry has already left to upload more videos. I take another shower, because who knows when I'll get another chance, and coax the boys to stuff their sleeping quilts in their packs. When Curry returns, we go out to breakfast and walk to Grandma Lani's house, a two-story gabled structure, sided with rolled asphalt material in an imitation brick pattern. It hasn't changed much since last I saw it, thirty years or so ago. Small yellow poppies grow along the front, but none of the large red ones I remember. On those childhood visits, we'd gather around the kitchen table, and Grandma would mix my older sister and me each a glass of Tang and cut us a slice from the fruitcake she kept in a red tin in the cupboard. A plastic curtain beyond which I never ventured hung in the doorway to keep the heat from the oil burner from leaking out into the rest of the house. My dad tells me the house was so cold in the winter that if you brought a glass of water to bed with you, it would have a skim of ice on the surface by morning. Even though she was barely five feet tall, Grandma Lani made me nervous, with her cap of curly gray hair, strong Austrian accent, and the cardigan sweaters she wore even in summer, with a tissue stuffed up the sleeve. She pronounced my name the Austrian way—*Ahn-dray-uh*, with a rolled r.

The house looks empty and sad, and I try to imagine raising kids in it, in this high mountain town where winters get so cold your laundry breaks, after having lived and raised children in war-torn Europe. While our hike through five hundred miles of Colorado's mountains may seem like an extreme experience for a family to go through, it's nothing compared to the journeys millions of immigrant families have taken to seek a better life in this country. After World War II, economic prospects in Europe were bleak, with thousands of people out of work or living in refugee camps. Because my grandfather came from Yugoslavia and had not changed his nationality when he moved to Austria and married my grandmother, the family was eligible for relocation to a host country. In the summer of 1951, my grandparents sold or gave away most of their possessions and moved to a refugee camp in Salzburg, followed soon after by one in Bremen, Germany. An epidemic in the camp kept the family quarantined until December, when my grandparents and their seven children, ranging in age from ten months to twenty years, boarded a Navy troop ship. Over nearly two weeks the ship tossed on stormy seas, and the passengers did not emerge on deck until they glided into New York Harbor on calm water, the lights of the city welcoming them to their new home.

Less than two months after they arrived in the city, my grandfather and my dad's two oldest brothers were hired to work in the Yak Tunnel and mining complex, and the family traveled by train to Leadville and moved into this house, which my grandparents later bought from the mining company. My uncle tells me that the mountains rising around Leadville reminded the family of Austria, where the older kids had learned to ski before kindergarten because that's how they got to school. But the 1950s were largely bust times for the mines, and my grandfather was in and out of work until after the Korean War, when the mine he worked for closed down and he took a job as a janitor at the Miners Union Hall. The two oldest sons had trained as electricians in the mines and eventually moved to Denver. Only one of my dad's siblings stuck with Leadville and the mining industry, working for Climax until retirement. My grandfather lived in Europe through both world wars, losing an eye at age seventeen when soldiers threw fireworks into a bonfire. He worked in dangerous conditions like hydroelectric tunnels and mine shafts. But it was fatal injuries from an accident with a piece of mechanical equipment in the Union Hall's bowling alley that killed him. On her own, Grandma finished raising the younger kids and stayed in her home for most of the next thirty years.

I line my kids up along the curb and take their picture, Grandma Lani's asphalt-brick house standing forlorn behind them. Gentrification hasn't hit this part of town, a block away from downtown, but it's on its way. Across the street, a tiny pink bungalow is for sale, with an asking price of more than $200,000, though its water system is only usable in the summer. Deep pockets are snapping up houses and apartment buildings and turning them around as vacation rentals. Meanwhile, descendants of miners and many Latinx residents, who make up 40 percent of the county's population, will likely be squeezed out by the town's newfound fortunes.

This should be a touchstone moment for my kids—a link to their past, a connection with their maternal grandfather's side of the family, but I'm not sure this sad little house has made much of an impression. I expect it's the last time I'll ever see it, and I bid it a silent, melancholy goodbye, feeling like a failure as a mother and a daughter for raising my kids so far away from my family, from their heritage. We return to the motel, pick up our packs, then stop at the post office and grocery store, head out of town, and start hitching. We trudge along the edge of the asphalt, the hot sun beating down on us as the few cars going our direction fly past. After a long while, a dark-haired woman in a blue minivan with a cracked windshield pulls over, and we pile in. She tells us she's lived in Leadville for twenty-one years.

"It doesn't snow like it used to," she says. "The snow used to come up over your cars. You had to dig them out. You had to swim through the snow. Not anymore."

It's the same story everywhere—climate change, social change, environmental change. Nothing is the way it used to be, sometimes for the better, sometimes for the worse. It's good if Leadville sees a little economic revival, but not so good if people like this kind woman don't benefit. And warmer winters and less snow means more bark beetles and more people vying for less water. What will these mountains, these towns be like in another twenty years? Another hundred?

The woman drives us a few miles out of town, dropping us near the entrance to the trailer park where she lives, and we hop out and resume hitching. Car after car after car zooms by as we trudge along the hot shoulder, thumbs out. We have miles to go to the pass. I'm starting to worry we'll have to walk the whole way when two guys in a pickup truck pull over. We shove our packs in the back and climb in after them. At the pass, we eat lunch beside the Tenth Mountain Division monument, shoulder our packs, kick the dust of town off our heels, and head down the trail.

PHOTO 1. Andrea and Curry on the Continental Divide near Georgia Pass on their first Colorado Trail hike in 1996.

PHOTO 2. Milo, Emmet, and Zephyr cross the Continental Divide near Georgia Pass.

PHOTO 3. Emmet, Zephyr, and Milo regale each other with stories as they hike together through a Douglas fir forest.

PHOTO 4. Zephyr bounds across a boulder field in the Tenmile Range.

PHOTO 5. The boys contemplate a swim in one of the Porcupine Lakes in the Holy Cross Wilderness.

PHOTO 6. Emmet treks toward the summit of the highest peak in Colorado on the North Mount Elbert Trail.

PHOTO 7. The boys make their way down the steep slope beyond Hope Pass.

PHOTO 8. Milo, Emmet, and Curry cross Snow Mesa on a glorious, post-thunderstorm morning.

PHOTO 9. The whole family at the high point of the Colorado Trail below Coney Summit.

PHOTO 10. Zephyr, Milo, and Emmet rest on a rock beyond Carson Saddle.

PHOTO 11. Summers are short in the Colorado high country, as attested by this lingering snow field in the Weminuche Wilderness.

PHOTO 12. Emmet and Zephyr look out over Junction Creek Valley from Gudy's Rest on the last day of their thru-hike.

PHOTO 13. Curry, Milo, Zephyr, Emmet, and Andrea celebrate completing the trail at the Junction Creek trailhead near Durango.

6

FALSE SUMMIT

It was another cloudless morning,
one of the many here on which one
awakes early, refreshed, and ready to
enjoy the fatigues of another day.

—ISABELLA BIRD

DAYS 13–16: JULY 22–25, 2016
Tennessee Pass to Mount Elbert

We hike up a gentle grade, through lodgepole forests that have seen a fire
in the past—charred, knee-high stumps interspersed among large live
trees. No birds sing in the heat of the afternoon and no breeze stirs the
treetops. Nothing breaks the silence of the woods, but chatter fills my
head. At the grocery store, I discovered that my debit card was blocked
because of a suspicious purchase made since we've been on the trail. I
called the bank to order a new one, but I can't stop wondering how it was
compromised. Will the replacement arrive in time? Do I have enough
cash? What will happen with bills on automatic payment? Even Henry
David Thoreau was plagued by town worries following him down the
trail. "I am alarmed when it happens that I have walked a mile into the

FIG. 7. Old-man-of-the-mountain (*Tetraneuris grandiflora*)

woods bodily, without getting there in spirit," he wrote. "But it sometimes happens that I cannot easily shake off the village. . . . What business have I in the woods, if I am thinking of something out of the woods?" I try to shake off the village and bring my spirit back onto the trail.

We're heading toward the Holy Cross Wilderness area, named for the Mount of the Holy Cross, a peak that retains snow throughout the summer in a cross-shaped crack. One of my favorite places from our hike twenty years ago, I remember its lush valleys, naked peaks, and ridges of raw, jagged rock towering over turquoise alpine lakes. At that point in our hike, in late August, autumn had moved into the mountains, but in the Holy Cross, summer had been given an extension, with wildflowers in full bloom, especially paintbrush in shades of crimson, rose, wine, and orange. The trail merely cuts through the southeast corner of the wilderness area, and it took us less than a day to hike through. I'd vowed to return and explore the area at a more leisurely pace, but we've never been back. This time our planned campsite falls within the wilderness, so we'll at least have a few extra hours to experience its wonders.

As we follow the old road that forms the trail here, we pass a solo thru-hiker and a couple who have left their kids at home while they try out backpacking for the first time. In the late afternoon, the trail diverges from the road and within a mile enters the wilderness area. The land has a wild, untouched feeling to it, with big, old trees and mossy ground. We pass the remains of an ancient, dilapidated cabin—no more than a few logs forming four corners—and I wonder about the trappers, loggers, and prospectors who found their way to remote, out-of-the-way places such as this, where summers are short and winters extreme. What made them settle here? How long did they last? Did they appreciate the beauty of the place, or did they see only terrifying wilderness to be tamed, or animals, trees, and mountains to be churned into money? Did they make an offering and pray to the local god or goddess, as Thoreau wished the loggers of his time would do: "I would that our farmers when they cut down a forest felt some of the awe which the old Romans did when they came to thin, or let the light to a consecrated grove (*lucum conlucare*), that is, would believe that it is sacred to some god."

We wind our way along a stream, then the trail climbs steeply. As I trudge upward I vow never to go hiking again. Clouds move in and the temperature drops. Rain coming. No butterflies urge me along the trail, but the bright bunches of yellow arnica, pink and red paintbrush, and blue larkspur remind me of butterflies and metamorphosis and that this is supposed to be hard.

The forest we climb through feels ancient, sacred—not in the Christian way implied in the wilderness area's name, but in a way much deeper and holier than religion. Huge gray granite boulders dot the hillside. Towering fir trees march up the steep slopes, their trunks so thick two people could wrap their arms around them and barely graze fingertips. Low green plants with tiny leaves carpet the ground. I see another thru-hiker lumbering up the trail ahead of me, and I take comfort that I'm not the only one struggling on this slope. But I don't want to catch up with him. The banal talk of fellow hikers would break the spell this forest is casting. I'm starting to transcend. When we hiked the trail twenty years ago, I had hoped for a "spiritual" awakening, although I didn't know what I meant by "spirit" or how to get in touch with mine. I understand now I was searching for transcendence, to rise above pain, exhaustion, frustration, heat, cold, rain, and snow and appreciate the beauty of my surroundings, to feel at one with the natural world. Looking back, I'm sure I had moments of transcendence—those images that stuck with me years after we hiked the trail, including here in the Holy Cross.

I pass the other hiker on a sharp bend in the trail. He and Curry are talking and I'm able to slip by with only a "Hi, how's it going?" The trail continues up, up, up through the afternoon. Curry passes me, and I catch up with Zephyr. We plod along together. At the top of the climb, the trail skirts a wide meadow, the Porcupine Lakes shimmering at the far end. Curry's setting up the tent between the nearer lake and a copse of ragged fir trees. Milo and Emmet, stripped down to underwear, crouch on a rock, summoning the courage to swim in the cold water.

"They call these lakes?" Zephyr asks as we make our way toward the pools, each about the size of a farm pond. Then he looks toward Mount

Galena towering over the meadow, jagged and snow frosted, and concedes, "Well, to be fair, Maine has lakes. Colorado has mountains."

We join Emmet and Milo at the pond. The twins and I plunge into the icy water, but Milo doesn't join us.

"I saw a leech over there," he says by way of excuse.

"Meh, a leech won't hurt you," I say, but he stays on the rock.

Later, while rice noodle ramen soaks in cold water and our underclothes dry on a line, I explore a low hill carpeted in wildflowers. I move from penstemon to paintbrush to lousewort, photographing and sketching. This is how I wish every evening was—a majestic campsite and time to revel in it. The clouds that gathered as we hiked have cleared, and the setting sun casts a pink glow on the sharp, snow-dotted ridges to our east. As evening cools, mosquitoes descend in clouds, whining and looking for bare skin. We swat and squirm and slurp rubbery noodles as fast as we can, then complete our camp chores in record time and dive into the tent.

The temperature drops overnight, but the cold doesn't drive away the mosquitoes. They swarm even more thickly at daybreak. We try to hurry through our morning routine, but it takes longer than usual to get ready, and we don't start hiking until almost eight. The trail climbs and climbs, angling diagonally up the mountainsides in half-hearted switchbacks. It's impossible to rest because mosquitoes and biting flies descend when I slacken my pace. As I creep along, I envision throwing myself against the near-vertical hillside and clawing my way up, a method of travel that would surely be easier than this slow, slow climb. I curse every Maine friend who has said to me, "Western trails are so much easier than eastern trails because of the switchbacks."

The day grows hot as we travel through meadows of wildflowers, each more colorful than the last. Paintbrush in red, orange, yellow, and pink. Blue chiming bells and purple asters. Fir and spruce trees towering over masses of yellow sunflowers. We head downhill for a while, toward a cluster of small lakes, and far too soon the trail takes us out of the wilderness area toward Turquoise Lake.

Twenty years ago, we'd taken a detour off the trail here and stayed two nights at a campground on the west end of Turquoise Lake, riding into

Leadville for our resupply with a pair of government geologists. I don't remember how exactly we got to the lake, or how far away from the trail it is, but I assume it can't be far, and I'm looking forward to swimming on this hot day. But when we come to an intersection with the side trail that would lead us to the shore, Curry vetoes the idea.

"Have you looked at the map?"

"No, I haven't looked at the map. You have it in your pack."

"The lake's at least a mile from the trail."

He turns and continues down the trail. The boys follow, and I fall in line. Even if I wanted to run after him, shouting, it would be pointless. Though we get along well most of the time and agree on most things, when we don't, we argue in circles, never getting anywhere, never resolving anything. He's made his mind up that a two-mile round-trip detour is out of the question.

As we hike, I fume, annoyed at the Colorado Trail planners, who didn't build the trail to the water's edge, furious with Curry for force-marching us on three seventeen-mile days so he could use the internet but refusing to take a side trip for a swim. My hike has been absorbed by his hike, just like my life has been absorbed by his life—living a mile from his childhood home, known to most people as "Curry's wife," trapped in Maine because he got homesick whenever we tried living in Colorado. After a silent lunch, Curry and Milo power hike ahead while Emmet, Zephyr, and I follow, making our slow way toward Mount Massive Wilderness area.

Mount Massive, Colorado's second-highest peak, at 14,429 feet, is my favorite mountain. Named not for a dead white guy, but for its appearance, a hulking pile of rock whose ragged flanks reach in all directions, almost a range unto itself. Alluring and foreboding, the mountain looms over Leadville, withholding and releasing clouds, wisps of fog, black thunderheads. We won't be climbing Massive this hike, but Curry and I climbed it last time. We had camped the night before in a subalpine meadow, perched on the mountain's right knee, crawling into our tent as a tempest swept the slope. Thunder and lightning rocked the meadow, hail pounded our tent, and I cowered with each flash and boom, waiting for a bolt of lightning or dislodged boulder to flatten us.

We survived the night, the next morning dawned clear and crisp, and we headed cross-country to meet the summit trail. As we hopped over the first tiny stream I tripped over my hiking poles and fell in, suffering a bruised shin, a wet boot, and scraped finger. Though I managed to cross the next two trickles of water without incident, my boots grew wetter and wetter as we slogged through swampy hummocks of grass and willow. Once out of the marshy area, we climbed up through fir forest and an ancient clear-cut, where trees had been cut at chest level, the remaining stumps withered to sinewy, splintery wood. No new trees had grown in to replace them.

Beyond the ghost forest, we climbed alpine meadow slopes, angling toward the ridge where we expected to meet the summit trail. During a snack break at a rocky nubble, we watched an older couple work their way upward, he with a fluffy beard and funny hat, speeding ahead, she much farther behind, looking like she wished she were elsewhere. As we climbed toward the saddle, rain came down, followed by soft balls of ice, somewhere between snow and hail.

The weather cleared momentarily as we met three young couples on their downward journey, looking wet and miserable. They'd turned back at the saddle when the graupel started. We forged on, pausing at the saddle long enough to snap a photo before hunkering under a rocky overhang as the real weather hit. Inside our shelter, we lunched on cheese and crackers as more little ice balls blanketed the talus slope below. A wintery chill came on the wind, and we huddled close together until the boulder above us started dripping meltwater, driving us back onto the trail. As we hiked upward, my fingertips stiffened red around my poles, but soon a window opened in the umber clouds, letting in blue sky and sunlight. We continued along the ridge, over several false summits. As we neared the peak, a coppery weasel poked its pointed nose out from a pile of rock and regarded us, strange creatures climbing a mountain in the snow.

From the summit we could see blue-black clouds hovering over Mount Elbert, Massive's neighbor to the south, dropping a curtain of rain and slinging lightning bolts onto the other peak. We lingered long enough to take a picture before heading down the mountain, passing the older couple, still doggedly working their way upward despite the ominous skies. From the rocky nubble where we sheltered earlier, we struck out cross-country, taking the most direct route to our little tent on the mountain's right knee. Exhilarated by our successful climb through wind and snow, we gratefully crawled into our blue oasis.

Today we will pass by around the region of the mountain's ankles. Our schedule doesn't allow for more than one sidetrack, and we plan to attempt Mount Elbert in two days. I don't mind. Though climbing Massive was thrilling, I'm happy to let the mountain loom over me as I hold onto the memory.

The trail takes us uphill through an arid landscape of pink gravel, lodgepole pine, and sparse groundcover, and the sun shines from a clear blue sky.

"We're back in the desert again," Emmet says, and indeed this area feels much like the Buffalo Creek burn area, only with trees.

Though the sun doesn't beat down with the intensity it did at Buffalo Creek, the day is hot, and Emmet is wearing dark blue rain pants because he got his shorts wet at Porcupine Lakes.

"Emmet, do you want to stop and change? Your shorts are probably dry by now."

"Nope."

I ask again several times throughout the day, and each time he declines. Emmet has an amazing tolerance for discomfort. He's never bothered by the high neck of his backward shirt rubbing his throat. He wears his backpack diagonal across his back so he can tilt his head back to look up. Many evenings, he pulls off his shoes to reveal socks bunched up in wads around his toes. Tonight when he takes his rain pants off, granola bar wrappers will fall out of the legs where he stuffed them in lieu of pockets. Yet he never complains of being uncomfortable.

The trail winds up, up, up around the flanks of Bald Eagle Mountain. When we see blue sky appear through the trees on the slope above, we think we're near the saddle, but instead of making one last switchback up and over, the trail marches straight ahead, toward a higher part of the mountain and more switchbacks. After this happens several times, the trail dips downhill for a distance. I pause to check the data book.

"I think that was the saddle. It should be downhill from here."

But the trail turns a corner and climbs uphill again.

"I knew it was too good to be true," Zephyr says.

Finally we crest the saddle and angle along the contour of the slope and into Mount Massive Wilderness area, where we find Milo and Curry sitting next to the trail. They hop to their feet, saying another hiker told them there were nice campsites past the stream a short way down the trail. They set off and we follow. Though we're hot and tired and haven't stopped for a break since lunch, we're eager to get to camp and settle in. The trail crosses a stream, but the campsites appear small and sloped, so we hike on. The next stream cascades over an even steeper hill through dense trees, with nowhere to camp. Curry checks the map and points to an area of widely spaced topo lines.

"Looks like we should be able to find a flat area to camp here."

We hike another mile along a steep hillside, but when we come to the place, we find it's not as flat as it looked on the map and is overgrown with dense vegetation.

"We could camp here and go back to the last stream for water," Curry says. "Or we can go back and camp at that first site."

"Where would we camp here?" I say, gesturing at the thick shrubs that cloak the slope on both sides of the trail. I drop my pack, sit, and flip open the data book. There's another stream in half a mile, but no campsites.

"Well?" Curry jiggles his hiking poles impatiently.

"How long did you and Milo sit down after that long, hot climb? Because we haven't had a break all afternoon."

"That's not my fault. You just kept hiking."

"You said we would camp near the stream, not hike two more miles."

Zephyr drops his pack and runs down the trail.

"Where are you going?" I call after him.

"To see if there's a campsite by the next stream."

We sit in stony silence. Milo and Curry waited for nearly an hour. They're rested and bored, anxious to move on. I'm hot and exhausted, too tired and irritated to think. This trip has spun out of my control. I feel like I have no say in how far we hike each day, when or where we stop, how long we spend in town, whether we take a side trip, because I'm the slow hiker, not the leader, not the one who carries the map and covers the miles with ease. Not the man. I know I have a tendency to want to dictate the terms for how events unfold, and I know I have a sense of ownership over this hike. But I'd settle for more give-and-take and less tug-of-war, especially since it's a war I'm losing.

I sit quietly, drink water, eat a granola bar, and puzzle over our options. I don't want to backtrack two miles to the first, inadequate campsite and cover those miles again tomorrow. I'm also worried about Zephyr; he's been gone a long time. We need to hike on and look for him soon. If we reach the stream and find no place to camp nearby, we can carry water to a dry site farther along. I'm too annoyed with Curry to talk to him, so, without a word, I shoulder my pack, pick up Zephyr's, and hike on.

Even though Zephyr's pack isn't heavy, it's awkward to carry. I shift it from one aching arm to the other. After about a quarter of a mile, I drop it on the side of the trail. He'll have to come back and get it himself. Before long, he meets us coming back down the trail. He reports that the area near the stream is too steep and forested for camping and heads back for his pack. At the stream we fill all the water bottles and bladders and continue another mile or so to a point where the land uphill from the trail smooths out in a flat area of open pine forest.

Curry sets up the tent while I make dinner. Milo asks to borrow the lighter from the emergency kit I carry so he can melt the end of a cord.

"How come you don't have a lighter, too, Papa?" he asks.

"Because Mama won't let me have one."

"You're welcome to have a lighter. Go to the store and get one. Or do you need me to buy everything for you, including your underwear?"

"Stop yelling at Papa." Milo stretches his cheeks down in the way he does when he's trying not to cry. He can't stand to hear us argue.

"Why do you have to be so miserable all the time and make everyone else miserable, too?" Curry says.

"So I'm not allowed to have an opinion?"

"We should all just let things go," he says.

This should be the crescendo, the moment we hash out our differences, our frustrations with each other, but Curry's already signaled his desire to drop it, silencing me with his implication that I don't have legitimate complaints. I've lost this argument, as always. The boys, as always, take their dad's side. Four pairs of eyes glare at me. I forced this trip on them. I made them endure flimsy gear and cold food. I wouldn't let Papa have a lighter or a pair of underwear.

I need to get away and there's only one place to go—into the woods. I storm uphill, through the forest of sparse pines, rehearsing in my mind all the things I should have said. Halfway up the slope, I come to an odd-looking pile of pink granite rubble downhill of a four-foot hole in the ground. Farther uphill, a mound of yellow sand reveals an even larger crater. These odd, isolated signs of past prospecting activity distract me from my litany of complaints, and I climb on, looking for more. At the top of the hill, three trees grow out of a tumulus of pink stones. Beneath a three-legged structure of weathered wood, a USGS marker is embedded in a rock.

I wander around the top of the knoll, wondering what these odd rock piles and the wooden structure mean. I'm aware that if I go down the back side of the hill I could get lost for real. But I'm not ready to return to camp yet, so I head toward the trail at an angle from the path I followed up. I find a gnarled old pine with one dead leader, the bark missing from a third of its trunk, a woodpecker hole drilled in the side. It's a beautiful tree, its twisted limbs reaching higher into the sky than all the nearby trees, even those growing higher up the slope. The tree, still alive despite its damage, whispers to me, "Persist." I continue downhill and come across two more craters and an old road. Again I wonder if those who cut trees and blew holes in the hillside ever stopped to wonder at the majesty of this place, of Mount Massive looming in the distance, or if they only saw gold and green.

I follow the old road to the trail and head back toward camp. A young couple passes by. The man, dark hair pulled back in a ponytail, hikes close on the heels of the woman, who wears braids and glasses. I recognize them from the Holy Cross Wilderness, where they had set up their blue-green tarp tent on the far side of the Porcupine Lakes. They look about the same age Curry and I were when we hiked this trail the first time. They duck their heads shyly when I say hi. I want to shout, "Don't do it!" Whatever they're contemplating—living together, marriage, kids—it's too much trouble. I've been joking with people that twenty years ago Curry and I hiked the Colorado Trail together and *still* got married. Now the challenge will be to stay married after hiking it a second time. Right now that seems doubtful.

Resentment scrapes against my soul, like a sharp file. Resentment over the fight about the lighter, about him dragging us over long days for his convenience, about having done all the preparation and packing for this trip without help or thanks from him. About him focusing on his own desires and needs, while I'm left to make sure the kids are safe, healthy, and happy. Over the fact that I'm not allowed to express my feelings. Other resentments, years of them, come curdling to the surface: being trapped in Maine; having had to work a miserable job while he built his business; imbalances in our domestic roles—a division of labor that, after children, solidified along the gender lines we had both grown up with despite the *Free to Be You and Me* utopia of equity I'd been led to expect. Now we've dragged that imbalance to the wilderness with us.

As I head back along the trail toward our campsite, my legs feel leaden in a way they didn't when I wandered over the hillside. The trail itself adds weight, the collective troubles of all those who have gone before— Archaic and Prehistoric peoples, Native Americans, explorers, prospectors, mountain men, loggers, miners, hunters, hikers. They've all climbed onto my back for the ride. These mountains have seen their share of tragedy—the Utes driven out of their homelands by white settlers, miners dead in horrific accidents, Baby Doe frozen in her cabin, my grandfather injured at the Union Hall. Some people believe emotion infuses place. Perhaps those who tried to scrape a life from these mountains left a mark on the land, a weight pressing down on those of us who travel through for amusement. I add my own small measure of unhappiness to the mountain's collective burden.

Rain pours in the early morning, letting up while we get dressed but resuming with lightning and thunder as we emerge from the tent. It's what we expect at the foot of a mountain that makes its own weather. No one mentions last night's argument. After my ramble on the hillside, I returned to camp and washed dishes and prepared breakfast in silence. Then I read to the kids while Curry plugged in his earphones to edit his video. This morning we are cordial but cold. Once we start hiking, the rain dissipates. Curry and the boys speed down the trail. I hike alone. The trail eases down a gentle slope through sparse forest. Late in the morning, another thru-hiker catches up to me. We exchange pleasantries and I expect him to pass, but he is as slow as I am and stays a short distance behind.

I've felt shamed by my speed-hiking husband and sons and the thirty-mile-a-day hikers I've read about. Except when my hiking partners were toddlers who stopped to pick up every rock and caterpillar along the trail, I've been the slowest hiker in almost any group. I believed I was bad at hiking because I was slow and that in going on this hike I would set a good example for my children, showing them it's possible to enjoy things even when we're not good at them. Now I see the real lesson is for me, about not measuring myself against others. It's fine to move at my own speed. Each hiker has a different pace. Some are sprinters, other marathoners, others slow and steady tortoises, like me. But that doesn't make me a bad hiker.

As I round a switchback, I startle a lone mule deer. He bounds uphill, covering a dozen yards in a few leaps then stops to look back at me. His smooth, pale-brown coat looks soft and clean. His big ears stand alert in front of two-pronged antlers. We regard each other for a minute or two, then he leaps away, up the hill and out of sight. I continue along the trail alone, daydreaming about other hikes I'd like to take—preferably by myself. Many thru-hikers travel solo, for good reason. The work of fitting one's hiking style with another person's (or four other people's) and balancing the needs, expectations, and priorities of members of a group is as exhausting as the hiking itself. I never considered taking this trip without my family; I wouldn't want to be apart from my children for that long, and I wouldn't want them to miss out. But now I daydream about some day in the future, when they're grown and I can strike out on my own, unencumbered by responsibility.

Perhaps Curry and I should have learned how to work together over the last twenty years, but we are no better at communicating now than we were the first time we hiked the trail, and we're still fighting over the same crap. He hikes fast; I hike slow. He wants to hurry and get there; I want to slow down and be here. He wants to put in miles; I want to enjoy a pleasant campsite. He can't sit still; I could lie on my back watching clouds all day. But our first Colorado Trail hike was made up of much more than disagreements about goals and hiking styles. We also sat back-to-back in camp, leaning on each other as we wrote in our journals. We lay side-by-side in the tent, talking and dreaming. We shared the work of setting up and taking down camp. We enjoyed each other's company enough to make plans for the future. This time we aren't experiencing those moments of connection that eclipse the aggravations.

The trail climbs steeply up to a ridge, one of Massive's knees. Below the saddle, we pass the green-blue tarp tent of the Shy Couple, as I've dubbed the pair I saw last evening. We stop to rest on a log with a view of Mount Elbert, whose summit is our destination tomorrow. The boys strike out downhill at full speed, leaving me to hike alone again. Later, I catch up with Emmet and Zephyr at a stream crossing. They're leaping back and forth across the swift, narrow creek. I pause and try to absorb their delight in this moment, the wild abandonment of their activity, their obliviousness to miles and schedules and goals, to fights and frustrations. But I feel anxious about the time and still out of sorts over last night's argument. After a while, I urge them along, and the three of us hike together to the trailhead, where we find Curry and Milo waiting on a log, the tent stretched out to dry in the sun. Halfmoon Creek runs shallow and wide along the road, and Emmet and Zephyr take off their shoes to wade in the cold water and skip stones across its surface. The afternoon is getting on and we have a long way to go to get to a campsite, but again I check my impulse to hurry them along. These moments of playfulness are what they're going to remember about this hike, the whole point of being here, and I wish I could share their joy.

After the tent dries, we cross the road and climb up steep switchbacks as dozens of people pour down. I hope that because tomorrow is Monday the mountain will be less crowded. After we pass the junction with the North Mount Elbert Trail, the crowds thin out, and a day-hiking couple heading toward the trailhead pauses to chat.

"We're just fake hikers," the man says after I tell them about our hike.

"But you get to go home to hot food and showers and soft beds," I say.

They laugh and tell us about a nice-looking campsite next to a stream a couple miles down the trail. We find the site, a sliver of flat land on the steep slope, just big enough for our tent, bordered on one side by the trail, a narrow, fast-flowing stream curving around two sides, and tall, dense trees hemming in the fourth. We sponge off with icy stream water and do our camp chores among thick swarms of mosquitoes and little flies that Emmet has taken to calling "raisins."

"Go away, raisin!" he says when one lands on him.

"Tell your raisins to leave me alone," I say as I shoo away a half-dozen.

"They're not *my* raisins," Emmet says.

It's still light when we crawl into our tent, partly to escape the insects and partly to rest for tomorrow's climb. I read two chapters of *Treasure Island* to the boys then go out to pee one last time before bed. I have to cross the trail and head uphill into the trees to get the requisite distance from the stream, but a hiker is coming down the trail, so I busy myself picking up discarded hats and pack towels, pretending to tidy our campsite. We chat for a few minutes about his hike and ours, then two more hikers come along. One of them looks at our enormous tent and back at me.

"Are you with the family of six we've heard about?"

"Five. We lost one along the way."

"Oh, man, I'm really sorry."

"I'm kidding. There's always been just five of us."

We chat about our hikes and our plans for climbing the mountain tomorrow and wish each other well as they head down the trail.

It takes us as long to get ready in the morning as on a regular day, even though we only have to eat our cold oatmeal and toss lunch, snacks, and warm layers into our packs. We don't hit the trail until seven o'clock, late for mountain-climbing. But the sky is clear cerulean, and I hold out hope that we can summit the mountain and return to camp before the inevitable afternoon thunderstorms roll in. When we reach the trail junction, an older gentleman hands us each a postcard listing Colorado's fifty-four mountains over fourteen thousand feet.

"After you finish this one," he says, "you might decide you want to hike more."

At 14,433 feet, Mount Elbert is the highest mountain in Colorado and one of more than a dozen fourteeners accessible from the Colorado Trail. I've never cared for the phrase "peak bagging" for mountain climbing. It implies an adversarial relationship with the natural world—conquering and owning a mountaintop—and a checklist attitude toward wild places. I want to approach a mountain with humility. It's the *only* way to approach a mountain, which stands thousands of feet taller than a human, has preceded us by millions of years, and will outlast us by millions more. But I love standing on top of a peak, the highest point for miles around, buffeted by the wind, with views of mountains stretching to the horizon in every direction.

After our snowy climb up Mount Massive twenty years ago, we were treated to three days of clear weather. The first of these we spent hiking from our campsite on Massive's flank to a base camp near the junction with the South Elbert Trail. We got up with the sun next morning, cooked breakfast, filtered water from an old beaver pond, and set off up the mountain. The trail ascended steeply through a golden-green aspen grove. We passed a few groups on the way up through the forest, but nowhere near the hordes we saw coming down the mountain yesterday. The trail was badly eroded, resembling a road where vehicles got off track, leaving three or four deep ruts in the alpine meadows. After a long but fairly easy hike up the grassy shoulder of the mountain, we reached the summit and were greeted by an icy blast of wind from the northwest. We donned extra layers, enjoyed the view, ate lunch, and chatted with other hikers, trading stories and being congratulated on our thru-hike. Around twenty people shared the peak with us, and, to my surprise, I enjoyed the social experience on top of the world. After a few more photos, we headed down the trail, broke camp, and made our way to the town of Twin Lakes, where a hot German meal and a featherbed awaited us at the Nordic Inn, our first night indoors in twenty days.

Today we'll follow a different route up the mountain, the North Elbert Trail. According to the data book, each trail gains the same elevation over the same distance, and so should be about the same level of steepness and difficulty. The trail starts out gently, switchbacking through the woods, but soon grows steeper, angling straight up the slope. Emmet and I hike together through the thinning trees. This trail is as badly eroded as the South Elbert Trail, the braided pathways of many hikers' feet forming ruts. When we stop to rest in the last patch of spruce trees, three gray jays descend on us, perching within inches of the log we sit on. Experienced camp robbers, these birds know where to look for handouts, but we deny them bites of our granola bars, every calorie precious to us. Emerging from the trees, we find the others resting in a meadow of fading yellow buttercups and withered old-man-of-the-mountain sunflowers. We flop down and gaze north toward Mount Massive, along whose skyline fluffy white clouds are gathering. After a few moments' rest, we resume the climb, Curry and Milo trooping ahead while Emmet, Zephyr, and I trudge behind. Across the valley I can see the South Elbert Trail wending its gradual way up the mountain, its ascent so gentle that a mountain bike makes its way up among the climbers. I wish we'd taken that trail.

People stream past us up the mountain, defying my hopes for a quiet day. An estimated twenty thousand to twenty-five thousand hikers summit Elbert each year, and it appears that about half of them have chosen today to make their ascent. A dude wearing only shorts and sneakers with a tiny water bottle strapped to his wrist runs uphill past us, his long hair bouncing as he goes. It's a clear day, so far, but mountains are unpredictable; the weather can turn in a moment, altitude sickness can strike, a loose rock can turn an ankle. But this guy is a symptom of a new approach to the outdoors: mountain as giant fitness center, the world's biggest Stairmaster, where hazards don't exist, people are obstacles, and reverence for—or even awareness of—the natural world has no place. I try to adopt a more generous assessment—maybe he's running to the top to meditate or collect weather data—but later in the morning he runs down, pinballing off upward-climbing hikers, including my children, confirming my impression of a jackass.

We climb higher and higher and slower and slower. Farther up the slope, the wildflowers appear fresher, having bloomed later than their more withered brethren downslope, I assume. Already people who passed us on their way up earlier are coming down. The fluffy white clouds that we saw over Mount Massive drift across the sky. I hope they stay fluffy and white. I catch up with Milo sitting on a rock at a switchback. He tells me he feels light-headed and has a headache, probably a mild case of acute mountain sickness. I give him ibuprofen and urge him to drink water and eat a snack. After a few minutes he says he's okay to go on, but I stick close behind to keep an eye on him. Ahead, a nubble of red earth mottled with green rises above us. The cloud-dotted blue sky shines beyond it, but it's too soon to hope for the top of the mountain.

Curry, waiting for us farther along the trail, confirms my pessimism: "False summit."

It's an apt metaphor for life—whenever you feel you've surmounted your greatest personal challenge, like raising small children or working a terrible job or hiking a difficult trail, you find an even taller and steeper obstacle to climb on the other side, like teenagers or unemployment or an even steeper portion of trail. I've left the job that was killing me. I've given myself permission to live the life I want, if only for this summer. But I'm still me, with all my faults and failings, and I still need to figure out how to move forward, and be happy, within the confines of marriage and a family and a life that's destined to be in Maine for at least the next decade. So far I haven't done well in communicating my needs and desires. I've let go, for today, those other frustrations and resentments, setting aside the desire to resolve them in favor of the immediate, physical, and just plain easier goal of climbing the highest mountain in Colorado. But eventually I'll have to face the future.

We hike on until we reach a pile of rocks at the edge of a big cirque of reddish stone. The steep headwall sloping down from Elbert's summit is dotted with patches of snow whose meltwater drains into a green tarn at its base. The clouds have merged and darkened, spitting tiny balls of ice on us, and the wind whips down the slope.

"Let's go back down!" Emmet shouts. "I don't want to get blown off the mountain."

We huddle near the rock pile and put on warm clothes. A patch of blue gleams over Elbert's right shoulder, and I hope the clouds will blow over and allow us to reach the top. But the gray mass overhead doesn't budge. Thunder rumbles to the north. A blue-black cloud trails a veil of virga over the valley between Massive and Elbert. The flow of people has reversed, most of them now pouring downhill, although a few continue doggedly up, including a couple in jeans and leather jackets, their pocket radio blaring. One of the descending hikers tells us the clouds look even worse on the other side of the peak, so we join the downward stream of disappointed climbers.

Emmet, who had trudged up the mountain like his feet were made of lead, turns into the horse who smells the barn and gallops downhill. I stick with Zephyr, who is studying the rocks we walk over in search of signs of past lightning strikes. When we reach the trees, we step off the trail and pull lunch out of our packs. A woman Curry met earlier in the day gives us two big handfuls of fresh cherries from her orchard. A light rain patters down, and after lunch we hurry to camp. It's only two in the afternoon, and Curry wants to put in more miles. But there's no good reason to pack everything up and hike for an hour or two only to set camp up again. We have a short distance to go tomorrow, and the kids and I want to relax and enjoy the rest of the afternoon, so we decline the suggestion and crawl in the tent. It's a small victory, but I feel I've regained some agency over this hike.

The boys and I write postcards and play rummy and I read them a few more chapters of *Treasure Island*. We emerge long enough to eat cold beans and rice before scrambling back inside to escape mosquitoes and "raisins." We didn't make it to the top of the highest mountain in Colorado, but none of us is too disappointed. We're warm and cozy in the tent, where we've spent a whole afternoon enjoying each other's company, a scene that almost exactly matches what I pictured when I first dreamed up this hike two years ago.

FIG. 8. Alpine spring beauty (*Claytonia megarrhiza*)

7

WATERSHED

A withdrawal from man's society into that of nature is our greatest safety
valve (and also one of the most immediate reasons for retaining our
wildernesses, great and small). The benefits of wandering are there for
anyone who makes the time and cares to develop an observant eye.

—ANN HAYMOND ZWINGER

DAYS 17–18: JULY 26–27, 2016
Mount Elbert to Hewitts Gulch

We wake with town in the air and get an early start. We have about five
and a half miles to hike to Twin Lakes, where we'll meet my two aunts
who are serendipitously vacationing there. But instead of enjoying the
gentle downhill hiking, I worry about next week, when we'll head into
unknown territory—the Collegiate West route. This eighty-three-mile
length of trail was added to the Colorado Trail two years ago, forming
a keyhole loop halfway between Denver and Durango. Beyond Twin
Lakes, hikers can take the Collegiate East route, which, for the most
part, follows the original path of the Colorado Trail, skirting the Collegiate Peaks along the range's base, or they can take the Collegiate West
route, which sticks close to the Continental Divide and entails climbing
a high pass each day.

We've been taking it easy since Leadville, hiking eight to eleven miles a day. What if we can't manage sixteen-mile days over rough terrain? Do I even want to hike big mile days, or finish this hike at all? This question nagged me our entire first Colorado Trail hike—why am I here and why should I keep hiking? I never came up with a satisfactory answer. Now I mentally revisit my motivations for hiking: To immerse myself in my heart's home. To spend time in nature, away from "real" life. To have close, undistracted time with my children. So my children develop a close relationship with the natural world. To press a reset button on my life. To find happiness. Oddly, getting closer with Curry was one of my goals on the first hike, but nothing about our relationship made it to my list this time around. I'd taken it—us—too much for granted to recognize that even a twenty-year-old companionship requires work.

The trail travels through lodgepole forests, the ground littered with withered gray trunks piled like pick-up sticks, then descends into a woodland of aspen trees so old and big their normally smooth white bark has grown rough and gray, split into a diamond pattern at the base of the thick trunks. Through the trees, we can see the two lakes on the valley floor, one smaller than the other, a narrow isthmus separating the two. When we come to a sign for Twin Lakes with an arrow pointing straight downhill, Curry, dreaming of coffee, starts to take the spur.

"Wait," I say. "If we go into town here, we'll have to climb back up that steep trail late this afternoon." I'm worried about making our miles next week and want to get as far as we can today.

"Why would we do that?"

"We can't just skip five miles of trail."

Though I'm not a purist, skipping that much trail seems like downright cheating. Besides, the morning is pleasant and the hiking easy. We continue on, Curry casting a wistful glance down the spur.

Around a bend, we come upon a dry hillside of big, widely spaced trees with reddish bark and cones with little forked tongues. Douglas fir! I haven't seen this tree since the first week on the trail. Around another bend we come upon a stand of ponderosa pine, which we haven't seen in a while either, and I feel as if I'm welcomed by familiar friends.

As we near the highway, we find a handmade cardboard sign taped to a pair of hiking poles beside the trail. CT *Thru-Hiker? Hungry? Thirsty? Need a Ride? Trail Magic.* An arrow points left, to the nearby campground. Curry wants to pass by and head to town and coffee, but the kids and I are drawn by the irresistible pull of trail magic, and we make our way to a campsite where we meet trail angels Frankie and Hugie, recent empty nesters who sold their house in Wisconsin and moved into a camper van. They'd planned on hiking the Colorado Trail this summer, but Hugie developed heart trouble, so instead they've brought magic to the trail. While we chat, they lay out food on the picnic table. Emmet, Zephyr, and Milo help themselves to drinks and eat an entire box of sandwich cookies. Curry and I each take an apple. Frankie asks the boys what the best part of hiking the trail is.

"The sunsets," Zephyr says.

"And the worst?"

"Pooping in a hole."

"The best thing is trail magic," says Emmet, "and the worst thing is cold oatmeal."

"I think the best and worst things are the same, and that's that you only get to see your family." Milo says. "It's pretty awesome, but it also is kind of tiring sometimes." I know exactly how he feels.

Hugie passes him the cookies. "You'll remember this the rest of your lives."

"You'll cherish these moments," Frankie adds. "And bring your kids out here someday."

Milo tips back his soda. "We'll see about that."

Hugie offers to fire up the grill to cook burgers, but it's only ten in the morning and we plan to have lunch with my aunts. We thank them and hike the last half mile to the highway, which we cross via a concrete underpass, the boys making echoing sounds as we walk through.

"Hey, Milo," Emmet says, "this looks like a place where Batman would fight crime."

"And it's also like in Harry Potter five," Zephyr adds.

I love the way that fantasy and reality intertwine for the kids out here, and even though they're talking about scenes from movies, it's their imaginations that bring these images to life for them.

When we reach the other side of the tunnel, I call my aunt Sharon, leave a message, and suggest we wait a few minutes, to give her a chance to return my call. But Curry is desperate to get to town, so we put out our thumbs. The first car to pass pulls over. The driver gets out and, looking at a pickup truck parked nearby, asks us if we've broken down. Curry starts to tell him we need a ride when a boxy silver van stops. A tall, slender woman with strawberry blonde hair hops out of the driver's side and says, "Hey, do any Lanis need a ride to town?" It's my aunt Sharon.

"These are our relatives," I say to the other driver. "Thanks anyway."

He drives off and we arrange ourselves and our packs in the van, squeezing onto a bench seat spanning the back. Georgine's wheelchair is strapped into the front passenger area. She suffers from a degenerative muscular disease and has been bed- and wheelchair-ridden for years. She lives with my grandma and gets out rarely, but each summer Sharon takes her on a trip to the mountains. By lucky chance, they happened to be staying in Twin Lakes this week. Their lodge is next door to the former Nordic Inn, where Curry and I stayed the night in a fluffy feather bed after our Mount Elbert ascent. I'm disappointed to learn it's now called Twin Lakes Inn and the German restaurant has been replaced with a barbecue joint.

We cram our packs into my aunts' room, plug our devices into every outlet, and dump our resupply box onto their little dining table. Curry sits in a corner editing video while the kids help me sort snacks and meals into stuff sacks. I switch out maps and journals, refill sunblock, soap, and first aid supplies, wash food containers and water bottles, and load extra food, last week's maps and journal, and a big pine cone Zephyr found into the emptied-out resupply box for my aunts to take back to Denver.

"I'm sorry we're taking up all your space and making such a mess," I say, but Sharon and Georgine laugh.

"This is the most fun we've had all week," Sharon says.

There's no laundromat in Twin Lakes, so we'll have to go another week with dirty clothes. But I take a luxurious shower before we pile back into the van and head to the nearby town of Granite for lunch. At a small cafe the boys order burgers and I dig into a grilled cheese sandwich with avocado and mushrooms with sweet potato fries on the side and a sparkling grapefruit drink. For days I've craved potato salad, and while they don't have that on the menu, I relish my dish of coleslaw, as well as Curry's, Emmet's, Milo's, and Zephyr's, since they all hate mayonnaise.

Murals of aspen groves decorate the walls of the cafe and quotations from nature writers are painted on the tabletops. Our table has a quote from *Journey on the Crest* by Cindy Ross: "Returning home is the most difficult part of long-distance hiking. You have grown outside the puzzle and your piece no longer fits." When the twins were small, a friend gave me Ross's book *Scraping Heaven*, about her family's multiyear section hike of the Continental Divide Trail, beginning with the Colorado Trail when her kids were one and three years old. The book gave me the first inkling of hope that family life could include adventure, could consist of more than diapers, play dates, and car seats. It took our family a lot longer than Ross's to get here, but we've finally made it.

Back in Twin Lakes, we find that a thieving chipmunk has broken into the packs we left on the patio and has been nibbling on the homemade granola bars my mom sent in the resupply box. The boys chase it away then take showers while Sharon and I walk to the general store, where I pick up postcards and a giant bag of potato chips, then go in search of a mailbox so I can send out last week's postcards. Twin Lakes is a tiny village—its population of less than two hundred dwindles to even fewer during the winter, when the highway to Aspen over Independence Pass closes for the season. The town originated as Dayton in 1866, enjoyed a brief heyday as the Lake County seat, before that honor was transferred to Granite in 1868, then faded to little more than a ghost town. The discovery of silver over the pass brought new life to the town when a toll road was established connecting Leadville and Aspen, with Twin Lakes at its hub. Many buildings in town date from the late 1800s, including my beloved former Nordic Inn, and the village hasn't lost its historic charm to tacky tourist development.

When we return to the lodge, I tuck last-minute items into our packs while Curry uploads videos, Milo naps, and Emmet and Zephyr explore outside. After a while, Emmet runs into the room. "I just saw a fox or a squirrel. It ran up into a tree and now the magpies are attacking it."

We follow him around to the front of the lodge, where an enormous cottonwood grows. Half a dozen black-and-white birds hop among the tree's branches, chattering and shrieking, with more flying in from around the neighborhood. A high limb stretches almost horizontal and a furry thing with the body of a weasel and the face of a kitten dips in and out of what appears to be a hollow at a thickening of the limb. Georgine flips through her field guide and identifies the creature as an American marten. Judging from the magpies' ruckus, we guess it's feasting on a nest full of eggs or young. The marten pays no heed to the birds' distress and continues to raid the hollow in the branch. We watch for a while, then return to the room to finish packing. Emmet and Zephyr continue to explore the yard and come back to take me to see more of their discoveries—a recently shed snakeskin on a stone wall and a dead duckling near the stream. The twins, homesick for their pet ducks, give the duckling a proper burial.

Once we have everything packed, I sit down and pull on a stretchy ankle bandage to support my right foot, which has been aching for the last few days.

"Can I wear that?" Zephyr asks.

"Do your feet hurt?"

"No, but they feel weird."

"My feet feel weird, too," Emmet says. "But maybe that's because they're clean."

I laugh. Poor Dusty isn't used to clean feet.

Sharon and Georgine drive us to the east end of the lakes, where the boys clamber on a tall yellow gate to pose for photos before we say goodbye to our relatives and head across the dam. Heavy gray clouds loom overhead, spitting rain, and wind whips across the lakes, tearing at our pack covers and spinning us sideways.

These lakes were born near the end of the Ice Age, during which the sharp peaks and bowl-shaped cirques of the surrounding mountains were carved by a twenty-mile-long, fifteen-hundred-foot-thick glacier. The glacier's leading edge dropped loads of rock and silt here in the valley, forming a terminal moraine. As temperatures warmed, the glacier melted back and the moraine dammed the flow of meltwater to create the lower lake. Paused in its retreat, the glacier dropped another load of debris to form a recessional moraine, the spit of land that divides the lakes. The first man-made dam was built in 1897 to expand the lake's storage capacity for irrigation. The dam we cross now was built in 1978, one of five constructed in this region of Colorado by the Bureau of Reclamation as part of the Fryingpan-Arkansas Project, which stores, diverts, and transports water to the east side of the Continental Divide. The project also created three hydroelectric generating plants, including the Mount Elbert Plant on the north shore of the lower lake.

The plant generates power from water stored four hundred feet uphill from the lakes, in the Mount Elbert Forebay. The water sluices through penstocks, turning two massive turbines to generate two hundred thousand kilowatts of electricity. Much of the water in the forebay comes from Turquoise Lake near Leadville, but supplemental water is pumped back up the penstocks from Twin Lakes. While it takes more energy to pump water up to the forebay than is generated by water coming down, the power is generated during peak demand times and water pumped up during periods of low power usage. When we passed through Twin Lakes on our first hike, Curry and I went on a tour of the plant, which extends down from a modest concrete structure into the earth to a depth equal to a fourteen-story building. The project struck me as absurd, something engineers dreamed up just to see if they could do it, not because it made sense to use electricity from polluting coal plants to pump water to generate less electricity from a supposedly renewable source. I can't help but imagine that if all the effort and ingenuity that energy projects like the Mount Elbert Plant required had been put toward conservation and efficiency instead, the climate crisis we're facing would be less dire.

On the far side of the dam we enter the trees, escaping the wind, and follow the south shore of the lower lake. As we near the narrow divide of land between the two lakes, we come upon a mini ghost town. In 1879 John A. Staley built a hotel here for wealthy visitors to the Twin Lakes area. Four years later, millionaire James V. Dexter purchased the hotel and named it Inter-Laken. Over the following two decades, Dexter expanded the hotel and added other buildings, but he struggled to make the inn profitable. After the dam was built in 1897, rising lake levels washed out the bridge and part of the road to the hotel, further exacerbating the resort's problems. After Dexter died in 1899, the hotel became a boarding house, eventually closing in the 1910s. In the 1970s, the Forest Service and Bureau of Reclamation moved some of the buildings to protect them from the rise in water level caused by the second dam and stabilized or restored others. We mount the stairs of the wrap-around porch of one of the restored buildings, Dexter's Cabin, built in 1895 for the owner's family. Inside the square, log-sided structure, the floors and wainscoting are made up of alternating stripes of dark- and light-stained wood, and doorframes and window moldings are carved with sunbursts. A tin bathtub takes up most of a tiny closet. We make our way up a steep, narrow staircase to the hexagonal cupola and gaze out over the lakes. This charming building is exceedingly modest by the standards of today's wealthy, but the view is priceless.

Beyond Dexter's Cabin, we pass the ghosts of the other resort buildings—a huge log barn, several small sheds, and the original hotel, painted white, with *Inter-Laken* in large brown letters, its windows boarded over. Across the meadow we pitch our tent in golden grass beside the upper lake. Still full from lunch, we eat a small dinner of cheese, crackers, and potato chips. Zephyr explores the isthmus, and Curry puts in calls to his business and learns, through conflicting stories from his office and project managers, that things aren't going well. After telling me about the situation, he seems to forget about it. He has an amazing ability to not sweat things he can't do anything about. I, meanwhile, toss and turn all night, worrying about the next section of trail.

I get up early and watch pink light creep down the mountains to our west. A hint of fall is in the air, with Canada geese honking on the lake and a film of frost on the tent. Today is going to be hard, perhaps the hardest of the trip. We'll climb Hope Pass, three thousand feet up in less than four miles. Gudy Gaskill's guidebook tip for the alternate to this section reads: "Those [who] climb Hope Pass know why it is so named: 'Hope

I will never have to pack over that again.'" Twenty years ago I dubbed it "Hopeless Pass." When Curry and I hiked over it, after two relaxing days in Twin Lakes, we hiked in misery, him in a bad mood and me sick to my stomach. My body felt weak, and my feet moved in slow motion up the steep, closed-in trail. I try to push past experience out of my mind as we set out from the shore of the lakes.

South of our campsite, the Colorado Trail splits in two. The left fork heads toward the Collegiate East, the way we went twenty years ago, except now the route circumvents Hope Pass. We take the right fork, onto the Collegiate West route, which heads over the pass and into the heart of the Collegiate Peaks Wilderness area, and what I hope will be the more remote route. I'm ready for some solitude.

The trail winds up a gentle grade through sagebrush flats and into an aspen grove, the trees' leaves shivering in a faint breeze. Among the aspen grow Douglas fir, sagebrush, and leggy orange paintbrush. Are the aspen taking over from the sage, or the other way round? I hear twittering in the trees and look up to see a blue-gray gnatcatcher land on a branch. It's a tiny little wisp of a bird—slate-gray on its back, pale gray on its breast, with a long tail and white eye ring. It flies off, hovers in the air, and lands again. I would like to settle here with a pair of binoculars, a wildflower guide, and a sketchbook. I could spend an entire day on this hillside, observing birds, drawing flowers, and speculating about forest succession. But today I'm here to hike. Straight up.

We cross a couple of small creeks and proceed on an old jeep road. Like other old roads the Colorado Trail makes use of, this one was built on the principle that the shortest distance between two points is a straight line. In this case the line goes straight uphill beside Little Willis Gulch, a swift creek, all rapids and cascades. I can't imagine what kind of vehicle ascended this road. In the walking meditation I read this morning, Thich Nhat Hanh tells the story of climbing a mountain in China, taking a breath with each of the 1,080 steps. I don't breathe with each step—I'm a slow enough hiker as it is—but I try to concentrate on the movement of air in and out of my body.

The air near the stream is cool and damp and the trees grow tall on the steep hillside. No flies or mosquitoes buzz or bite. I don't expect to see butterflies in the deep shade of the trail, but a moth flutters across my path, my spirit guide for the day. Green plants and shrubs grow in the understory and the ground is blanketed in fine emerald moss, the damp cool green more like the Pacific Northwest than the Rockies. The sacredness of the place engulfs me, and I walk in peace, one step, one breath, at a time, nothing in the world but me and the trees and the mossy ground. After half a mile or so, the trail takes a left turn and angles across the steep slope, away from the gulch. I bless the trail builders who made this single, long switchback, this reprieve from the straight-up path of the old road. With each step away from the streambed, the air grows warmer and drier, the vegetation more sparse. Lichen replaces moss. Green plants give way to bare gravel. By the time I round the bend in the switchback, I have left the Northwest and returned to Colorado—dry, dusty ground, bright, warm sun.

The trail winds back to the creek and again heads straight up, toward tree line. My right foot hurts and I creep up the steep climb. I find Zephyr sitting in an avalanche meadow, looking tired. We hike together through thin stands of spruce and fir, stopping briefly to inspect the collapsing remains of a cluster of ancient log buildings. Beyond the trees, we find the others and eat lunch near a green pond, among wildflowers blooming in a profusion of pink, yellow, blue, and purple. A few minutes' rest and a handful of crackers and cheese recharge Emmet and Zephyr, and they leap off the boulders that dot the meadow, but I'm content to sit, resting my foot and enjoying this place, such a different experience from last time I hiked the pass.

After lunch, Curry, Milo, and Emmet once again speed ahead while Zephyr and I make the final ascent together. Two trail runners pass us, dripping sweat and carrying nothing but hydration packs. I'm sick of people going fast, setting speed records. I want to hear about the slowest Colorado Trail hiker, like Thich Nhat Hanh, taking one step per breath.

We make our way along switchbacks that wind across a talus slope, pausing to look back at the view of Twin Lakes and Mount Elbert. Pikas squeak at us from behind rocks. The wildflowers are fading from their summer brilliance, but fuzzy-topped bistort, pink elephant's-heads, and spiky, pale yellow bundles of alpine thistle are still going strong, and an alpine spring beauty blooms beside the trail, its tiny, white, five-petaled blossoms nestled in a rosette of succulent-looking gray-green leaves with a wash of burgundy in the stems. Near the top of the pass, a stone cairn with a wooden post peeks out over the slope, with bits of ragged colored fabric fluttering from it.

Zephyr looks at the tattered rags. "Why would anyone need a scarecrow up here?"

At the top of the climb we see it's not a scarecrow but a string of Tibetan prayer flags. They look tacky and out of place here, and superfluous. The mountains are prayer enough, holy beyond any human-imagined gods, stretching back millions of years before bipeds set foot on this pass and deep into the future, beyond any depredations we may perpetrate on their slopes.

The moment we mounted Hope Pass on our first Colorado Trail hike stands out in the picture-postcard album of my memory. After the long, grueling climb up Little Willis Gulch, crossing the pass was like stepping into another world. Behind us lay the familiar—the little pond where we ate lunch, the paired water bodies of Twin Lakes, the mountain ranges we had already crossed. Quail and Hope Mountains towered over us on either side. Ahead of us, blue mountain ranges rose one after the other, to the edges of the earth, and the thin, brown trace of the path, winding below the ridge, looked as if we could follow it along the top of the world all the way to the Andes. The stomach pain, the strain of climbing that endless gulch, the misery of the day evaporated. I sensed the vastness of those endless ranges, but instead of feeling small and insignificant, I felt light and strong, like I could dance across the mountaintops on tiptoe, one with the wind and the clouds. I experienced the transcendence I had been searching for. We had entered the heart of the Rocky Mountains, and I never wanted to leave.

Today the pass offers the same view, but the sublime intensity of the experience is missing. My kids sprawl on the grass below the saddle. I don't begrudge their presence—after all, I brought them here, and I hope they're sensing some of the wonder I experienced last time I was here. But a short distance away Curry sits talking with a couple of day hikers. The polite thing would be to join my husband and talk with these people, but I don't want to be polite, and I don't want to waste this moment gabbing, so I sit with the boys and try to block out the chatter and enjoy the view. The sun shines bright from an intense blue sky. A few cottony clouds bob across its surface. From the valley below, mountains rise in steep-sided humps of gray stone, scooped out in glacier-carved cirques, their lower reaches cloaked in blue-green trees. At the far end of the valley, more mountains rise, snow clinging in cracks and crevices, a herd of soft white clouds brushing their summits. I am at once buoyed and anchored by the view, alive with a sense that here is where I belong.

Author Helen Macdonald writes in her book *H Is for Hawk* that the chalk landscapes of southern England "bring an exhilarating, on-tiptoe sense that some deep revelation is at hand. This makes me feel guilty . . . because I know that loving landscapes like this involves a kind of history that concerns itself with purity, a sense of deep time and blood-belonging."

Standing on Hope Pass gives me the same "exhilarating, on-tiptoe" feeling, and I am guilty too, not because "deep time and blood-belonging" have any bearing on the heart-opening sensation I have looking out over the endless blue mountains before me, but the opposite. I know my access to this view is dependent on the removal of those who truly belong in what they called the "Shining Mountains." Once the mineral wealth in these rocks was discovered, the Utes were pushed farther and farther west, until they were driven to reservations in Utah and southwestern Colorado by 1881, their lands declared open for white settlement. After killing and driving out the Native peoples, white settlers killed off important links in the ecosystem. The last grizzly bear in Colorado was killed in 1979, the last gray wolves were exterminated by 1940, the last wolverine was sighted nearly a hundred years ago, and the last wild bison was shot in 1897.

The land itself is not what it was before white men riddled the hills with mine shafts, cut whole forests for charcoal and building materials, dammed and diverted rivers, released droves of livestock into the valleys and high meadows, and laced the landscape with roads and highways. But without those roads, many built for access to timber and minerals, we wouldn't find our way this deep into the mountains. Hiking would be a different experience, too, if at any moment we might round the bend to come face-to-face with a thousand-pound bison or a hungry grizzly sow. And if the Utes had not been driven out by the greed of our ancestors, we would be trespassers on this land. Perhaps we are trespassers still. We are able to enter the wilderness because essential elements of the wilderness have been removed or destroyed—Indigenous inhabitants, wild creatures, remoteness, inaccessibility. Breathtaking though the view may be, I gaze upon a land diminished.

The trail does not skirt the mountains all the way to the Andes, but plunges into Sheep Gulch. The switchbacks run diagonally across the slope rather than perpendicular to it, making for a steep descent, and the trail is surfaced in loose rocks and slippery gravel. The boys, zig-zagging down the trail ahead of me, look so small and vulnerable, and they grow smaller with every switchback. My heart contracts, and I follow, my knees aching with each step as I slip and slide down, down into the valley. The hydration-pack runners pass, going back up. They're drenched in sweat and look miserable. I try to imagine what compelled them to climb Hope Pass twice in one day.

Late in the afternoon I find the others waiting at a stream crossing on a steep hillside. Curry proposes we fill our water containers and hike until we find a level area where we can camp. I suggest going back the way we came a few hundred yards to a meadow that slopes gently down from the trail to the edge of an aspen grove. It's early, and it never feels right to hike over ground you've already covered, but we've gone well beyond where we planned to camp, and the data book shows the next campsite six miles on, much farther than I want to go. Curry begrudgingly agrees, and we head back to the meadow.

While Curry sets up the tent, the boys and I return to the stream to collect and treat water. Back at camp, Emmet, Zephyr, and Milo lay their sleeping mats out in the sun and play war and poker. When they grow tired of cards, they play a few rounds of a game in which one person says, "I won a snake," another person says, "I two a snake," and so on, until somebody says, "I eight a snake," and the other players reply, "You ate a snake?" The game is suited for children too young to understand odd and even numbers, but the three of them play over and over, roaring with laughter each time one of them eats a snake. Then they invent a game of naming a fish for each letter of the alphabet (i = "interesting purple jellyfish"). I love watching the boys laugh and be silly together, and I experience a rare feeling of rightness. Despite the challenges of the last few days, in this moment I know that we're doing exactly what we should be doing. We belong here, in the wilderness, together.

8

PEAKS AND VALLEYS

The world is mine: blue hill, still silver lake,
Broad field, bright flower, and the long white road
A gateless garden, and an open path:
My feet to follow, and my heart to hold.
—EDNA ST. VINCENT MILLAY

DAYS 19–23: JULY 28–AUGUST 1, 2016
Hewitts Gulch to Monarch Pass

Light comes early to our meadow and we get an early start, winding gently around hillsides of aspen and sage, bristlecone and ponderosa. Hummingbirds trill and hover, dipping their long bills into red paintbrush. The wide trail has a level surface of packed earth or, where it traverses talus fields, stones laid flat and smooth as patio pavers. Craggy mountains surround the forests, and Clear Creek meanders through willows and alders along a broad, flat valley floor walled in by the steep slopes of mountains. I truly have arrived. I could hike like this forever, on smooth trail with stunning views.

We've entered terra incognita. After crossing Hope Pass and descending

FIG. 9. Broad-tailed hummingbird (*Selasphorus platycercus*)

to Clear Creek Road yesterday, we headed west, away from the original route of the Colorado Trail. When we hiked that section twenty years ago, in early September, autumn had arrived in the Collegiates. Golden aspen leaves shimmied overhead and the slopes of Mount Princeton were spangled green, gold, orange, and crimson beneath an achingly blue sky. Though the sun warmed the afternoons to a sweaty heat, wind sweeping down the mountains brought a wintery chill. I continued to struggle with my reasons for finishing the trail. It seemed that all we did each day was hike, eat, sleep, set up camp, break down camp. I appreciated moving through a constantly changing landscape, but even my plodding pace was too fast. I caught only glimpses of the landscape while I stared at the trail, weighed down by my pack. I did not want to live life the way we hiked the trail. "I do want to surmount peaks," I wrote in my journal, "but also wade in streams, smell the flowers, and drowse under trees along the way."

Again our hike is more rushed than I'd like. Yet it's far slower than "real" life. We don't have to hurry to school and jobs or cram the activities of three kids into a tight schedule. That constant need to rush from place to place compounds the stress created by a miserable job and drains joy from family life. At home, too, I'm gripped by a near-constant ache of longing for my kids where they were smaller and a breathless grasping at the current moment, all too aware of how quickly time passes. Out here I don't feel nostalgic about either the past or the present. Though I daydream about immersing myself in a meadow or forest for days, I'm much more aware of this gift of slow time than I was twenty years ago, and I soak in as much as I can at two miles per hour, appreciating each moment in the wilderness and with my family as it comes.

Late in the morning we enter the Collegiate Peaks Wilderness area. The trail switchbacks uphill, gently at first, following the edge of the deep gorge that Clear Creek cascades down and crossing the creek at the base of a waterfall. Near tree line, the trail grows steeper, and I puff my way up. Zephyr waits for me at the edge of the tundra, and we make our way toward Lake Ann together. As we zigzag up switchbacks, he points to blue sky peeking above the slope and says, "We're almost there." I appreciate his encouragement and the juxtaposition of my child as my guide.

Lake Ann is a clear turquoise tarn at the base of a gravelly cirque below the last of a cluster of mountains called the Three Apostles. Curry, wet from a swim, sits on a slope uphill from the tarn, digging a lunch bag from his pack. Milo lies in the sun beside him. Zephyr and I circle the shore to where Emmet stands ankle-deep in the swampy shallows. I plunge into the lake and shriek obscenities as the water envelops me. It's shockingly cold, as cold as the snow it melted from, so cold I will die if I stay in a moment longer. I surge out into the blessed sun and rub my numb skin with a pack towel. Zephyr points to a boulder sticking up from the surface a few yards from shore.

"I'm going to swim to that rock."

"No, don't." He would freeze and I couldn't save him. He plunges in, gasps, and paddles back to shore. Milo has come around the lake to join us, and he and Emmet dip in and burst back out.

After lunch we wind our way up a steep talus slope dotted with purple sky pilot and topped with a cornice of snow. The view beyond Lake Ann Pass is not as awe-inspiring as that from Hope Pass. The mountains appear more distant and rolling, a blue haze blurring their outlines. A blue pool in the distance shows the mark of man: Taylor Park Reservoir, dammed in 1937 for storage and diversion of irrigation water to Uncompahgre Valley. Many prospectors and miners turned to the land's surface when their mining ventures failed or after the easy placer gold played out. Land speculators, railroads, and local politicians extolled the homesteading potential of the high plains and mountain valleys, pooh-poohing warnings about the challenges of farming in arid and semiarid regions and claiming that "rain follows the plow." One of the most enthusiastic purveyors of this fallacy was William Gilpin, first territorial governor of Colorado. Unusually wet weather through the 1880s gave credence to the myth, and settlers poured west on the promise of 160 acres and a sod house.

But drought hit the region in 1889 and 1890 and again, with a vengeance, in 1894. Homesteaders abandoned their dryland farms or turned to grazing livestock, and it became clear that agriculture in the Great American Desert would require irrigation. Colorado's first non-Indigenous agriculturalists, Spanish American farmers who moved north from New

Mexico, brought with them their traditional acequias, cooperative irrigation systems of canals and ditches. Early white settlers' efforts also included digging ditches, generally on an individual basis without the communal aspect of the acequias. Seeing financial potential, corporations got in on the irrigation game, creating larger canals, but it soon became clear that to make agriculture possible across a large swath of the West, the government would have to get into the business of storing, diverting, and distributing water, and Congress passed the Newlands Act in 1902, giving rise to the era of big dams and diversions. One of the earliest projects built with the newly established Reclamation Fund was a tunnel that moved water more than five miles from the Gunnison River through the depths of Vernal Mesa to Uncompahgre Valley.

In its language and, perhaps, in the minds of early proponents, the Newlands Act was intended to benefit small family farms through development of projects via a revolving fund, with beneficiaries repaying the costs, thus funding the next project. In practice, the act primarily benefited big agribusiness and urban developers, running roughshod over residents of areas to be flooded, Native American tribes, and acequias. Further, the costs of projects would never be repaid. Dam proponents bemoan any water that runs through the natural river channel to the next state, the sea, or Mexico as "wasted." Yet the western states have the most wasteful water use practices in the world, and vast amounts of diverted and stored water is lost through evaporation from reservoirs, ditches, and flood-irrigated fields. Excess water that runs off fields raises the temperature of rivers and brings with it soil, salt, nutrients, and chemicals. Colorado's rivers and streams are clogged with more than nineteen hundred dams with a total capacity of 7.5 million acre-feet of water storage.

At the pass, Curry talks with a day-hiking couple who grumble about the number of people who flock to the Collegiates to climb fourteeners. I'd hoped this section would be less populous, but it appears we'll be overrun with peak baggers and day hikers complaining about peak baggers. Twenty years ago, in the Collegiates, I inadvertently almost bagged a peak when I missed a turn. After breaking for lunch, Curry and I had studied the book and map, figuring the three-mile ascent and descent that remained would take about an hour and a half, putting us in camp by mid-afternoon. After the first two miles or so of gradual rise, Curry set off to scout a campsite between Brown's Creek and Little Brown's Creek. A short distance later, I reached a junction with Little Brown's Creek Trail. Thinking it was what the guidebook described as a well-marked intersection where the Colorado Trail joins Brown's Creek Trail, I signed the register, wondering why Curry had not also signed it, and hiked on.

The trail continued to climb, even though the book described it as descending beyond the junction. It climbed. And it climbed. And it climbed. By the time I neared a ridge, I was furious with the Colorado Trail, guidebook author Robert P. Denise, and mountains in general. But Curry's diamond-patterned boot tracks marked the dusty trail, so I continued on. The trail dropped to the creek and ascended again without crossing. I couldn't understand why Curry hadn't chosen one of the many campsites I passed. I looked for our little blue tent around every corner, but the slopes grew steeper and the creek disappeared underground. I continued to climb toward tree line, which didn't make sense, since our planned campsite was below ten thousand feet.

Then I heard a muffled, far-off cry. "Ahn-dree-aaah!" It came from downhill. Had I passed the campsite? What about Curry's boot-prints? I paused to listen and heard it again. "Ahn-dree-aaah!" Curry was downhill. I was lost. All the anger washed out of me, replaced by fear and confusion. I ran down the trail, crying and calling to Curry. When I saw him coming around a bend, I rushed into his arms. I had passed by the "well-marked" turnoff, which would have taken me to camp in fifteen minutes, instead hiking three pointless miles up Mount Antero, following another hiker's diamond-patterned boot tracks. Curry took my pack and we jogged to camp. The next day I got my longed-for day off. We lounged in camp, relaxing, repairing gear, reading, and finally just *being* in the wilderness.

From the pass, the trail winds around a steep slope of grass, talus, and scree before descending into spruce forest and, lower down, lodgepole. We exit the wilderness area and find ourselves hiking on a motorcycle track, a badly eroded rut filled alternately with fine, slippery dust, skull-sized boulders, fist-sized rocks, and mud. All difficult to walk on. After an hour or two of slipping, sliding, and stumbling, we take a break. When we hike on, I set out behind Milo, trying to match his steps. He walks with his toes pointing outward at an angle, moving loosely, his limbs like wet spaghetti, his joints made of springs. His footsteps are steady and even, each stride the same length as the last. Within the first dozen steps, I swat a mosquito, scratch the back of my calf, stub my toe, and lose him as he saunters steadily on.

We spend a cold, wet night camped near the stream in Prospector Gulch, a deep, buggy hollow whose steep slopes block both morning and afternoon sun. In the morning our hike begins with a long descent down the motorcycle rut through a dense spruce forest. Midmorning, the trail levels out at the edge of a flat-bottomed valley, and our view opens up. Texas Creek meanders along the valley floor, winding among tall grasses, willows, and beaver ponds. Rounded hillsides blanketed in spruce rise beyond, and a craggy gray peak towers over the head of the valley. I pause at the edge of a pond with the huge mound of a beaver lodge in its center. Three great blue herons perch on an expanse of mud. A big dragonfly zooms past. Two couples heading in the opposite direction pause to chat. They're hiking the Collegiate East and Collegiate West routes as a loop and will finish at Twin Lakes in a couple of days.

We gaze at the pond, hoping for a moose to make an appearance, then I wish the foursome good luck and hike on. At the far end of the valley, the trail climbs into an airy forest of widely spaced pines. As the trail climbs, backpackers and day hikers pass by, heading in both directions. The trail goes up and up and up until we reach a long, rolling meadow dotted with scrubby trees. Wildflowers carpet the meadow, including the first fringed gentian I've seen this hike—a deep purple fluted tube with a ruffled fringe on the edge of each petal. Zephyr and I make our way up the final switchbacks to Cottonwood Pass together.

"Zephyr, you haven't picked me a strawberry in a long time," I say.

"I haven't picked *me* a strawberry in a long time."

"Maybe they're out of season. Or maybe we're out of their habitat."

"Yeah, unless there's a super wind- and cold-resistant mountain strawberry."

We crest the pass and Zephyr hurries to catch up with the others on the descent to the road. Cars wind up and down in an endless stream and pack the parking area. A woman standing outside a van asks where I'm going. She's holding a baby, and several more kids sit in the vehicle. I tell her about our hike, hoping we'll inspire her family to get out on adventures. I also hope she'll take pity and pull a bag of chips or cookies out of the van, but she doesn't, and I move on, weaving among people milling around the trailhead, and climb a stark hillside of boulders and scrubby grass. I find Curry and the boys crouched in the lee of a stone wall, but I'm not ready to rest and I continue on. After a few minutes, Curry, Milo, and Emmet pass me, but Zephyr hangs back. We come upon a white-tailed ptarmigan, a little brown chicken-like bird of the tundra, and her clutch of chicks that blend almost perfectly with the ground.

The slope drops steeply to our left, into a deep, green valley dotted with turquoise ponds and patches of spruce. Gusts of wind carry needles of cold. We catch up with the others sitting on the edge of the trail, talking with an older couple who are heading toward the parking area after a day hike. The woman wears a flowered scarf over her head and has an Austrian or Swiss accent. She says her husband has always wanted to hike from Cottonwood Pass to Monarch Pass.

"That's where we're heading!" I exclaim, but they look skeptical.

The couple heads back to the trailhead and we continue on our way. Zephyr hikes with me for the afternoon, telling me about the houses he plans to build when he grows up—one old-fashioned Norwegian style outside and high-tech inside, the other a Hobbit hole, with gardens, orchards, and farm animals. He describes the dishes he'll cook for Thanksgiving, recounts Calvin & Hobbes comics, and tells me his plan to dress like the graphic novel character Big Nate and walk past the author Lincoln Pierce's house in Maine. I listen and respond to questions, but mostly save my breath for hiking.

The trail's a narrow thread stitched along the edge of the Continental Divide. A steep slope drops to our right. Bright, fat heads of old-man-of-the-mountain sunflowers bob on short stems. A ribbon of silvery water winds along the valley bottom. In comparison to the lush, flower-filled meadow on the other side of the pass, these hillsides are sparse, with shorter grass, fewer flowers, and more rocks than vegetation. The trail crosses talus and scree slopes and boulder fields where the rocks vary in texture and color, from lumpy to smooth, gray to buff, black to silver. The ascent is gradual, but the uneven, rocky surface makes for difficult walking. Stones jab through the soles of my shoes, stub my toes, and trip me up. The wind pushes and pulls us. As we wind along the final traverse before reaching Sanford Saddle, I feel queasy and dizzy. I try to keep my eyes averted from the steep slope that drops to my right and focus instead on moving forward.

It's late in the afternoon when we cross the saddle, slipping and sliding along the lower edge of a cornice of snow. More patches of snow dot the cirque and red algae stain the meltwater tarn. The ridge blocks the relentless wind, but it also blocks the lowering sun and the air is chilly. I want to cry but I don't know why—perhaps from tiredness, hunger, vertigo, or relief that we're out of the wind and off the steep slope. If I were alone, I might indulge in a good cry. But I've got to keep it together; it's late and we need to get moving. I sit on a rock at the side of the trail and compose myself. We have a long way to go before camp.

We pull on warm layers and descend into Mineral Basin. A narrow creek hemmed in by willow bushes flows down the center of the valley. Craggy mountains rise on all sides. Tufts of leggy spruce trees dot their slopes. The sun is setting and I don't know how far we have to go. I contemplate what to do if we don't find camp before dark—we could hike with headlamps or put on all of our clothes, eat granola bars for dinner, and huddle all night in our sleeping bags beneath a spruce tree. Neither is an appealing option. I'm endangering my son by being such a slow hiker, and I try to pick up the pace. Before long, we come around a bend and see the gold pyramid of our tent a mile or so down valley. Relief floods my body—we won't have to hike in the dark or sleep under a tree. Energized by the sight, Zephyr and I almost skip down the basin to our campsite. It's the most spectacular we've had. Our tent nearly fills a tiny patch of grass that's hemmed on three sides by lichen-encrusted boulders and by willows on the fourth. Rugged mountains surround us, their peaks brushing the indigo sky. There's no sign of another soul.

In the middle of the night I go out to pee. The sky appears immense and low to the earth, close enough to touch. Stars blanket the inky blackness, their points nearly touching, and the bright swath of the Milky Way streaks down the center, like a gauzy scarf draped from horizon to horizon. I find the Big and Little Dippers, and I'm tempted to retrieve the star chart that's tucked in my journal in the tent. But instead I stand beneath the blaze of stars, hugging myself because of the cold and out of a sense of deep contentment. This is what I suffered through a twelve-hour hiking day for. A meteor streaks diagonally across the Milky Way, and I crawl into the tent and go to sleep.

Zephyr and Curry rise early and exclaim over the sunrise and a weasel that runs through our campsite, but I'm too tired to even peek outside. I stay wrapped in my quilt until 6:30, and when I emerge, the sky is clear, the air crisp. We eat breakfast, pack up, and head down Mineral Basin. Today's walking meditation was about walking mindfully and happily for your ancestors, to keep their troubles and sadness from crossing generations. "Happiness is not an individual matter. As long as the ancestors in us are suffering, we can't be happy and we will transmit that suffering to our children and their children," Thich Nhat Hanh writes. As I switchback up a flower-covered hillside, I force my mouth into a smile, a test to see if I'm happy. My chapped lips split, but my cheeks don't work as hard to smile as they did two weeks ago. Still, I can't tell if I'm happy. I'm not sad, angry, frustrated, or resentful, but what does happy feel like? I focus on one foot moving in front of the other up the switchbacks. I breathe in, out, in, out. I walk mindfully. But am I walking happily? If I'm not happy here, now, in this beautiful place, making this trek I longed for for years, where and when can I be happy?

I think of Grandma Meyer, trapped in the brain-cage of dementia, having forgotten everyone and nearly everything, including how to stay sitting up. I think of Grandma Lani, living through two wars, raising seven kids, migrating to a foreign land, carrying on after her husband's death. Were they happy? I would not consider either of them cheerful, but cheer and happiness are not the same. Perhaps they were content, with their lives of marriage, motherhood, caring for house and home. There weren't many options for women of their generation, although Grandma Lani had gone to cooking school and had cooked for the inn her family ran before she got married, and Grandma Meyer worked in a factory during the war and later cleaned houses to supplement the family income. Cooking and cleaning would never make me content, let alone happy, but did women of their time find joy in caring for others, as they exercised creativity at the stove and sewing machine, or did they resent their lack of options?

When my kids were young, I felt so much frustration over the never-ending repetitiveness of childcare and housework and the stress of trying to be a full-time hands-on mom while working an unsatisfying job. I learned to hold anxiety and depression at bay by engaging in creative projects. Those projects were also domestic—paint a chair, knit a hat, do a craft with the kids—but as long as I could create something tangible that I didn't have to do again the next hour or day, I could maintain a level of, if not happiness, at least non-misery. As my kids grew older and less interested in projects, and when my job went from dreary to night-marish, I could no longer knit or bake myself out of despair. This hike was as much about escape as it was about connection. Inherent in my desire to connect with my children and reconnect with the wilderness on this trip was a need to escape the hamster wheel of domestic chores.

I do feel closer to the wild here, both the wild world and the wild within me, and I feel closer to my kids than I have since they were little. But the frustrations of the trail are parallel to those at home—the burden of keeping others safe and happy, the redundancy of camp chores, the apparent imbalance in both power and responsibility between Curry and me. Because I worked part time in order to be with my kids when they were young, more of their care, and more of the care of the household, fell to me. That pattern continued when I returned to work full time, and it has followed us into the wilderness. One thing the trail has taught me is that while family has felt unduly burdensome over the last fifteen years, it's not *motherhood* that's the problem. Rather it's the pressures that come from outside, some of them general, abstract pressures from society to "have it all," which really translates to *do* it all, perfectly, and some specific and tangible, like the constant rush to get kids to school or pick them up from sports. Out here, with those pressures removed, I'm finding joy in hanging out with my kids and witnessing them interact with the wilderness and each other. This joy is what I need to bring home with me, while leaving the frustration behind.

The trail winds along the Continental Divide, stony ridges towering above and shimmering streams and lakes dotting the valley below. I join the boys on a rock, where they're resting and watching a marmot. When we get up to move on, Milo has climbed three switchbacks toward the saddle in the time it takes me to shoulder my pack. Later, I tell him we should change his trail name to *The Flash*. He looks pleased but says he'll stick with *Flaky*. The twins and I follow Milo over a shoulder of Emma Burr Mountain, at 13,538 feet, one of the highest points on the Continental Divide. So few landmarks in these mountains are named for women, yet I can find no record of who Emma Burr was and how she came to have a peak named for her.

On the other side of the saddle the trail meanders among boulder fields and talus slopes. A pika runs by with a bouquet of paintbrush and daisies in its mouth, disappears under a rock, comes out empty-mouthed, and darts back to the flower patch.

"I bet a pika would like to live in a horse barn," Zephyr says.

"They seem to like rocks," I say.

"But they could learn to love a hay bale."

The trouble is that a hay bale or a horse barn would be too warm for a creature that likes it cool. Pikas favor talus fields high on mountain slopes, where rocks shade the ground and slow the melting of snow. Beneath the rocks, temperatures may be as much as twelve degrees cooler than at the surface, forming an air-conditioned retreat for a tiny critter that can die from exposure to heat. Researchers have documented a decline in pika populations in California and the Great Basin, which they attribute to the warming climate. A study of sixty-nine pika populations in the Southern Rockies, however, found that pikas persisted in all but four historically active sites. For now the pikas are holding on here in Colorado's mountains, which is good news not only for hikers who enjoy hearing the little lagomorph's friendly chirps as we make our way through its territory but also for the entire tundra ecosystem.

Ann Zwinger, in *Land Above the Trees*, points out that the simplicity of the alpine world renders it vulnerable. "When food chains are complex and elaborate," she writes, "as in a lowland community, a shift in any one component is less felt, the change is easily absorbed in the interwoven web, and the community retains its essential stability. When the food chains are short, the alteration of a single member results in a prompt and drastic change in the rest of the chain." The loss of the pika would make life harder for the weasel and hawk. For now, the cool talus fields provide refugia for pikas, but warmer temperatures, lower snowpack levels, or less moisture could mean hunger for predators and silence in the boulder lands.

As we reach the final switchbacks, the grade becomes steep again, the bends of the switches angling straight up the slope. Zephyr waves to me from above. A ferocious wind tears down the mountain. He doesn't like being whipped by wind on exposed hillsides, and I try to hike more quickly to catch up, hoisting myself forward with my poles over widely spaced stone steps on the near-vertical turns in the trail. Butterflies flutter past, tossed by the wind—orange with black dots, saffron colored, brown-and-orange checks, black with red bands, white with black stripes. They urge me up the hill.

My morning meditation comes back to me, and I realize I don't have to be happy all the time. I can be cold, wet, tired, hungry, hot, awestruck, amazed, exhilarated, annoyed, angry, or just focused on climbing up and over a ridge to be with my child. This experience is about challenging my body, my mind, my heart, my spirit. I can find happiness looking back in retrospect. I don't need to be a smiling, constantly cheerful person. On the other hand, I don't want my face to freeze in a frown. I smile as

I catch up with Zephyr a few switchbacks from the top and we finish the climb together.

"Almost there!" he tells me as he rounds the final bend.

"Nearly to the top," I call back to him. This mutual encouragement with my eleven-year-old son, this makes me happy.

When we get over the saddle, he points to the long ridge of mountains undulating ahead of us. "That's where we have to go."

The trail snakes along the slope of the mountain to the far end of the valley where it winds over another pass. As we hike along the steep drop-off I feel dizzy and nauseated again. I plant my poles firmly and try not to look down. On the other side of the pass, the trail winds steeply down a forested hillside. I look back and see two hikers and a dog behind us. I hurry, hoping to stay ahead of them. I'd hoped today would be the one day we'd have the trail to ourselves. As we near the bottom of the valley, a loud roaring fills the air. Four-wheelers or motorcycles, out of sight at the base of the hill, zoom on and on, an endless roar of two-stroke engines. They've passed by when we reach Tincup Pass Road where Curry, Emmet, and Milo wait for us.

"You just missed about a dozen four-wheelers," Curry says.

"No, I didn't." It would be impossible to miss that deafening noise.

We cross the road and collect water at Chalk Creek. The ATVs roar by again. All the way up the steep climb, the infernal noise continues as the machines chase each other up and down the road. I send mental ill-wishes to the riders—deafness from the noise, impotence from the vibrations. Curry, Milo, and Emmet trek ahead, and together Zephyr and I climb winding switchbacks up a mirror image of the steep forested hillside we came down. Near the top of the climb, the trees give way to a rolling meadow. The cottony clouds that have scudded across the sky all afternoon have coalesced into the blue-gray mass of a looming thunderstorm, and we stop to cover our packs as rain begins to spit. I can still hear the jackasses on the ATVs. Maybe the rain will drive them away. We step aside for a group of mountain bikers heading back to the road.

"We didn't want to get caught up here in this storm," one of them says.

"Good idea," I say.

The meadow is wide open, with few trees, a bad place to be in a thunderstorm. I hoist my umbrella and smile. The bikers head down the trail, and we hike on, the roaring of engines on the road below growing louder and more belligerent. Rain does not deter them but increases the fun. As we approach an exposed, grassy hillside, the rain pours down harder and thunder rumbles in the distance. Soft ice balls pelt us as we crouch among the last of the willows, waiting for a break in the weather. Zephyr peeks out at me from beneath his blue umbrella.

"Look, I'm a toadstool," he says. I'm glad he's taking this thunderstorm in stride, even enjoying it, without fear.

After the ice pellets let up, we emerge from the bushes and make it across the grassy meadow before thunder rumbles again. When it does, we shelter beneath a cluster of spruce trees. After a long span of quiet, we get ready to move on, but thunder shakes the air again. We wait a few minutes more and the same thing happens. Each time I think it's safe to leave the trees, thunder growls. But it appears the worst of the storm is staying east of us, caged in by two rolling green and brown mountains shaped like a pair of humped dinosaurs, so we hike on, one eye on the clouds. Lightning flashes between the dinosaurs. I count seconds until thunder—thirty-five. Does that mean the lightning struck thirty-five miles away or three-point-five? I can't remember the formula, but either seems far enough and we keep going. We approach a grassy hillside that climbs to a wide-open saddle with no trees or shrubs to shelter beneath.

"Zephyr, we need to haul butt over that saddle."

"What does that mean?"

"It means go fast."

He scrambles uphill ahead of me, looking tiny and vulnerable in his blue raincoat, his pack bobbing in its highlighter-yellow cover. His closed umbrella swings from his wrist. I will my legs to move faster, and I catch up with him on the other side of the saddle.

"Are you hauling butt?" he asks me.

"I'm trying."

We trot down the hill and continue on, through more undulating willow and grass meadows, toward another, bigger climb at the far end of the valley. The noise of ATVs still follows us, carrying over the mountains, the riders not one bit daunted by hail and lightning in their quest to shatter the peace. A hole appears in the clouds and slanted sunlight illuminates the meadow wildflowers. We take off our raincoats and Zephyr points to more clouds beyond the end of the meadow.

"It's raining on the other side of the pass."

But when we climb over the saddle, we find the rain has moved on and the golden light of evening fills the valley. At the bottom of the slope, Curry, Milo, and Emmet are setting up the tent near Tunnel Lake. The saddle, finally, blocks the roar of the ATVs, and we hike to camp in blessed quiet.

The sun rises in a clear blue sky, yesterday's thunderstorms relegated to memory. We hike through more alpine meadows, willows, and scrubby trees, from Tunnel Lake over Tunnel Pass. Today is our last full day on the Collegiate West route and, I figure, our last chance to hike in solitude. We didn't see another soul after the mountain bikers we passed yesterday, and no tents shared the valley last night. Surely we have finally hiked far enough to escape people. But as I descend from the pass, I hear hikers behind me. I hike more quickly, determined to go one day without sharing the trail.

The trail drops to the flat, smooth grade of a railbed. We've reunited with the route of the Denver, South Park and Pacific Railroad. Having lost out to the Denver and Rio Grande in the lines' race to corner Leadville traffic, the South Park continued to plug on, building track toward Gunnison and its aspirational goal of California. In 1880, workers began boring a 1,772-foot tunnel under the Continental Divide here. The tunnel took two years to build, and before it was done the Rio Grande had laid rail over Marshall Pass and reached Gunnison, once again beating out the South Park. Trains traveling through the tunnel endured accidents, avalanches, and collisions. One avalanche killed thirteen people in the railroad settlement of Woodstock, including six children from one family, and at least four crew members suffocated in the tunnel, which was abandoned in 1910 and later sealed off.

A short detour to the left would take me to the west portal of the tunnel, but I don't take it because I'm irrationally, obsessively determined to stay ahead of the hikers, even though there's little chance of my hiking more quickly than anyone even on a good day, and today my right foot aches worse than ever. The railbed is wide and flat and should be easy to walk on, but walking on level ground hurts even more than climbing uphill.

Except for the flat railbed cut out of the hillside, most signs of the railroad are gone, but once in a while the rotting remains of old ties appear in the pathway, and in other places the roots of living trees grow across the trail in neat, parallel lines, having filled in the spaces where ties rotted away. I limp along, trying to move my foot in a way that's not painful.

Pikas peek out from tumbled talus and squeak at me. Fat brown marmots sit on their haunches and whistle. Tiny least chipmunks dash across the trail. On the slope across the valley, three-quarters of the spruce trees are dead. Over the last several years the spruce beetle has taken over from the pine beetle as Colorado's primary forest pest, with more than 1.7 million acres impacted. The outbreak has abated slightly this year as large-diameter Engelmann spruce have been depleted. Like the mountain pine beetle, the spruce beetle is a natural element of the forest ecosystem that has been super-charged by warming temperatures and reduced precipitation. The southwest quarter of the state, where we'll be hiking for the rest of our trip, has been hit especially hard. We'll see a lot more skeletal trees in the weeks to come.

Three hikers catch up with me when I stop to read an interpretive sign about trains derailing at "sawmill curve," the most dangerous spot along the South Park line. I say hi and hurry ahead while they take their turn reading. They catch up again at the next sign and again I hurry on. I can't avoid stopping to talk with a lone woman traveling in the opposite direction. She's hiking the Collegiate Loop for a research project about women going into the wilderness to overcome trauma, and this is her first backpacking trip, aside from a trek in Patagonia. She says she's found the Collegiates isolated by comparison.

"Really? It's like Grand Central Station to me."

She's one of the few solo female hikers we've seen on the trail, and I imagine that being a woman alone puts a different perspective on solitude. She tells me she plans her campsites so she's near other hikers at night, and I wonder whether this would make me feel more safe or less so. On our first Colorado Trail hike, I once experienced the fear particular to women hikers. I was hiking alone, miles behind Curry, when I came upon a cattle gate. As I struggled to pry the loop of taut wire over the log post, three men dressed in blue jeans and cowboy boots came along. They fastened the gate for me and asked what I was doing way out here by myself. I knew instinctively to lie.

"My boyfriend's a little ways behind me."

"I wouldn't let my daughter hike out here, in the middle of nowhere," one of the men said.

Perhaps they were just three concerned citizens, fathers themselves, who believed the world was dangerous and the best place for young women was at home where their fathers can keep an eye on them, but his paternalism was as creepy as a proposition. I thanked them for the help with the gate and hurried down the trail, faster than I'd ever hiked in my life. I'd like to think a lot has changed in twenty years, and that a woman alone in the wilds is not an aberration. But though we've seen a few solo women hikers and several women as halves of couples or in pairs or small groups, most of the hikers we've come across have been men, and I know that fear always lingers in the periphery of consciousness for a woman alone. I wish this brave young woman luck with her hike and her project and continue down the trail.

Curry and the boys wait for me at the point where the trail joins a jeep road. Tents and screen houses are set up in every clearing in the woods and trucks rumble over the road. The three hikers I'd tried to avoid catch up and stop to chat. Two of them hail from New Hampshire and one from Massachusetts, the first New Englanders we've met on the trail. Soon two more hikers join us. They've all heard about us, the "family of five hiking the Colorado Trail." We walk together up the road of ankle-twisting round stones ranging in size from clementine to grapefruit. Where the road ends at Hancock Lake, the other hikers continue on, but we stop to take a swim before making the easy climb over Chalk Creek Pass, our rough halfway point at mile 245.4.

We stop for lunch beyond the pass, on a grassy bench that looks out over a verdant meadow sloping toward a forest of dead trees. A creek threads through the meadow, pooling in several small, unnamed lakes, like a necklace of turquoise beads draped over green velvet. The mountains that wall the valley on either side are gray with a greenish or reddish cast and they undulate in a series of rounded peaks and saddles, like many-humped dragons. Beyond the foot of the valley, hazy blue mountains rise in the distance, their forested slopes drifting in and out of shade cast by fluffy white clouds.

Curry slices cheese into rectangles and we pass around crackers and packets of nut butter. The boys dole out flakes of turkey jerky, and I toss back a handful of dried chickpeas. Once we finish the "healthy" part of our meal, I pass out the goodies: a gummy vitamin, two chewy sour candies, and one lollipop each, plus a treat from my friend Yvette. She sent trail magic for my mom to add to each of our resupply boxes, and this week's surprise is maple-flavored hard candies.

"Who misses Maine?" I say as I toss each person a leaf-shaped candy. While Curry and Milo say they do just so they can get candy, both Emmet and Zephyr respond enthusiastically.

"I do! I do!"

I know they're telling the truth because each evening when we've settled into the tent they say, "I miss Maine. I miss my ducks." I want to say, "Are you crazy? We're in one of the most beautiful places on earth and you miss boring old Maine?" But instead I hug them and tell them we'll be home soon.

Emmet unwraps his candy and says, "Can we bail on the trip when we reach Monarch Pass?"

His question takes me by surprise. The kids have complained little, and even though they're homesick, I didn't suspect anyone wanted to quit. Despite the pain in my foot I want to finish, and now that we've passed the halfway point, right on schedule, it looks like we might actually make it to Durango. But I'm not a tyrant. If mutiny threatened, I'd consider changing course.

"Does anyone else want to bail?"

"No!" Curry and Zephyr shout. Milo, while less emphatic, does not want to throw in the towel, either, so I give Emmet a little pep talk as we head down the valley.

Wildflowers grow thick among the tumbled boulders at the edges of the ponds. The trail follows a pleasant, gradual grade downhill as we work our way from one valley into another. We enter a forest where at least two-thirds of the spruce trees are dead, the ground springy with a thick layer of red, yellow, and brown needles. As usual, our group has stretched out along the trail, but Curry stays behind me and we hike together through the afternoon, pointing out interesting sights and telling each other about things we've noticed over the last few days. I feel a softening behind my breastbone, an easing of resentments and frustration. Most days, all we talk about is when to stop for lunch, where to camp, and whose turn it is to get water. I enjoy having a real conversation and appreciating the trail together. We haven't had this kind meaningful interaction this whole trip, which is probably why we get so irritated with each other.

At the bottom of the valley, the trail joins a road for a short distance and then climbs through the forest on a series of switchbacks. I assume this section of trail was built to skirt the road or a mining claim. On a topo map, the mountains and valleys in this area, as in much of the West, are riddled with shaded oblongs, as if a cartographer with a rectangular stencil and a number two pencil had too much time on his hands. These are mining claims, twenty-acre parcels of land transferred from the public trust into private hands for a small filing fee and a few hours' worth of labor.

The General Mining Act of 1872 established a "right to mine," affirming mining as the highest and best use of public lands. The law, which also enshrined the "first in time, first in right" and "use it or lose it" rules previously established by mining districts, may have been appropriate for prospectors with pickaxes but is far too simplistic when applied to multi-billion-dollar corporations. The right to mine presumption of the law prevents public lands agencies from considering competing interests such as timber, grazing, recreation, scenery, or watershed or wildlife protection when granting hardrock mineral mining permits. In Colorado, nearly 280,000 mining claims were recorded as of 2010. After five years, a prospector can "patent" a claim, outright purchasing both the minerals and surface property for a fee of $5 per acre. Before Congress placed a moratorium on patenting new mining claims in 1994, around 3.1 million acres of public land were transferred into private hands. Even without patenting, claims tie up the land, and if the federal government wishes to put claimed land to another purpose it must pay the claimant fair market value for the minerals in the ground.

The system is subject to abuse, with people staking claims on which they've built summer homes or through which they've cordoned off prime trout fishing streams. When mining does occur, nothing in the act requires environmental controls or cleanup and federal agency rules lack teeth. Also, unlike mining for gravel, fossil fuels, or fertilizer, the government receives no royalties from hardrock mines that extract billions of dollars' worth of resources from public land and leave behind messes that require billions of dollars in taxpayer funds for cleanup or waste management. Nationwide, Forest Service lands harbor around 27,000 to 39,000 abandoned mine sites, with up to 150,000 additional abandoned mines on Bureau of Land Management lands.

We see some evidence of mining activity as we hike on: a private property sign, slopes of yellow tailings, an old road the trail crosses over and over again as we climb uphill and down and back up again. Usually switchbacks take a hiker up and over a ridge or saddle or to the top of a mountain, but these go up and down without seeming to go anywhere, built, I'm certain, for the torture of hikers. Neither the data book nor the map does justice to this spaghetti pile of trail. I can hear Zephyr, two or three switchbacks ahead of us, singing, "I believe I can fly!" I smile, amused, and I'm determined to adopt the same optimism on this exasperating tangle of trail. But when we catch up with him, I hear his actual words: "I believe I can die!"

We haven't seen Milo and Emmet for a long time, and I worry they may have taken a wrong turn at one of the many crossings of the old road. At the bottom of a steep descent, we arrive at the Middle Fork of the Arkansas River. A "Bridge Closed" sign is tacked to the end of a single handrail which rises from a single log that spans a wide ravine with the river rushing far below. A pile of lumber waits nearby for a crew to come and repair the bridge. Zephyr and Curry scurry over the log and I scoot sideways, holding the rail with both hands. There's still no sign of Milo and Emmet. Did they shimmy over the log or are they wandering lost among old mining roads?

From the valley bottom, we begin the long, steep, winding climb toward Boss Lake, passing a half-dozen hikers and anglers. Not far up the climb, we finally catch up with Milo and Emmet, and we all hike together as the trail skirts Boss Lake and crosses the dam. Bright tents are pitched at intervals along the opposite shore. It looks like a lovely place to camp and I'm tired. We could add our own tent to the collection. But camping now would make tomorrow's hike longer and Curry's not ready to stop, hellbent on getting as much of a jump on tomorrow's miles—and the food that lies at the end of them—as possible. At the end of the dam, we pass a square hole cut deep into solid rock. A sign tacked above the open shaft says "Danger!" in big red letters and lists the possible hazards of abandoned mines. Curry, to whom "danger" translates as "welcome," sidles to the edge of the shaft to get a better look. Fortunately the boys have already hiked ahead and don't join their dad in trying to fall in. When we reach the dirt road, we find them waiting on a log bench.

I sit beside them, and Milo says to me, "I don't really want to be here."

He's been so easygoing this whole trip, the last to complain, that I'm surprised to hear him say this. But we've had a maddening hike all afternoon, over, around, and through dense, unbroken forest with nothing to draw one's attention away from aches, pain, and discomfort. Clouds have been gathering since we descended from Chalk Creek Pass and now a gray sky broods overhead. We have an hour or more to hike before we stop to eat cold food and sleep on the ground. I put my arm around his shoulders and sympathize. I don't really want to be here in this exact location. But I don't want to be home either.

We get up and hike on, reaching Hunt Lake in a little more than a mile. The dark pool of water in a dense forest of dead trees swarming with mosquitoes does not make for an inviting campsite. Curry studies the map and points out flat ground near the next, unnamed lake, a mile or so up the mountain, the last source of water before Monarch Pass, eight miles on. The data book doesn't mention a campsite there, but Curry's confident there will be one. So we keep climbing. Zephyr and I hike together, our feet dragging. The trail gets steeper and rockier. The wooly clouds drizzle rain.

We leave the dead spruce behind and climb into an area of talus and boulder fields. The ground is so steep, so rocky, so uneven that I expect to see the others hiking back down the trail, having been unable to find flat, bare ground big enough for the tent. After a while, Curry does come down the trail toward us, but he's alone and not carrying a pack. He takes Zephyr's and the three of us trudge the last half mile to the campsite, a tiny patch of grass barely bigger than our tent near a tiny snowmelt tarn. The lake sits at the base of a moraine, below a cirque carved out of Bald Mountain. The map shows another, larger tarn behind the moraine, but I'm too tired to hike up to see it. I'm too tired to even go see our own little lake, which the boys tell me has blue sand in the bottom. I'm too tired to do anything but eat my cold dinner, mix tomorrow's cold breakfast, and crawl into the tent as the cold drizzle turns into a downpour.

"You know, it's okay if you don't love every minute of this hike," I say to the kids, thinking I'm sharing a nugget of wisdom they can carry though their lives. "Even awesome things suck sometimes."

"Yeah," Milo replies, "and so does this."

I laugh. So much for my wisdom. A thirteen-hour, fifteen-mile day with a painful foot sucked. The last few hours of hiking, through miserable switchbacks and the dismal forest of dead trees sucked. But now we're fed, warm and dry, talking, laughing, playing cards, and reading *Treasure Island*. I have another revelation, though I don't share it with the kids: even sucky things can sometimes be awesome.

The clouds drain themselves dry overnight and we wake early to a luminous blue sky, anxious to get to Monarch Pass. My parents will meet us there with our next resupply, and, reportedly, there is a snack bar at the pass. The boys have been talking for days about what they will eat when we get there—hot dogs, chicken tenders, potato chips. I tell them not to get their hopes up—the snack bar might have nothing but candy and chips—but they elaborate on their food dreams as we slurp cold oatmeal.

Bald Mountain, a peak that appears to be a pile of loose stones, looms over our campsite to the west, the morning sun gilding its rough surface pink and gold. A smattering of rocks clatters down the hillside, and I look toward the sound, expecting the mountain to tumble down on us, but it is still, massive and brooding. Another shower of pebbles rains down, and we make out the tiny figures of six bighorn sheep ankling along the ridge between peaks. I get out my camera to zoom in for a closer look, but a "low battery" warning flashes on the screen and the camera dies. I put it away and watch as the tiny sheep travel along the top of the talus. They make it look so easy.

We break camp and hike over a shoulder of Bald Mountain onto the Continental Divide. As I crest the divide, a cold wind blasts from the west and I stop to add layers. The boys take off, anxious for their fantastical feast. I don't much care about food, though I still crave potato salad. More important than eating, for me, are showers and laundry. It's been six days since I last showered and eleven since we did laundry in the back-washing machine in Leadville, and I really, really want to get clean. But the nearest town, Garfield, doesn't even have a post office, so I don't expect a laundromat.

Curry hikes behind, herding me, I assume, so I will move faster. We travel high above tree line, through undulating meadows of rock, dry grass, and patches of low wildflowers. The sky is a deep cerulean with little puffs of cloud bobbing across. Mounds of cloud fill a distant valley, like whipped cream in a bowl, and wisps of fog drift over the hillside. The trail follows the Continental Divide, which here is broad and flat, sloping gently toward the south and dropping sharply to the Waterdog Lakes to the west and into the headwater valleys of Galena and No Name

Creeks to the east. Blocky, lichen-covered stones of a pinkish-buff color litter the saddle. They appear to be part of the natural boulder-scape of the tundra, but a pair of interpretive signs informs us the rocks are the remains of a prehistoric game drive. Now that I know the rocks were placed intentionally, I see a faint sense of linear arrangement, along with the abandoned feeling of the stone walls that weave through our woods in Maine.

Sites such as this appear in at least thirty locations on high ridges and passes throughout Colorado, where drive lines of low stone walls or cairns funneled game toward restricted areas, where hunters hiding in pits could ambush them. The walls here are estimated to have stood three feet high. Wooden posts set at regular intervals in some of the lines may have served to hang leather flagging that fluttered in the wind to frighten animals and direct them along the drive. Anthropologists estimate that this site was most heavily used between about one thousand and five thousand years ago, during the Archaic and Prehistoric periods, with possible more recent usage by the Utes. Traces of multiple lines appear on this ridge, and varying lichen cover on the rocks suggest they were built at different times. Differences in construction and locations imply that hunting strategies, target game species, and cultures changed over time. Anthropologists speculate that game drives may have been a regular summer activity that took place to provide bands with meat for the winter and that big drives may have occurred periodically, bringing together different tribes from over extensive ranges.

The interpretive signs here are the first formal indication along the trail of people living in these mountains prior to the influx of prospectors, miners, and settlers 150 years or so ago. The existence of Indigenous peoples has largely been erased from the landscape. With a few exceptions—Arapahoe National Forest, the Sawatch Range—the mountains, rivers, and places we've passed through so far bear Euro-American names. But these mountains were inhabited by Archaic and Prehistoric peoples and Native Americans for thousands of years prior to white settlement. Over those millennia, the Indigenous peoples left the land largely unmarred, while in the century and a half since the Utes were driven out, we have altered the landscape in dramatic ways—dams, rail beds, strip mines, clear-cuts, housing developments, highways, tunnels, bridges. Permanent though they seem, these scars are also temporary.

On November 24, 1864, a regiment of 675 cavalrymen led by Colonel John Chivington attacked a camp of around 750 Arapahoe and Cheyenne Indians along Sand Creek in eastern Colorado. The soldiers besieged the camp at dawn, indiscriminately striking down people as they fled in panic and confusion, killing around two hundred, at least half of them women and children. Seeing troops shooting into lodges, White Antelope, a Cheyenne chief, stood in front of his lodge, arms folded, and sang the death song, "Nothing lives long, only the earth and the mountains," until he was shot down. White Antelope foresaw the fate of Indigenous peoples: they would be killed, driven out, or confined to reservations and denied their historic homelands and sources of material and spiritual sustenance.

After perhaps two thousand years of living here, the Ute are gone from their Shining Mountains. Their predecessors of twelve thousand years or more vanished before that. We, too, will not live long. Our dams will breach, our mines and highways and McMansions will sink beneath layers of sediment or lava and ash, fossilized in the belly of the earth. Even the mountains will wash away once again. Only the earth will remain.

FIG. 10. Quaking aspen leaf (*Populus tremuloides*)

9

RANGE

Who can travel the miles who does not put one foot in front of
the other, all attentive to what presents itself continually?

—MARY OLIVER

DAYS 23–28: AUGUST 1–6, 2016
Monarch Pass to Nutria Creek

We follow the Continental Divide, skirting peaks and crossing smooth
saddles before dipping down toward tree line, where our surroundings
change from cool, blue mountain to dry, reddish hillsides with widely
spaced bristlecone pines springing from gravelly soil. As we approach
the Monarch Mountain ski area, dead and dying spruce replace the
pines. The trees give off a sour, pungent smell. They smell like death.
The trail joins a dirt road that skirts the top of the slopes. The road has
recently been widened and graded, trees cut, rocks blasted, reddish
soil raw like a wound. Monarch is one of Colorado's less commercial
ski areas—independently owned, closed during the summer, not in the
business of real estate development. No condos march up neighboring
hillsides. No fake Swiss village occupies the valley. Still, the gash of the
road, the barren slopes, and the dead and dying trees depress me after
the near-pristine wilderness we've hiked through over the last week.

Beyond the ski area, Curry and the boys take off and I hike alone.

One final climb takes me over a steep hill to Monarch Pass. Across the busy highway, down the road a few hundred yards, and below a tramway that climbs the slope beyond, sits the Monarch Crest gift shop. Inside, I find the boys at the snack bar, eating their second lunches. I order a cheese sandwich, chocolate milk, and potato chips. The boys return to the counter again and again to buy hot dogs, nachos, chips, cinnamon rolls, bags of candy. After I finish my sandwich, I wander the store, squeezing between racks crammed with t-shirts, mugs, rocks, toys, and western-themed kitsch. I buy postcards and a new hat for Emmet, who lost his earlier this week, then retreat to a quiet corner of the store. Zephyr and Emmet join me for a moment, but they can't sit still and hop up every few minutes to look around and buy souvenirs. Emmet returns with a fake arrowhead necklace, a worry stone, and a heart-shaped stone pendant on a chain, which he presents to me. Zephyr buys a souvenir spoon for my mom and a tin of mints with my dad's name on it.

Emmet hops up again. "I want more knickknacks."

"You know you have to carry anything you buy."

They go to admire the three-foot-tall amethyst geode and return, grinning, to tell me their grandparents have arrived. I emerge from my hidey hole and we head to the nearby campground and set up camp in a pleasant, tree-fringed meadow. My parents lay food out on the picnic table while we wash our clothes and ourselves in icy pump water and sort out next week's food. In a box of extra supplies I find a blessed pair of brand-new, clean underwear. My mom takes Curry back to the store to pick up the devices we left to charge and my dad and I walk around the campground, looking at wildflowers. Then I put my aching feet up while he cooks burgers. Milo and Emmet lounge in camp chairs, but Zephyr, who needs to rest his sore knee and groin, runs around, chasing chipmunks and jumping off rocks and picnic tables. After dinner we crawl into the tent, full and exhausted, ready to face the second half of our hike.

My parents drive us to Monarch Pass late in the morning. After one last trip into the store, we hit the trail, following a level course across the steep hillside. Emmet and I hike together and he tells me about the trail he's going to build someday.

"People will ride inside a car that goes along a cable."

"Like the tramway at Monarch Crest?"

"Yeah, but there will be a treadmill inside, so you still get exercise."

Hiking the trail has inspired Emmet to make the world a better place—or at least conform to his expectations. After our stay in the crappy motel in Leadville, he imagined a nicer hotel. When we ate in a restaurant with poor service, he designed a better restaurant. When we received a surprise medical bill, he contemplated better ways to provide health insurance. I hope this idealism follows him back to real life.

The trail sticks close to the divide, traversing a hillside of loose gravel covered in dried grass and faded wildflowers, dotted with sparse bristlecone pine. Later we come across a long-dead forest—whitened gray knobs of wood all that remain of trees that died maybe fifty or a hundred years ago. Emmet hikes ahead, leaving me alone with a mood as bleak as the landscape. I feel sick from overeating and nagged by the bills and deadlines a brief return to civilization reminded me of. Anxious and unsettled, I drag weighted feet down the trail. Around a bend, a patch of purple harebells brightens the scenery and my spirit a bit. Around another bend, a hillside dotted with more harebells and contrasting red fairy trumpets and yellow sunflowers, aflutter with butterflies, clears the rest of the town worries from my mind.

As I hike on, a young bearded man scrambles down the hillside ahead of me, roll of toilet paper in his hand. I pass his red pack, propped against a tree and a while later come upon a young woman with dreadlocks sitting by the trail. She giggles as I approach.

"Are you with that family?" she asks.

"Yeah."

"That's such an amazing vacation."

"Thanks," I say, though "vacation" doesn't seem adequate to describe this journey.

She giggles again and points to the Colorado Trail logo patch sewn to the side of my pack. "Is that a *really old* Colorado Trail patch?"

"It's an original patch," I say. "My husband and I hiked the trail twenty years ago." She's about the same age Curry and I were then, which means she was a toddler while we were hiking the trail. To her, I, like my patch, must seem *really old*.

"I know. He told me. That's so cool."

"Yeah," I concede. It is pretty cool. I wish her well and hike on. She giggles.

Curry and the boys wait for me on a flat saddle of land that drops steeply away on two sides. Here the Continental Divide actually looks like the dividing line between watersheds. The Collegiate East route climbs up the steep east face to join the Collegiate West. Approaching the divide on that trail twenty years ago was like coming upon the edge of the world. All I could see beyond the crest was the ash-gray sky, and I half expected the other side to drop off into the swirling abyss where heaven meets earth. We have only a few miles to go, so we lounge in the grass, enjoying the view. The flat top of the crest looks like a stage or movie set, with a painted backdrop of distant mountains. Over and over, Emmet and Zephyr run to the edge and pretend to fall off what appears to be a cliff, then crawl back up, like a Monty Python skit. Curry takes video and Milo and I crack up every time they disappear over the edge and reemerge. When they grow tired of the game, they join us on the grass.

"Did you see that couple hiking?" Zephyr asks. "He had an avocado in the side pocket of his backpack!"

"Do you think that they'll camp at the shelter, too?" Emmet asks.

"I hope not," I say. "She's too giggly."

A short while later, the couple passes by. We exchange greetings and, when they're barely out of earshot, Emmet says, "I see what you mean about the giggling."

We collect ourselves and hike toward Green Creek Shelter, Curry and the boys, as always, galloping ahead. The day Curry and I camped at the shelter on our first Colorado Trail hike had been overcast, foggy, and rainy. That morning, we'd stuffed damp sleeping bags, rolled up a wet tent, and marched into a dank day. Except for golden leaves in a few aspen, all was gray and dreary. We climbed toward the divide through pounding hail, hurrying the last two miles to the shelter, where we rolled out our sleeping bags in the lean-to, built a fire in the pit, and warmed up with hot chocolate. I hope the shelter is still there and isn't already filled with hikers.

I emerge from the woods into a big, grassy meadow, the silvery glint of metal corrugated roof winking at me from the distant trees. The shelter faces away from the trail, and as I come around it I find Curry and the boys hanging out on a log bench that runs along the front. The lean-to is here and intact, mostly, but the floor is gone, leaving bare, sooty ground. I'm a little disappointed, but not much. It's darker than I remembered, surrounded by dead spruce with an assortment of old junk littering the ground.

Milo studies the graffiti that covers the log walls. "Did you guys carve your name here?" he asks.

"Probably not." I scan the markings. The oldest is from 1975, but I don't see any from 1996. Curry and the boys pull out their pocket knives, find unmarked patches of log, and get to work adding their own tags: ZEPHYR CT '16. Flaky. DUSTY CT '16. Family of Five '16, with a two-peaked Colorado Trail symbol.

When they're done we collect water from a shallow seep down a side trail and prepare dinner. Even though we won't be camping in the shelter, we're drawn to hanging out here. Another hiker joins us, a tall man with a long ponytail and the cheerful drawl of his native Missouri. He introduces himself as SpecOps. We swap stories as we eat and he sets up camp. I point out the dead trees around his tent, but he says, "I figure when it's my time to go, it's my time to go."

We head across the meadow to set up our tent. I can't find the baggie that holds my toothbrush and the toothpaste gummies. Hoping it got stuffed in one of the food bags, which are packed and ready for hanging, I beg a squirt of toothpaste off Emmet and swish it around my mouth.

In the middle of the night I wake to Curry scrabbling around in the tent. "What's going on?"

"A water bottle leaked all over my spot."

I hand him my towel and go outside to get the boys' towels out of their packs. It's perfectly still, the sky awash in stars. I hand dry towels to Curry and take soaked ones to wring out and hand back. Once he's gotten the tent floor as dry as it's going to get, I crawl in and lie awake, worries from earlier in the day drifting back through my brain. In the morning I search for my toothbrush, but I can't find it anywhere. Curry is cranky from his wet night. I'm exhausted from lack of sleep and infuriated that every time I forget something in the midst of packing gear for everyone else, it's something of mine. Zephyr has caught our bad moods and is uncooperative about getting ready. When I speak sharply to him, he storms down the trail.

The morning's hike takes us through another ghost forest, pale blue mountain bluebirds and a tiny yellow Wilson's warbler flitting among dead trees, and then into dense woods, first spruce, again with many dead and dying trees, then lodgepole, with most trees showing signs of pine beetle infestation. Mountain bikes and motorcycles have eroded the trail into a trench surfaced in either slippery dust or ankle-turning loose rocks, with an occasional mud hole for variety. The dull forest and unpleasant trail drive me into my head. Anxiety about my debit card, bills, and health insurance continues to haunt me. I'm also worried about the upcoming portion of trail. The hiking won't be as difficult as the Collegiate West, but this section was one of the most challenging twenty years ago for other reasons: rain, snow, and cows. Then, as we hiked away from the Green Creek Shelter, fog and rain wrapped us in a wet blanket for three days. On the third night it snowed. Two days later I was wracked with intestinal distress. Today the sun shines brightly, but I'm concerned about getting my family through the cow-infested zone without anyone getting sick. I've narrowed the possible sources of my illness to four. The first is a piped spring from which we collected water without filtering it. When I come upon the pipe midmorning, I fill bottles, but sterilize the water.

In the afternoon, we hike through a dark, brooding forest. The woods are completely still, with no sound of breeze or bird. I sense spirits hovering. These trees affected me the same way when we hiked here last time; I referred to them in my journal as "soldiers frozen in time." On that day, we escaped the murky forest for an evening, taking a detour to camp in a meadow with a cold stream a few inches wide chortling between mossy banks. The sun emerged as we collected water, gilding the grassy slopes around us, and, I hoped, foretelling good weather. I was still frustrated with the hike. I felt like my experience was limited to the brown strip of trail, the sound of my own footsteps, and the clang of my ski poles. I wondered what I was missing and how to find it. A return of sun and time spent in that meadow reminded me of why I had wanted to go on a long hike in my beloved mountains and temporarily rejuvenated me.

Today we don't find the meadow with its happy little stream. Instead, we camp in a hollow beside Tank Seven Creek, next to a patch of brilliant magenta fireweed. As I prepare dinner, Zephyr finds dried rushes, cuts them six inches long, and gives us each one for a straw. The young couple we saw yesterday are camped nearby, and the man, Nightmare, visits our camp while we eat. He tells us that he's hiked the Appalachian Trail but this is the first long hike for his partner, Pinecone Mama. Zephyr makes him a straw.

"Wow, that's so cool. Hey, Wolverine," he says, "can you make a straw for Pinecone Mama, too?" It's the first time anyone's used one of our trail names. Zephyr smiles and sits up straighter on his log as he whittles another straw.

It rains off and on through the night, and though it's only partly cloudy when we wake up, rain is threatening again by the time we start hiking. Curry snarls as he rolls up the wet tent.

"Rain makes everything miserable."

"I'd think you'd be more waterproof, being from Maine," I snarl back.

Curry stomps off, down the trail, leaving the rest of us to finish packing. Maybe the memory of hiking through days of rain on this section of trail twenty years ago affects his mood. After the brief reprieve in the meadow, clouds returned. "The tent's wet. The food's wet. My sleeping bag is soggy. My clothes are damp. My boots are cold. Time for the sun to reappear," I wrote. Clouds swirled, going nowhere, dropping low to the ground and lifting, thinning to almost-brightness, then swelling together in thick masses. Spruce trees held back the rain then released it, drip after incessant drip onto the drooping tent. The only bright spots those days were the aspens, whose yellow foliage intensified against a backdrop of dreary skies.

The day we ascended through Cameron Park, a long, narrow meadow that follows the course of Tank Seven Creek, Curry and I discovered the maggot-filled remains of a dead calf in the stream's channel. The second possible source of my illness was water we collected downstream of the carcass. As we hike though Cameron Park, I watch for bodies in the creek. I haven't gone far when I catch up to Emmet, washing his hand with water from his bottle. It's unusual for him to drag in the morning.

"What's up, bud?"

"I accidentally kicked a rock and it landed in a cow pie and the juice splashed my hand."

Cameron Park is littered with cow pies the size of throw pillows, each one topped with a crater filled with greenish liquid. Over the next few days we'll follow the Continental Divide along the rolling Cochetopa Hills. Cochetopa means "pass of the buffalo" in Ute. Today, buffalo are in short supply, replaced by a slower, dumber ruminant that lacks the fierce majesty of the American bison. Though the Cowboy Mystique maintains a firm grip on the American West, the real cowboy era spanned only a couple decades of history. While cattle brought by early Spanish settlers and the oxen that had towed miners' wagons grazed Colorado's prairies and parks in earlier years, the territory did not see massive herds until the 1860s and '70s.

Near the end of the Civil War, when Texas found itself with an excess of cattle and northern states suffered from a dearth of beef, cattle and their drivers began the long trek north through the vast grasslands of Kansas and Nebraska, toward railroad terminals from which the animals were shipped to market. Cattle were also driven into Colorado, where they fattened on grass before being shipped east by rail. By the 1880s, the great cattle drives were already in decline, due to a combination of factors, including obstacles in the form of fenced homesteads and irrigation ditches, quarantines imposed at state borders, and depleted grasslands. The end of cattle drives did not mean the end of cattle in

Colorado, however. Stockmen had established large river-bottom ranches through manipulation of the General Homesteading Act of 1862, which was intended to give away 160-acre plots of public domain lands for the establishment of small family farms. By amassing multiple homesteads, ranchers were able to secure water rights for growing winter feed, cut off access to other users, and graze their cattle at no cost on vast areas of public land surrounding their holdings.

Unlike wild ungulates, which travel continuously, cattle congregate in and along creeks, consuming grass beyond its ability to regenerate, trampling streambanks, compacting soil, and polluting water. Cattle-trampled streams tend to grow wider and shallower, increasing water temperatures and rates of evaporation at the expense of fish that prefer cold, deep pools. Water quality goes down and fecal coliform bacteria, cryptosporidium, Giardia, and Listeria go up. As riparian vegetation is reduced or eliminated, water tables drop and small mammals and birds lose habitat. Without the erosion control, water absorption, and bank stabilization of riparian plants, flooding increases, as does spring run-off, with a corresponding reduction in stream flows later in the season. Upland, understory plants are replaced with woody vegetation, which fuels forest fires. Cows also displace native grazers and spread invasive species, which outcompete native plants. To protect their herds, ranchers and government agents shoot, trap, and poison wild predators.

In 1906, the U.S. Forest Service made the first foray into regulating livestock by establishing a permit and fee system for grazing on Forest Service land. Other federal lands did not come under regulation until passage of the Taylor Grazing Act of 1934 and subsequent amendments. Partly spurred by low beef prices during the Dust Bowl, the act set fees for grazing public lands but established those fees well below market value, and it did not initiate a reduction in stocking levels or make any provision to protect riparian areas or wildlife. Grazing fees on public land continue to lag far behind those on private land. This year the fee for grazing a cow and calf on federal public land is $2.11 per month, compared with around $22 per month on private land. The fee formula ensures that the rate charged for grazing on public land does not increase either in terms of inflation or real dollars. About half of U.S. Forest Service land is available for grazing and around six thousand permit holders run livestock on seventy-seven million acres of National Forest. As with timber harvesting, the Forest Service spends far more money on managing and administering grazing permits than they take in for fees, bringing in only 11 percent of costs last year.

As Emmet and I hike up the cow-pie meadow, he asks, "Would you rather have a cow or a dog?"

"A cow, I guess."

"Cow pies are disgusting. But dogs fart a lot."

"Cows give cheese."

"And milk and butter," Emmet adds. "If we had a yard big enough, I'd like a cow." I don't tell him that our twenty acres in rainy Maine is plenty big enough for a cow.

"Do you think a cow would protect the ducks against foxes?" he asks.

"I don't know. I've heard of guard llamas and guard donkeys, but not guard cows."

We reach the head of Tank Seven Creek with no sign of a carcass in the stream's channel, passing the second hurdle in my quest to avoid dysentery. We break for a snack and I explain to Emmet my system of food rationing. After one hour I eat a fruit leather, after the second hour a granola bar, both while walking. After three hours, I allow myself a sit-down rest and a strip of tofu jerky. Emmet's system is to eat a snack every time he stops to rest or wait, starting with his favorites (turkey salami sticks) and saving the worst granola bars (cashew cookie dough) for last. At this pace, he runs out of snacks by day four. Zephyr does the opposite, hoarding snacks to the point where his blood sugar drops and he gets cranky. Milo burns through his snacks not out of boredom or habit but because he's fifteen and hungry all the time, and I supplement his and Emmet's snack supplies from my own.

We enter a big meadow at the top of Sargents Mesa. A dozen tan cows and calves graze at the far end. The trail curves to the right, away from the herd, and Emmet says, "Aw, I wanted to pet them." After making a wide arc, the trail turns back in the direction of the cows, and Emmet says, "Oh, good, now I can pet them."

As we near a group of cows, they eye us warily. I don't expect them to stick around long enough for Emmet to pet one, and I don't expect him to have the nerve to do it, but I grip my hiking poles, ready to defend my kid. But the cows trot off as we approach, their tails swishing across their shit-stained backsides. We come upon a group of mostly calves, and Emmet says, "Maybe the calves will be less nervous." I study the two mama cows standing among the young, wondering which they belong to, which they'll defend with their half-ton bulk. But they all jog away as we get near. We hike on and chat about cows, movies, video games. Emmet tells me he doesn't like this hike.

"Have you seen anything interesting?"

"There was the dead chipmunk."

"And some live chipmunks?"

We name the wildlife we've seen: ground squirrels and chipmunks, marmots and pikas, mule deer and moose, squirrels and rabbits, bighorn sheep, gray jays, ptarmigan, a western tanager. His mood improves as the inventory grows, and we add a new animal to the list: Wyoming ground squirrels. The tawny-gray animals sit on their haunches and look at us with big, black eyes, like pint-sized prairie dogs. Ranchers don't like them because their burrows can create hazards for cattle and, supposedly, they compete for forage, though it's hard to imagine a fifteen-ounce rodent eating enough to deprive a twelve-hundred-pound cow of lunch. Golfers and homeowners don't like them because they make lawns lumpy. Chipmunk lovers don't like them because they may be out-competing the golden-mantled ground squirrel. The *Denver Post* expressed its aversion with the headline BAD WYOMING GROUND SQUIRRELS INVADING COLORADO'S WESTERN SLOPE. After more than a century of the systematic removal of hawks, owls, wolves, and other predators in support of the livestock industry, it's no surprise that rodents would spread across the state. A fact sheet from the Colorado State University extension service emphasizes the risk of bubonic plague spread by ground squirrels and winds up to near-hysterics over the potential of a colony of Wyoming ground squirrels enticing one of the state's few remaining predators: "Badgers have been known to attack people when threatened and with their medium size of 40–55 pounds . . . should be considered dangerous with their 'bad tempers' and fierce claws." The badger Curry and I saw twenty years ago at Elk Ridge was not much bigger than a house cat and appeared more near-sighted and shy than fierce. The fact sheet encourages control of ground squirrels through poisoned bait and fumigants, both hazardous to other life forms, including predators and humans. We have not yet learned to live with the wildlife that belongs to this land.

At the far end of the meadow stand the splintered remains of two cabins. When I came upon them twenty years ago, I felt as if I'd stepped back in time. That day, too, placid cows stared at me over their cuds as I waded through their excrement, the great-great-grandmothers, perhaps, of the cows we saw today. That evening we filtered water from stagnant puddles, the cattle-trampled headwaters of Long Branch Creek. That water, still brown after filtration, is my third suspect in the case of intestinal distress. Today we pass this dubious source without stopping.

At the edge of Sargents Mesa, the trail winds through a forest of dead spruce. Purple asters and magenta fireweed brighten the gloomy woods. On our first hike, when these trees were still green and alive, Curry and I had camped among them, and all night drops pattered onto the tent in a kind of water torture. We thought it was rain being caught and released by the trees, but when we unzipped the tent in the morning, we were greeted by white. Snow blanketed the mesa and heavy clouds hung low overhead. We packed up a sopping wet tent and hiked through veils of fog. Later that day the wind picked up, the clouds lifted, and we were treated to our first views in three days. We shed layers, and by the time we reached our campsite in Upper Razor Creek Park, the sky was clear, the sun beaming down. The park was cow-free, but there were plenty of signs of their recent tenancy—grass chewed to the nub, thistles and dandelions, trampled streambanks, and the ubiquitous cow pies. We filtered water from puddles of snowmelt collected in hoofprints at the headwaters of Upper Razor Creek. The water was a little fresher than the brown sludge we'd drunk the previous night but not the crystal clear Rocky Mountain spring water of a Coors commercial. Those snowmelt puddles account for my fourth possible source of illness.

Tonight we camp farther downstream along Razor Creek, the water still muddy and unpleasant from cows. I treat each bottle twice. We set up our tent in a small clearing relatively free of dead trees and crawl inside as rain starts to pour. We eat cold noodles in the tent and listen to hikers pass by throughout the afternoon. Curry edits his movie while the boys and I play cribbage, then I finish reading *Treasure Island* to them.

Twenty years ago, we woke to heavy frost at Razor Creek. It was mid-September, but winter was starting to flex its muscles. I battled stomach cramps as we hiked through a cool but clear day. Early the next morning, after we packed up our gear, the illness that had been waging war in my insides finally made itself known, barely giving me time to dig a hole. I hoped I could make it the thirty-nine miles to Gunnison. A guy from Oregon, in Colorado to trophy hunt at a ranch, picked us up. I clutched my stomach and tried to avoid looking at the bloody skull and antlers of the red deer he'd bagged while he talked in a surprisingly southern-sounding accent. "By the time the technology rolls off the assembly line," he said of his work in a Hewlett-Packard plant, "it's pert near obsolete."

In Gunnison, we bought groceries and sandwiches and checked into a hotel where I spent the day in bed, getting up only to use the bathroom. I felt better the next day, though not well enough to enjoy breakfast at a restaurant dubbed "the home of the giant pancake," where Curry ate a pancake bigger than his plate and I nibbled on dry toast. We replaced our water filter cartridge at a gear store and researched giardiasis symptoms at the college library, then spent another night in the hotel, avoiding freezing temperatures and more snow. The next morning I felt almost back to normal, and, pretty sure I wasn't suffering from giardiasis, we returned to the snowy trail.

At least it's not snowing now. And we've made it through the gauntlet of cow-shit creeks with no one getting sick. But it rains through the night, and when it's not raining the trees drip on the tent and a bird makes an unholy *wheet* sound. In Maine, from the time we open our windows in May until we close them in October, we're serenaded at night by frogs, toads, owls, coyotes, and crickets, but here the nights have been silent except when we camp near a road or a stream. So the bird's not only annoying, it's strange. What is it, and why in god's name has it chosen tonight to wail its tormented cry?

In the morning I emerge from the tent and find myself back in Maine. A shroud of dense fog has enveloped the world; I can only see as far as the trees nearest our tent. Curry holds up his phone and greets his followers: "Welcome to a crappy day. It's foggy. We're wet. We're cold. We're surrounded by dead trees. It can only get better from here."

The fog doesn't bother me as much as our schedule does. I'd planned our next resupply point, Creede, as a compromise between Gunnison, which is thirty-nine miles from the trail, and Lake City, which would have required carrying nine days' worth of food. But I allotted only a partial day in town, with a few miles of hiking in the morning and evening. I hadn't realized that from the "trailhead" there's a four-mile hike down a side trail and a jeep track to reach the road, where we'll likely have a slim chance of hitching the seven and a half miles to Creede on a Monday. There's no way we can get into and out of town in a day. We have to make up time and arrive a day early. According to the elevation chart in the data book, today's terrain will be relatively flat, with a long stretch of gradual downhill. If we hike an extra seven miles today, we can reach the trailhead on Sunday, improving our chances of getting a ride and giving us an extra half day in town.

"What do you guys think of hiking nineteen miles today?" I ask. Everyone responds with enthusiasm. Now we have our longest day before us.

The trail starts out wide, smooth, and perfectly flat, with mist in the air and stringy green usnea lichen hanging from the branches of dead trees. It is peaceful and lovely, and I hike alone, enjoying the gentle grade and the silence. Midmorning, I catch up with Zephyr, and as we hike on together, he tells me about a dream he had: "Because of the damaged ozone layer, all the people on earth came to a parking lot to be sent to the moon. I was eating an ice cream cone on my way to the parking lot, and I didn't get onto one of the space ships. There were three billion people who didn't fit in the ships and had to stay behind, and I became their leader."

He tells me how he stopped all pesticide use and coal mining and generated energy from solar panels and a type of wind generator that doesn't kill birds. He took down all the buildings except ones people needed to live in and assembled the remaining scientists to solve the ozone layer problem. "They took a sample and made a compound that they shot up to the ozone layer, only it had a mutation that caused the animals to evolve weird, like wolves with horns and stuff like that. Only animals in natural areas like national parks didn't evolve weird. And guess what happened to the people who went to the moon? They started mining it and built so many buildings it looked spiky." To solve this problem, for the people on earth, Zephyr had an image of the natural moon projected over the real, spiky moon. I can't tell how much of his tale is actually from the dream and how much he's making up as he goes, but it's entertaining and I'm pleased he's thinking about solutions to the world's problems, though also concerned that the fate of the earth lies so heavily on his shoulders.

Our nice level trail gives way to a steep climb that takes us through the rest of the morning. At the top, Zephyr says, "Now that I think about it, I'd rather have a nineteen-mile day in this," he waves his hand at the fog billowing around us, "than ninety-five degrees."

"Me too."

As we wind down the steep sides of the hill, I say, "It feels like we're hiking in Hawaii, doesn't it?" Even though I've never been to Hawaii, this side of the mountain has a tropical vibe, with deep ravines and steep hillsides. Tall sprays of magenta fireweed and yellow arnica grow along the trail, the lichen draping the trees looks like Spanish moss, and mist drifts along the slopes.

"No. Hawaii would be warm, with more flowers and no evergreen trees."

"Fine. It looks like Treasure Island." It has the dark, mystical feeling of a deserted, pirate-infested island.

The descent to Lujan Pass takes us on long switchbacks across a steep hillside. We drop from the dead spruce forest into lodgepole pines and then into aspen groves with waist-high grass. Walking into the aspens feels like an arrival, somehow. Perhaps because I spent much of my childhood camped in aspen groves, or maybe I'm anticipating the trail magic we've heard rumors about. Zephyr hikes ahead, and, as I near the pass, I hear voices and feel sure someone is there, cooking up hot chocolate and grilled cheese, but when I step out onto the Forest Service road, I find only Zephyr, sitting on a rock, talking to himself.

The wide, hard-packed gravel road winds in smooth switchbacks toward the highway.

"Wow," Zephyr says, "this road is nicer than a lot of paved roads in Maine."

It's not surprising that the Forest Service builds a beautiful road; it's as much a road-building agency as anything. Around 380,000 miles of classified roads weave their way through national forests, not counting federal and state highways and county roads. That's eight times the length of the federal interstate highway system and is enough road to circle the earth fifteen times. The majority of the roads have been built to support logging operations, and many continue to serve this function while others have been maintained for recreational access. A topo map of this area shows roads, both improved and four-wheel-drive, winding up drainages, zigzagging across slopes, encircling peaks. Only the highest ridges and summits are free of spidery black lines.

We cross the highway at North Pass, walk along the shoulder, and turn up the trail along Lujan Creek. A light drizzle oozes from the sky. Curry, Milo, and Emmet crouch under their umbrellas at the edge of the woods. We confer about the afternoon, decide to hold off on lunch until the rain lets up, and hike on through gluey mud and cow shit. Black cows and brown-and-white cows stare at us as we hike past. Any friendly feelings I felt toward the creatures early in the hike are long gone and I'm frantic to get my kids through cow shit country without anyone getting sick.

When the rain eases we stop to eat then climb a short distance over a forested nub of land and begin a long gradual descent on a wide pink-gravel trail between low pine trees. This is the easy, cruising trail I was looking forward to when I suggested a nineteen-mile day, but a few yards into the descent it feels as if I'm cracking my right shin bone against a coffee table with every step. I try to ignore the pain. We have many miles to go. Zephyr hikes with me, and I try to carry on my side of the conversation without letting on how badly my shin hurts, but it gets more painful as the afternoon wears on, and once in a while a bad twinge causes me to wince or gasp. Zephyr looks at me with concern, and I smile and say something cheerful.

The clouds thicken again and a light rain resumes. In the late afternoon the trail joins with Cochetopa Pass Road as it descends into Archuleta Valley, the treeless, rolling hillsides shrouded in mist reminding me of the open, sheep-grazed landscape of Ireland—a desert version of Ireland, with the greens more sage than emerald. Low plants of artemisia and rabbitbrush dot the hillside, small yellow sunflowers glow bright in the gloom, and the large cups of pink-and-white evening primrose blossoms droop from short stems. Zephyr and I catch up with the others at the bottom of the road, where the single-track trail resumes.

"We've got another half mile," Curry says, "if we want to make nineteen miles."

"I've got a really bad shin splint," I say. "I don't give a crap about nineteen miles."

We follow Los Creek uphill, hoping to get beyond the cow shit zone. But there doesn't appear to be an end to it, and we settle for a campsite in a high, open meadow beyond the crossing of Los Creek, two-tenths of a mile shy of our nineteen-mile goal.

Curry and I had camped near Los Creek twenty years ago, our campsite in an open meadow, possibly this same one, littered with green and red flakes of smooth, chert-like stone, leftovers from the prehistoric knapping of arrowheads and tools. The level ground with nearby water that made it an attractive campsite for us had also been inviting for those who came before. Prior to the 1850s, the Ute people occupied the mountain ranges of the land now called Colorado and Utah, as well as parts of what are now Arizona, New Mexico, Wyoming, and Nevada. Small family-based bands traveled into the high country during the warmer months to hunt game, collecting roots, seeds, and berries in the fall and migrating to milder valleys for the winter. Before returning to the mountains in spring, bands would gather together for the Bear Dance, an opportunity for elders to socialize and exchange information and for marriages to be negotiated.

The Ute were among the first Native Americans to incorporate the horse into their culture, acquiring the animals as early as the 1630s, reportedly when a group of Ute slaves escaped captivity in Santa Fe, taking Spanish mounts with them. Adoption of the horse allowed the Utes to expand their historic range. The tribal structure of small family units coalesced into larger groups as bands stayed together for longer periods of time and winter encampments grew. Fierce and feared warriors, bands of Utes raided Spanish villages and other tribes in the Southwest, and hunting parties traveled to the plains to hunt buffalo, bringing the Ute people into conflict with the Arapahoe, Comanche, and Cheyenne tribes while also bringing Plains Indian art and technology into Ute culture.

After the Treaty of Guadalupe Hidalgo in 1848 and the signing of another treaty in 1849, which established a boundary between the United States and Ute territory and allowed free passage of whites through the mountains, settlers from New Mexico encroached on Ute territory in the San Luis Valley. The discovery of gold in 1859 spelled the beginning of the end for the mountain domain of the Utes, through trickery, fraud, and whatever means the Colorado Territorial Government and the United States considered necessary to remove Indigenous inhabitants from their lands. The first treaty, which handed over the San Luis Valley to white settlers, was signed in 1863 by a band of Utes who did not live there. A treaty signed in 1868 that moved the Utes west of the Continental Divide was supposed to exclude whites, but it didn't stop a mining rush into the San Juans. With the 1874 Brunot Agreement, the Utes exchanged 3.5 million acres for $25,000. Though they believed they had only signed away the mines, the agreement restricted the Utes to a reservation.

A treaty signed in 1880 moved the Northern Ute bands into Utah and confined the three remaining bands—the Weenuchiu, Caputa, and

Mouache—to a narrow strip of land on the southern boundary of Colorado. This indignity was not enough for the people of Colorado and the state continued to try to expel the Utes for the next fifteen years, until the adoption of legislation that allotted the reservation to the Utes. In the western half of the reservation, the Weenuchiu chose to have their land held communally by the tribe, and this area became the Ute Mountain Ute Reservation. The eastern half was held in trust for allotments to individual members of the Caputa and Mouache bands. Allotments that weren't patented by members of the tribe were made available to white homesteaders, creating a checkerboard of ownership.

The Southern Ute Tribe established a tribal council and adopted a constitution in 1936 and the Ute Mountain Ute did the same four years later. The tribal governments successfully petitioned Washington in 1937 and 1938 for the return of 222,000 acres to the Southern Utes and 30,000 acres to the Ute Mountain Utes. The Utes in both reservations battled to claim their water rights through the twentieth century until the Colorado Ute Indian Water Rights Settlement Act was approved in 1988. In 2009, the Lake Nighthorse reservoir was completed to supply water to the tribes for irrigation and municipal and industrial purposes, but no federal funds were made available to transport water from the reservoir to the reservations. A 2009 memorandum of understanding with the state of Colorado restored to the Ute people some traditional hunting and fishing rights in the territory lost in the fraudulent Brunot Agreement. The tribes have faced the challenges of lack of water and other resources, along with years of the federal Bureau of Indian Affairs' policy to "civilize" Native Americans by destroying traditional culture and forcing white customs on them. Through lack of access to traditional hunting and gathering lands and systematic suppression of language, much historic Ute knowledge was lost.

I don't see any stone flakes in our campsite today, but I'm preoccupied with the pain in my shin and trying to finish camp chores before the gathering storm clouds bring another round of rain. I collect water bottles and dig the wand out of my pack.

"Want me to help collect water?" Curry asks.

"No, I want you to set up the tent before it starts to rain again."

"I thought I'd wait till after the next round of showers, to keep the tent dry."

"Please set it up now, to keep *us* dry."

He sighs but pulls out the tent bag and unfurls the roll of gold and gray nylon. The boys and I take the bottles down to the creek and wade into willow bushes upstream from the muddy, trampled crossing. The water is brownish-yellow and I swirl the wand through each bottleful for two cycles. Back in camp we eat dinner perched on rocks around a fire ring, trying to avoid dried cow patties, then I mix breakfast, Curry hangs the bear bags, and we crawl into the tent just as a deluge pours from the sky.

"Thank you for setting up the tent," I say to Curry, though I really mean, "I told you so."

We snuggle into our quilts, and Zephyr and Emmet squeeze between me and Milo as I start our next book: *The Adventures of Tom Sawyer*. After a few chapters, the twins migrate to their sleep spots. Zephyr says that when he gets home he's going to build a raft and float down the river near our house, and Emmet makes plans to whittle a corncob pipe.

"But what could I smoke in it?" he asks. "Lemon balm?"

He's conflicted between longing for the carefree, wild life that Tom led and eleven years of indoctrination about the evils of tobacco. I smile to myself. If he follows through and whittles his own pipe, I don't care what he smokes. I, too, long for my kids to enjoy a carefree and wild childhood.

Rain drums on the tent, and I remember the coyotes that howled and yipped throughout the night last time we camped here, a little glimpse of the prehistoric wild. The sky clears by morning, and Curry stays in camp to let the tent finish drying while the boys and I hike over a sagebrush flat with a view of the cliffs edging Cochetopa Dome in the distance. The trail is flat and should be easy, but walking on level ground hurts more than climbing uphill. Pain stabs with every step. Two-thirds of the way through our first hike, I got sick. Two-thirds of the way through this hike, I'm crippled with pain. Why does this have to be so hard for me?

I hear Curry's voice behind me. Thinking he's talking to me, I turn to hear him better and see that he's talking into his phone, recording today's video. If he joined me to talk about the view, the hike, the weather, anything, it would take my mind off my pain for a moment. But he's talking to his faceless viewers. An ache in my heart joins the pain in my shin, and I turn and trudge onward, tears pricking the corners of my eyes. I feel so alone.

The trail joins a Forest Service road, and the hard gravel surface intensifies the pain, sending a shockwave through my leg with each step. I sit on the side of the road and cry. When Curry catches up, he offers to take some weight from my pack, but there's nothing heavy in it—I traded the breakfast bag for Milo's sleeping quilt ages ago, and Zephyr and Emmet are each carrying half the lunch food. We walk together for a while and come upon Zephyr sitting by the road with his leg at a weird angle, his pulled groin muscle aching. Yesterday's nineteen-mile day did us both in.

After the trail leaves the road, we pass campsites with big tents and screen houses, tables covered with vinyl cloths, coolers, camp stoves, lanterns, all the trappings of car camping. I hope for the offer of a treat—potato chips or a bunch of juicy grapes—but most of the campsites are empty—the campers either out for the day or asleep in their tents. The few campers who are about stare mutely as we go by. A while later, we meet a hiker heading in the opposite direction. He's thru-hiking the Colorado Trail for a second time, having hiked north-to-south last year. He's curious about our gear and our family of five, and we commiserate about the livestock.

"I call these the Cowshitopia Hills," he says and we laugh in agreement.

We stop for lunch near a fenced spring in Van Tassel Gulch. SpecOps and a few hikers who passed us this morning sit by the trail. As we eat, we watch the others wriggle under the barbed wire and look for the water source. A guy with a dark beard wearing sunglasses, a straw hat, and a rain skirt made of house-wrap, comes down the trail and drops his pack next to us.

"Hey," Curry says, "you fell into our campsite!"

It's the bear who stumbled into our camp at Cataract Creek, whom we haven't seen since we hiked out that morning. He introduces himself as Dr. X.

Curry introduces us. "This is Wolverine. Flaky and Dusty are over there. She's Hey Mom, and they call me Ken Burns."

"Ken Burns? What does that mean?"

"You know, the PBS documentaries? Never mind." No one gets Ken Burns.

We finish our lunch and squeeze under the fence. We can't find the actual spring, where water bubbles up from the ground, only a small stream. SpecOps and Dr. X scoop water and cap their bottles. But large bones lying inside the fence tell me the enclosure is not entirely cow-proof, so I swirl the magic wand in our bottles. The water tastes good—fresh and cold and clear, like water we drank before cattle country.

Back on the trail, Zephyr and I make our slow way together through the afternoon. We're walking down a gravel road when we see something brown and leggy gallop down a grassy slope to a pond in the distance. It's too lively and agile to be a cow.

"I wonder if there are wild horses here," I say.

"Not a *wild* horse." Zephyr points to a truck parked on the edge of the road.

But there's a hill between the truck and the pond, and the animal came from the opposite direction. Besides, it seems unlikely anyone would let their horses run free out here. As we walk closer, two smaller brown leggy animals make their way down to the pond, and I can now see they are moose, a mother and twin calves. At that moment, the skies open and rain pours down. We put up our umbrellas and stand still, watching the moose as the ruts of the road turn into rivers around our ankles. After a few minutes, the rain lets up a little and we walk on slowly, trying not to disturb the moose. The trail leaves the road and skirts the edge of the pond. When the mother puts her head under the surface to collect a mouthful of pond weeds, we walk forward a few steps. When she lifts her head, we freeze. She looks at us. We look at her. She puts her head below and we walk a few more steps. She lifts her head. We freeze again. The babies watch us. We continue this way until, about halfway along the shore and directly across the pond from the moose, I slip in the mud and spook the babies. They scramble out of the water and the mother rears her dripping head out of the water and gallops up the slope, herding her young ahead of her and glancing over her shoulder at us.

Beyond the pond, we limp to Cochetopa Creek. When Curry and I hiked through this area last time, the sun shone from a clear sky but the wind held a tinge of winter. That night we camped in Ignatius Park, where we saw a bull elk near our camp and heard coyotes howling into the night. I tried to imagine the fenced, cowed, cow-pied, and over-grazed park as wild and free, native grasses waving in the wind, alive with bison, the frosted hills thick with elk, wolves, and grizzlies, where bands of Utes followed herds, hunted, gathered, literally worked for life. I couldn't help but feel we were traveling through a diminished landscape—nothing but the cows and us, in our synthetic skins, walking five hundred miles for no reason, eating out, taking showers, and staying in hotels when the going got rough.

We met a trio of Continental Divide Trail thru-hikers that day, two men and a woman. They'd started at the Canadian Border on the fifteenth of June and planned to arrive at the Mexican border by the first of November. They told us they averaged twenty miles per day and that about 15 percent of their hike consisted of bushwhacking and route-finding. They knew of only three others hiking the Continental Divide that summer. Among the dozens of thru-hikers we've come across this summer, a handful are hiking the Continental Divide Trail. By the end of this season, fifty-one hikers will have registered with the Continental Divide Trail Coalition as "3,000-milers." Back then, I was intrigued by the idea of hiking from Canada to Mexico. But, having struggled with days of eight to twelve miles, I knew I'd be miserable hiking twenty, if I could even do it. Now that an almost nineteen-mile day gave me crippling shin splints, I'm pretty sure I couldn't hack three thousand miles, but part of me still wonders *what if . . . ?*

Zephyr and I limp along the level trail along Cochetopa Creek for a long, long time. Rain comes and goes all afternoon. Dr. X approaches from behind on the narrow trail hemmed in by willows and says, "Hey

Mom, can I get past you?" It's the first time someone has used my joke trail name, other than my kids, who say "Hey Mom" a trillion times a day. I don't think I like it. Dr. X might be young—early thirties I'd guess—but not young enough for me to be his mom.

The data book says we'll reach a high point above the creek before descending to a ford. Each time the trail travels uphill I hope it's our high point. Each time I'm disappointed. Finally we crest the elusive high and emerge from the forest at the top of a steep slope. Two women have set up camp on a little shelf of open land near the edge of the drop-off to the creek. A chain strung across the trail holds back two prancing horses. One of the women opens the chain to let us through and the other woman tries to restrain her horse, but it skirts past and gallops down to the creek.

"How are you doing?" one of the women asks. "Your husband told me you had shin splints. I'm a massage therapist. This muscle is pulling away from the bone and tearing out little shards. That's why it hurts so much."

She shows me how to rub my lower leg muscles and says, "It's going to hurt more on the uphill."

"Actually, it hurts more going down," I say, "adding insult to injury."

The horse trots back up the steep, mucky trail and Zephyr and I start down. The woman shouts and we scramble out of the way as the horse lunges down and back up again, then we slip and slide to the bottom.

The bridge has washed out and the creek runs fast and wide between the steep walls of the valley. Curry, Emmet, Milo, and Dr. X wait for us on the other shore. Curry wades across barefoot and sits down with Zephyr to help him take off his shoes and the legs of his zip-off pants. He takes his pack, gives him a trekking pole, and holds his other hand as they teeter their way across slippery rocks beneath rushing water. I pull my wind pants over my knees but leave my shoes and socks on—they're already soaked from hiking in the rain and I'd rather have the traction of rubber soles on slick rocks—and ease into the river. The ice-cold water numbs my lower legs, and, for the first time all day, I feel relief from the shooting pain in my shin.

From the far bank, we climb a steep slope to a flat terrace of land.

Below, the creek meanders through a deep, flat-bottomed valley. After a short distance I catch up to Milo, standing and looking out over the valley. Beavers have dammed the creek in places, redirecting the flow in meanders and oxbows, creating a braided, tangled network of streams, streamlets, mudflats, and meadows.

"It's cool," Milo says, "the way the creek changes course."

I stand beside him, admiring the winding path of the creek. Milo's so fast I haven't had much opportunity to hike with him. I mostly see him at lunch breaks, when our conversations consist of "pass the almond butter," and in the tent at night, where he makes jokes about the dirty socks he and his brothers whip around the tent then falls asleep while I read. To know that he notices and pays attention to details of the natural world is worth the price of today's pain. I stand still, taking in the view with him, even though clouds are brewing and we need to get to camp before the next shower.

We don't make it, and it's pouring by the time we cross Nutria Creek and reach the flat grassy area where we plan to camp. Dr. X has already set up his small tent and is inside, warm and dry, but we missed the window, so we huddle under our umbrellas to wait it out.

"Why don't you prep dinner while we wait?" Curry says.

"Because we need to collect water." I'll get soaked if I move out from under the small circle of my umbrella. Everything in my pack will get soaked if I dig out the SteriPen and food bowls. I'm tired and in pain and I just want to rest for a while.

But the rain doesn't let up and Curry's mood grows surlier. He crouches under his umbrella, silent and radiating a cloud of dissatisfaction as palpable as the rain pouring down around us. In response, I grow chatty and chipper and extra patient with the kids. Emmet marches around our little huddle of bodies and sings a song about thanking the rain.

"When you see a flower, thank the rain! When you eat an apple, thank the rain!" The lyrics get more ridiculous as he walks a trench around us in the tall grass. "When a grouse flies into your window and breaks its neck and you eat it for dinner, thank the rain!"

I press my mouth to my knee to contain my laughter.

"Shh, don't laugh," Milo whispers, though he's also struggling to keep a straight face. "You'll make him self-conscious."

Curry's lips don't even twitch. The rain goes on and on and on. When thunder rumbles down the valley, we scramble into the shelter of the aspen grove up the slope. After nearly an hour of huddling under our umbrellas, a patch of blue sky appears. The sun, on the verge of setting, creates a rainbow, a full arc over the dead spruce on the hillside across the creek, as the last drops sprinkle down from the sky. We emerge from the shelter of the trees, soggy and cramped from crouching.

"Why are there so many songs about rainbows," Milo begins, and I join in. Before we set up camp or collect water or mix dinner, he and I sing every word of "Rainbow Connection," while admiring the view and enjoying this moment after the rain.

10

RESTORATION

To be whole. To be complete. Wildness reminds us what it means to be human, what we are connected to rather than what we are separate from.

—TERRY TEMPEST WILLIAMS

DAYS 29–31: AUGUST 7–9, 2016
Nutria Creek to Mineral Creek

We rise with the sun and take our time packing. Clear blue sky arches from one wall of the valley to the other. My shin feels better, and I walk slowly, stopping now and then to stretch. We travel along a bench of land above Cochetopa Creek, winding in and out of grassy meadows dotted with purple gentian and wide-spaced stands of bristlecone pine. The hillside across the creek is covered in the withered gray-brown skeletons of dead spruce. Only saplings and patches of aspen remain green. Even though we've entered the La Garita Wilderness area, hoof tracks and cow pies continue to mar the trail. Little streams that wash toward the creek have been trampled into mud holes. Each time we pass through a gate, I hope that we've escaped the bovine horde, but cow pies continue to plague the trail.

FIG. 11. Meadow fringed gentian (*Gentianopsis thermalis*)

The Wilderness Act of 1964 allowed livestock to continue grazing in designated wilderness under existing permits. A House Report attached to the Colorado Wilderness Act of 1980, which established or expanded more than a dozen wilderness areas in the state, prohibited public lands agencies from curtailing grazing simply for the sake of wilderness and allowed leaseholders to build and maintain livestock support facilities within wilderness and use motorized vehicles for stock management and emergency purposes. In other words, wilderness protections don't apply when it comes to grazing.

At the Eddiesville Trailhead, we pop out of the wilderness area and travel along the fence line of a ranch, one of those bottomland homesteads, a base property forever linked to grazing rights. I daydream about buying the place, evicting the cows, painting the brown trim of the house the purple-blue of gentian flowers, and welcoming thru-hikers. Beyond the ranch, we reenter the wilderness area and, after passing through two or three more gates, finally escape cattle country. The difference from one side of the gate to the other is stark. Tall larkspur and monkshood nod their deep purple blooms. Grass grows thick, brushing my legs as I pass.

Zephyr pulls seed heads off waist-high grass stalks. "What kind of plant is this?" he asks, as if a week of hiking through territory where every blade was nibbled to a stub has erased the natural form of grass from his memory.

After half a day of hiking, pain again shoots through my shin with each step. Zephyr picks wild strawberries and hands them to me as I hobble. After a while, he hikes ahead, out of sight, but before long I find him standing in the midst of a boulder field.

"I just saw a weasel catch and kill a pika."

He points to a crack between rocks at the base of the hills. My kids always root for the predator when they watch nature programs, so this incident doesn't alarm him. He climbs up to get a closer look at the crevice. The weasel pokes its sharp brown nose of the opening. Zephyr takes its picture and scampers back down to the trail.

We climb higher and higher up the valley. The trees grow sparse, and Cochetopa Creek abandons its meandering ways, becoming a torrent of clear, icy water. We plan to camp beyond the point where the trail crosses the creek. When I reach the crossing in late afternoon, I drop my pack and lower my legs into the frigid water, numbing my throbbing shin and aching feet. Curry comes down, laden with bottles. I scoop water and swirl the wand then hobble to camp. Our tent is set up in a little flat area among low willows and stunted fir trees. Two other tents share the neighborhood. One belongs to Dr. X, the other to an older man who plans to meet his son at the saddle and climb San Luis Peak in the morning. Spec Ops has hiked ahead to camp at the saddle for an early attempt on the mountain.

Twenty years ago, Curry and I camped an extra day in La Garita Wilderness, perhaps in this very spot. Fall had returned to the mountains that day, after our dip into winter. Sunny, clear days and cold, frosty nights replaced rain and snow, and we took a day off to enjoy the weather and the wilderness. We woke to the sound of elk bugling, an uncanny, long, lonely whistle, and I spent the day reading and writing while Curry crouched beside the stream, attempting to spear a trout with his pocket knife lashed to a branch. In the evening we went in search of the elk. We could hear bugling coming from uphill and climbed toward it. As we skirted a ridge, the bugling grew nearer and short whistles came from closer by but higher up. We crept along, trying to step on soft dirt, mossy patches, or large, stable rocks to avoid making noise.

On the open slope above us appeared the hindquarters of an elk—thick legs and the white rump that gives the elk its Shawnee name, wapiti. Elk are taller and bulkier than deer, and the bulls sport massive racks of antlers and manes of dark fur around their necks. Before Europeans arrived in North America, an estimated 10 million elk roamed most of the area that became the United States. Settlement, hunting, and conversion of land to agriculture had extinguished the Eastern subspecies by the 1870s and reduced the population in the West to fewer than 100,000 individuals by the early 1900s. With only about 500 to 1,000 elk remaining in Colorado, the state limited hunting between 1903 and 1933. During that time, 350 elk from Wyoming were reintroduced to fourteen different areas of the state. Today, Colorado's elk population of

280,000 animals is the largest in North America. With few remaining natural predators to keep populations in check, over-browsing and conflicts with humans have become problems, and the state has resorted to culling fertile females to manage elk numbers.

After seeing the elk's hindquarters, Curry and I took seats with a clear view and waited. The whistling sounded close by and the bugling drew nearer. Twigs snapped to our left and I thought I saw movement between two trees. I stared at the spot, my heart racing, my eyes watering from not blinking. The chatter of a squirrel made me jump. I heard Curry swallow and followed his gaze. Two cow elk emerged from the trees onto the slope above us. They nibbled at the ground as they worked their way toward the ridge. The smaller one raised her head, alert. After a moment she returned to grazing. The bull continued to bugle, but the females appeared indifferent to his call. When they reached the top of the slope, they headed away from him along the ridge, their white rear ends disappearing through the trees.

Hearing more crashing, we expected a pair of antlers to emerge from the trees to our west, but another cow elk appeared high up on the slope and disappeared behind a stone outcropping, followed by two more females. The bugling continued, sounding farther away and echoing off the slopes. After the sun disappeared behind clouds on the western ridgeline, we worked our way downhill to the trail. Another elk bugled from the southeast, and we hiked toward camp in anticipation of finding a bull next to our tent, but the calls faded into the forest across the creek.

That was in late September, the early part of a rut season that stretches through mid-October. Now, in early August, elk aren't yet thinking of amour, and none will serenade us tonight. I crawl into the tent to rest while Dr. X plays with the kids and shares snacks with them. It's a relief to have someone else absorb their energy for a little while. A hailstorm rolls down from San Luis Peak, and everyone retreats to their tents. Ice balls rattle on nylon and thunder reverberates off the peak. I hope SpecOps is okay at the saddle, where barbs of lightning must be dancing around his tent.

In the morning, I set off early, leaving packing, water treatment, and breakfast cleanup to Curry and the boys. It will take me a long, long time to cover our miles today, and I don't want to get left behind. The trail winds through open meadows of grass, sedges, and wildflowers alternating with dense willow bushes, their branches nearly obscuring the trail. San Luis Peak looms on the horizon with tall, volcanic tuff hoodoos marching up its grassy slopes like goblin armies.

Milo and Emmet pass me on the ascent to the saddle, then two women with whom we've been leap-frogging for the past two days pass me, followed by Curry and Zephyr. We all pause to rest on the saddle in the early morning sun. SpecOps has already summited the peak and is packing up his tent. One of the women prepares to climb, and another young man hikes up from the trailhead and heads up the summit trail. Of the fourteeners the Colorado Trail skirts by, San Luis would be the one to climb, only a mile and a quarter from trail to summit and, it appears, a smooth, gently sloping ascent. But today I'll be lucky to make it to the trailhead.

Walking downhill hurts more than uphill, and each step along the mountain's flank sends shocks of pain through my leg. *Universe, what are you telling me?* I shout inside my head. A little green and yellow butterfly sits on the trail, not moving. I pick it up and set it on a flower. It flutters away. *Slow down and pay attention?* Is that the message I'm not receiving? I'm already moving more slowly than almost anyone on the trail. I stretch my leg and look out over the view. More dead trees fill the valley. The mountains ahead look impenetrable, but so do the mountains we just passed through. It's an apt metaphor for life. I made it through and out the other side of a difficult period of life. The future, jobless with no real plan beyond the end of this trail, appears every bit as challenging. I don't know how I'll bring the small measure of joy I've found along the trail home with me. Yet there is always a path through, and sunlight on the other side.

The day after our elk-stalking twenty years ago, Curry and I found ourselves in winter again. We ascended San Luis Saddle in snow. As we dipped into the valley beyond, I heard the whine of an engine and assumed it was wind. But as we crossed a saddle north of a mountain called Peak 13,111, I heard another sound, like strange birds on the slope above. Looking up, I saw several figures on the south ridge of the peak and for a moment hoped I was at last setting eyes on mountain goats. But it soon became clear they were the commonest of species: *Homo sapiens sapiens*. Impressed they'd climbed nearly to the peak in such adverse weather, I marched forward with vigor, bolstered by their success. Another glance at the ridge showed a bright glint of light reflected off glass or metal, and I saw that two suvs, not strength or skill, had brought this gaggle of pirates within spitting distance of the summit of Peak 13,111 on a jeep trail that kisses the wilderness boundary.

Today I'm grateful to not be hiking in snow and to not be beset by gaggles of pirates on four wheels. Curry and the boys wait for me at Willow Creek Trailhead, a weathered signpost in the midst of a meadow. As we follow the footpath toward the jeep road, the others march ahead, leaving me to hobble alone. Two young women with a little dog pass, heading up toward the saddle. They sound concerned when they ask how I'm doing. Curry must have told them about my shin splints.

"Fine," I reply in as cheerful a voice as I can muster.

A mile and a half down the valley, the trail meets the jeep track, where Curry and the boys sit on the roadside. As we pass lunch food around, dark clouds congregate on the flank of San Luis. I take my cheese and crackers and eat while I walk down the washed-out jeep trail. I want to reach the road ahead of the rain. A caravan of at least two dozen off-road vehicles roars past up the track. They look like golf carts outfitted for elephant hunting—roll bars, knobby tires, camouflage paint jobs. Some are driven by children. An infant in a car seat is strapped into another. Heedless of the impending storm, they turn left at the trailhead and zoom up a steep track, heading toward the south flank of Peak 13,111. More pirates.

Clouds thicken. Drops spit. Thunder rumbles. The two women with the little dog catch up with us on the way down. Curry talks them into giving us a ride into town, and we reach their truck just before the clouds burst. Curry and Emmet crawl into the narrow space between the cap and a wooden platform that fills the bed of the truck. The dog and our packs go in after them. Zephyr, Milo, and I squeeze into the mini back seat behind the driver, Jo, and her passenger, Crystal. While they tell us about their work at the Creede Repertory Theatre and life in this high mountain town, I peer out the window, trying to pay attention to where we are so that we'll be able to get back tomorrow. The windshield wipers slap ineffectually at torrents of rain washing over the truck. Flashes of lighting cast a greenish glow on the sky. The rough gravel road winds between the steep walls of a canyon. Willow Creek cascades fast and silver-white alongside the road, with no guard rail to prevent us from plunging into the water. The truck stutters over washboards and Jo shifts into four-wheel drive as we skid down the steep grade. I grip the seatback and pray this isn't our end.

A cribwork of logs climbs up from the tops of the shallow canyon walls, as if we're passing between two massive cabins, only the walls hold back tons of earth moved from one part of a mountain to another. We're driving through the heart of the Creede Mining District. The last of the boom towns, Creede is situated at the southern terminus of several geologic faults into which mineral-rich fluids flowed during a period of volcanism that formed the Creede Caldera around twenty-seven million years ago. The rush to Creede began after the town's namesake, Nicholas Creede, discovered ore along East Willow Creek. Soon mines popped up along all the major veins radiating north of town, and, despite the drop in silver prices after 1893, mining carried on almost continually in the district for nearly a hundred years.

The road levels as it enters town, an acute triangle three streets wide and maybe ten long. Jo takes us to the south end, pointing out the post office and gear and grocery stores, and lets us off at an inn. She refuses our offer of gas money and arranges to give us a ride back to the trail tomorrow. We check in and drop our packs in a bright, clean room, then walk to the post office, where we collect our resupply box along with a package of five fancy chocolate bars sent by my friend Jennifer. Curry and the boys charge ahead through town while I limp yards behind them. The pavement hurts even more than the jeep road. On the way back to the inn, we stop at a food truck, and I rest at the picnic table while Curry and the boys eat sausage sandwiches, hot dogs, and fries. I poach a few of Milo's fries, but I'm not really hungry. All I want is to shower and lie down on the soft hotel bed and ice my shin.

Curry finishes his sandwich in three bites and licks mustard from his fingers. "Let's check out the gear store."

"My priority is taking a shower, doing laundry, and sorting our resupply box," I say.

"What about my priorities? I've been wanting to get underwear for four weeks."

"Your priority was eating, and you got to do that. I don't think you appreciate how long it takes to organize the resupply."

He sighs, stands up, and leads the way to the inn, me hobbling behind again. We change into rain gear and load our dirty clothes into Curry's pack, and he heads out to the laundry room and the gear store. The kids turn on the television and watch a cupcake baking competition. I get in the shower and scrub away two weeks' worth of dirt, sweat, and grime, then lay a bag of ice on my shin and put out an sos online: "Help! What can I do about shin splints? We have 11 days and 140+ miles left of hiking and I can barely hobble."

Over the next few hours, friends come through with a range of answers from discouraging (nothing you can do but wait it out) to helpful (stretches, ice, massage, tape) to impossible to find in a small town (supportive shoes, compression socks) to lifesaving (800 mg ibuprofen three times per day for eleven days). I put this last piece of advice, which came from a doctor, to work immediately, and when we go to the small grocery store to round out our resupply, I stock up on ibuprofen and athletic tape. I also buy extra treats for the trail—a canister of pink lemonade powder and tiny jars of lemon pepper and pumpkin pie spice to add some fun and flavor to our cold, dismal meals.

When I get up in the middle of the night to use the bathroom, I can barely walk. Not only does my right shin ache, the left one is starting to hurt too. The soles of both feet are tender and swollen, and it feels like my foot bones grind together with each step. I need new shoes if I'm going to finish this hike. But Creede is tiny, a literal dead-end town, connected to civilization by a single road. If I can't find shoes here, I'll have to hitchhike to Salida or Gunnison, each more than a hundred miles away. We'd have to stay another day, throwing off our schedule. I toss and turn, worrying. I want to wake Curry up and ask him if the gear store carries shoes, but it's three in the morning, so I lie in bed listening to the hum of the ventilation system and waiting for morning.

Hours later the others wake up and Curry assures me the gear store has a large selection of hiking shoes. With renewed optimism, I follow my family to the breakfast buffet. The food is homemade and nicer than most continental breakfasts—baked French toast, egg casserole, muffins. When the boys have eaten their fill, they return to the room to watch more TV while Curry and I chat with two other hikers, a couple a few years older than ourselves named Rick and Jean. They live in western Colorado, in the tiny town where Curry and I once spent a summer working for the Forest Service, and are good friends with one of the rangers we used to work with. They tell us that the baby the ranger and his wife had that summer is now eighteen. This news is dizzying. Logically, it makes sense; Milo is fifteen, and we worked there three years before he was born. Yet in my mind that kid is still the tiny baby in his mother's arms. Somehow other people's kids grow up even faster than my own.

Recent empty nesters, Jean and Rick have made time to thru-hike the trail. They plan to stay in Creede another day, so I don't expect to see them again. Trail life is so strange. We're out here, sharing the same intense, life-changing experience with so many people, yet we often don't say more than "Hey, how's it going?" to each other. With others we have lengthy conversations, over hours or days, before we hike on, not saying goodbye, not knowing if or when we'll see them again. Relationships are transient and conditional on being in the same place at the same time. Most of the hikers we've met along the way have either gotten ahead of us or dropped off the trail. We've likely seen the last of both Dr. X, who had planned to continue straight to Silverton, and SpecOps, who's taking a week off of hiking. Yet the moments of connection we've had have resonated despite their brief, temporary nature. I feel a small sense of loss with each person who vanishes from our hike and our lives.

We return to our room and reload our packs, then Curry, Milo, and I walk to the gear store, leaving Emmet and Zephyr in front of the TV. The store has an overwhelming display of hiking boots, lightweight hikers, and trail runners. I gaze at the array in confusion while Curry summons a saleswoman and explains my situation. She hands me three pairs of shoes, all sturdier than my trail runners but less bulky than boots. The first pair I try on are bright red and yellow. They look like something a kindergartener, or Ronald McDonald, would wear. But when I slip my right foot inside, I feel instant relief and I can walk without a limp. The second pair is too narrow. The third sends shooting pains up my leg. I try the ketchup-and-mustard pair again and again feel relief. I keep them on and browse the store while Milo and Curry pick out energy bars. On the clearance rack I find a fleece top to replace my sleep shirt, a twenty-year-old silk turtleneck that's falling apart, and I also finally find a lightweight nylon cap to replace the hat I hate.

Back at the inn, I shove my old shoes and hat in the box we're sending home, and we hoist our packs, bulging with a week's supply of food, and head downtown. As we pass a gas station, a woman filling up her van asks if we're hiking the trail and tells us she offers a shuttle service for hikers. In the restaurant, after we take our seats on the patio, two women picking up takeout tell us they plan to hike the trail with their kids and pack goats in a couple of years. One of them runs to her car and returns with a pack of cinnamon gum. It's a weird piece of trail magic— I've never chewed gum while hiking—but a sweet gesture, and I thank her profusely. Creede is the friendliest trail town we've visited so far. Jo picks us up after lunch and takes us back to the trail by a different route, through a part of the mining district called Bachelor Town, and drops us off at the Equity Mine. All that's left of one of the last-operating mines in town, which was worked from 1912 to 1988, are piles of yellow tailings behind a chain-link fence.

Emmet and I hike side by side up the jeep road.

"Do you feel clean and rested?" he asks.

"Yes. Do you?"

"Yes," he replies, to my surprise. Perhaps this is a new chapter in the life of Dusty.

Before long, he outstrips me, the two large bags of chips he bought in town swelling with altitude on either side of his pack. My shin feels much better with the new shoes, a couple yards of tape, and a handful of ibuprofen. But Zephyr's knee hurts, and he hangs back with me. A tiny chipmunk runs across our path.

"Why do you think least chipmunks' tails are twice as long as their bodies?" he asks.

The least chipmunk is the smallest member of the ground squirrel family, at about three to four inches in length with a tail that, while not twice as long as its body, is pretty long, especially compared to other ground squirrels.

"I don't know."

"Snow leopards' tails are twice as long as their bodies, so they can balance when they jump."

"Maybe least chipmunks are a kind of snow leopard."

Zephyr laughs and tells me more about snow leopards.

"They live in Mongolia and China where there aren't enough wild goats and sheep for them to eat because not-wild sheep eat all the grass and plants, so the snow leopards have to eat the farmers' sheep. So they get shot." He tells me snow leopards are camouflaged so well that a researcher tracking a radio-collared leopard couldn't see the animal right in front of him.

We hear a squeak nearby, and a little animal scurries past. "Was that a pika?" Zephyr asks.

"I'm not sure. I didn't really see it," I say. "What do least chipmunks say?"

"I think they say, 'pinecone, pinecone.'"

We find the others resting at the trail junction. A pair of thru-hikers stops for a chat. The man hiked the trail last summer, his girlfriend joining him for the first half. They've returned to hike the second half together. Emmet pulls two bags of candy he bought in town out of his pack and hands a mini Twix and a Jolly Rancher to each of the hikers. When we get up to hike on, Zephyr and I again lag behind. The mountains are long and humped, green on their lower slopes with tops that look from a distance like heaps of sand in shades of buff, red, and gray. The trail takes us over the saddle north of Peak 13,111, but doesn't descend into the valley on the other side. Instead it dips into a meadow and curves to the left, paralleling the Continental Divide and climbing higher. Zephyr points downhill, the way it seems the trail should go.

"Why doesn't the trail just go over there?" he asks.

"Because trail builders are sadists."

"Satanists?"

"No, sadists, people who get their kicks from making other people suffer."

The views, at least, make up for our trouble. Before us, the San Juans spread out to the very edges of the earth. To the north, rolling hills topped by craggy, pointed peaks appear as if they were squeezed from a pastry bag by a clumsy chef. The trail goes up and around a couple more humps of the mountain, reaches another saddle, and then descends a slope made of stones colored in Easter egg hues of blue, gray, green, pink, purple, gold, and orange, some polished to an oily sheen, others dimpled, pockmarked, or rounded by time. The trail heads straight downhill, no switchbacks, and Zephyr and I limp down the steep slope.

"Trail builders *are* sadists," he says.

Curry has set up the tent among sparse, dead spruce trees a short distance from the creek, perhaps the very place we camped twenty years ago, when I wrote, "Our campsite on a golden hillside by the trail was pummeled with rain and hail and tormented by thunder and lightning. Just in time, we had taken refuge in the blue dome, our safe haven, snail home, and true shelter."

I send Milo and Zephyr to get water and take my time mixing dinner. We've arrived in camp reasonably early, and now that I'm not in excruciating pain, I can relax and enjoy the view. Emmet, hyped on the two big glasses of Dr. Pepper he had at lunch, runs around the campsite, jumping off of rocks, and getting in everyone's way. When a hiker comes down the trail, he runs up the slope to give him candy.

A frantic squeaking of pikas from among the boulders on the hillside across the trail draws our eyes to the sky where a golden eagle drifts in lazy circles. Zephyr points to the ridgetop, where a single bighorn sheep picks its way along the rocky spine. The setting sun turns the hillside golden, and we chew cold al dente couscous and revel in the beauty of the moment. A warm feeling washes over me. I'm clean. I'm rested. I have new shoes on my feet. It feels good to be back on the trail with my family.

FIG. 12. Ponderosa pine cone (*Pinus ponderosa*)

11

TABLELAND

Those who dwell . . . among the beauties and mysteries
of the earth are never alone or weary of life.

—RACHEL CARSON

DAYS 32–36: AUGUST 10–14, 2016
Mineral Creek to Molas Pass

It rains on and off throughout the night and into the morning. We wake
late and get a late start. I begin a final countdown: Ten more bowls of
cold oatmeal. Ten more catholes. Emmet, Zephyr, Milo, and I hike out
together while Curry waits for the tent to dry. The boys, playing Harry
Potter trivia—*What is the name of Sirius Black's house elf? Which goblin
helped Harry break into Gringotts? Where did Harry end up when he first
traveled by flue powder?*—soon disappear down the trail. I catch up to
them about a mile later, sitting on boulders at the base of a climb. I settle
on a rock and join their game. *Who tortured Neville Longbottom's parents?
What is the name of the elf liberation organization Hermione founded?*

Curry comes hiking down the trail and scolds us, "You've been hiking
an hour and have only gone a mile."

We get up and work our way up the slope. Curry and the boys move
quickly ahead, and I'm left to hike alone until I come upon a couple emerging from their campsite in the willows. Tim and Derice, another pair of

empty nesters, tell me they've been section hiking the Colorado Trail for years and are finishing the last few sections this summer. They're the first hikers I've come across who travel my pace, and we walk together, chatting, through the morning, as the trail winds up a valley spiky with dead spruce, over and around ridges topped in red and green sand, and along the Continental Divide, here an undulating ridge of grassy tundra, loose talus, and cliffs of fractured stone. The wind comes up and dark clouds race across the sky. We find Curry and the boys crouching beneath their umbrellas beside the trail, and we join them as a thunderstorm charges down the valley.

When the rain lets up we part ways with the couple, who plan to camp nearby, and descend to Snow Mesa. We travel across the open, rolling expanse below the divide, which ridges the north end of the mesa. The trail climbs over low hills and dips into small ravines that rumple the mesa top and stretch into steep-walled valleys that gnaw away at the south end of mesa. After the third or fourth water crossing, I suggest we stop to find a place to camp. It's not clear from the data book whether we'll find more water before we have to descend the far end of the mesa.

"We should seriously assess your ability to finish the trail," Curry says.

"We've already hiked farther than we planned to today," I reply, "and taking it easy for a few days is part of what I need to do to be able to finish the trail."

"Fine, whatever."

He heads uphill, and I stomp after him. I can't believe he's suggesting I leave the trail, *my* trail.

The five of us fan out in search of a tent site. The mesa top is bare of trees, but the ground slopes steadily up from the trail and is lumpy with clumps of grass and low vegetation. Curry calls us over to show us a nest he almost stepped on. A scraggly baby bird pokes its head out of a pile of dried grass, perfectly camouflaged with the ground. I forget my irritation when I see the naked, vulnerable little bird. It's astonishing what harsh conditions life can thrive under. We scan the ground more carefully in case there are other nests and eventually find a flat spot on a terrace above the trail and below Baldy Cinco, a pointed peak rising from the steep ridge of the Continental Divide.

Fluffy clouds scud across the sky as we collect water and make dinner. A boom of thunder, like an explosion set off outside our tent, wakes me in the middle of the night. I lift my head and watch for lightning. The tent lights up at the same moment the next thunder cracks. One mile a second or ten miles a second? I still can't remember, but it doesn't matter. The lightning is right on top of us and we're in a tent with a metal pole poking up the middle on an open mesa, the highest object aside from Baldy Cinco. We're going to die and it will be my fault. For instigating this trip. For camping here. For putting my desires ahead of my family's safety.

I keep my head raised as the storm roars on, watching for flashes, listening for rumbles, counting off the space between each, as if constant vigilance can keep the lightning at bay and my children safe. The flashes and booms grow further apart, farther away. The rain lightens from a torrent to a drum to a patter. The storm rolls down the mesa and I finally lower my head and sleep.

We rise early. No one else woke during the night. No one saw the lightning or heard the thunder dancing around our tent. No one but me feared morning would not come.

"I couldn't remember whether a second between lightning and thunder equals a mile or ten miles," I say when I tell the others about the storm.

"Well, the speed of sound is about 760 miles an hour," Milo says. "So that's five seconds for every mile." Which means the lightning, flashing less than a second before the thunder, was less than a thousand feet away, though how much less it's impossible to say. It sounded like inches.

While we eat breakfast, Zephyr points to a tiny shape moving up the ridge on the left flank of Baldy Cinco. I squint my eyes, hoping to see a bear or coyote, but the animal that comes into focus is a moose. It's an odd place for a moose to be—high and dry. It must be making its way from the swampy south end of the mesa to another watershed over the divide. We watch it lope in its ungainly way around the shoulder of the ridge and out of sight.

After breakfast, we cross the gold-green expanse of mesa in the calm left behind by the storm. Turquoise blue sky stretches from horizon to horizon. Fluffy white clouds drift over its surface here and there, all innocence, not acknowledging they will spend the day gathering together and growing into another storm. As we near the western edge of the mesa, the San Juan Mountains rise up on the horizon, blue and purple and red, illuminated by the morning sun, patches of snow still lingering on the sharp peaks, truly Shining Mountains. A light but steady wind fills my ears, and I can imagine the nearest person is hundreds of miles, perhaps centuries, away. Despite the night spent terrified we'd be fried in our beds, I'm happy to cross the mesa now, in the quiet of early morning. If we'd crossed yesterday afternoon, I'd have been tired, sore, and grouchy, we'd have been rushing to beat the storm, and clouds would have obscured the view.

I catch up with Curry and the boys as we approach the mesa's edge.

"It was so peaceful walking across this morning," Curry says.

I take this as a tacit apology for being an ass about stopping yesterday, but I can't help rubbing it in a little. "I'm glad we didn't do it last night."

At the edge of the mesa, we come upon a couple and their twelve-year-old daughter resting after climbing up from the valley. We chat about the throngs of people taking over the mountains and about hiking as a family. Their daughter is one of the few kids we've seen all summer. The dad, a mountaineer, names some of the distant peaks we've been admiring.

"See that crooked, sharp one? That's Uncompahgre." He points to a red mountain glowing in the morning sun. "That one's either Redcloud or Sunshine." I love these mountains' names—much nicer than dead presidents, ivy league colleges, or genocidal explorers. Uncompahgre is an alternative name for the Taviwach band of Ute. Redcloud Peak was named by a poetic U.S. Geological Survey topographer in 1874 for its sweeping slopes of red. The source of Sunshine Peak's name is a mystery, but this morning it is fitting, with the sun illuminating its ruddy face.

The trail into the valley is steep and badly eroded, a chute filled with loose rocks the size of toasters. We descend into trees, tall dead spruce, small live ones. Two backpackers pass going down, then another. Where did they come from? I thought we had the mesa to ourselves last night. More hikers head up the trail, wearing clean clothes and carrying day packs. So much for the mesa being hundreds of miles and years away from other people. An older couple passes me on their way up.

"Were those your two boys up ahead?" the man asks in a Texas accent. "They're about a mile ahead of you."

I detect a slight reprimand in his tone. He must have seen Milo and Emmet but didn't connect them with Curry and Zephyr, hiking after them but ahead of me.

"They always are," I say.

"That's a good place for Mom, bringing up the rear," the woman says.

After you're done wiping their rears, I think.

"You probably have the heaviest pack," the man adds.

"Nope. I keep giving them all the weight."

"Good. That's the way it should be."

As I continue toward the trailhead, more people surge past, heading up, and a few backpackers stand at the edge of the road near the Spring Creek Pass picnic area, thumbs out for rides to Lake City. Twenty years ago, we left our tent set up near the road and hitched from this spot. A guy with a ponytail and John Lennon glasses picked us up in a small pickup truck. His name was Jerry, and he ran an organization that sets up yurts in the backcountry for cross-country skiers. After we finished our town chores, Jerry drove us back to the trail in a growing snowstorm, and, as we climbed out of his truck, he handed Curry a joint, one hippie to another. Though I've never liked smoking pot, that night, with snow accumulating on the tent and the temperature dropping, Curry and I passed the joint back and forth and talked and laughed late into the night, warm, safe, and a little stoned, in our tiny blue dome.

Today it's hot and sunny at the trailhead, no snow in sight. We rest by the outhouse and entertain ourselves watching a woman prepare for a trail ride. After an elaborate process of packing and strapping, she mounts one horse and leads another up an old jeep road, and we roust ourselves and follow her up the gently rising dome of Jarosa Mesa. Over the mesa, the trail dips into a valley, climbs over a saddle, and descends through dead spruce into another valley. This one is dotted with hundreds of sheep, the shepherd riding along the forest's edge on a black pony.

We make our way down to the meadow and set up camp well away from the shepherd's camp and his flock. But after we retire, they migrate to our end of the meadow, surrounding our tent. Big white sheepdogs loom nearby, and the sheep mill around, making ridiculous noises, their bells ding-donging. They sound more like people pretending to be sheep than actual sheep. A few dozen say *maa*, and a dozen more reply *baa*. They all quiet down, long enough to allow me to doze off, then one cries *maa!* A few answer *baa!* More cry out *maa* and *baa* and *moo* and *boo*. A dog barks. Another replies. More sheep *baa*. Then they all quiet down for a few moments only to start up again.

John Muir referred to sheep as "hoofed locusts" for their tendency to eat every green growing thing to its roots. A decline in populations of wild sheep in the nineteenth century was due primarily to overgrazing and diseases spread by domestic sheep. While the original Mexican settlers of the southern part of the state grazed some sheep, the industry took off with the discovery of gold that brought prospectors, miners, and a demand for mutton and wool. The number of sheep in Colorado increased from 110,000 in 1880 to more than two million six years later. With the great drives of cattle arriving at the same time, cattlemen and sheepherders came into conflict. Cowboys, driven by ethnic animus and the twin beliefs that sheep destroy grasses intended for cows and cows will not drink from water fouled by sheep, formed the Cattle Grower's Protective Association. Bands of "Night Riders" tried to intimidate wool growers off the land, often resorting to violence, as in 1896, when ranchers killed two Mexican shepherds and clubbed to death three hundred sheep in northwestern Colorado, and in 1915, when they tied up a shepherd and drove two hundred sheep off a cliff near Crested Butte. Like cattle, sheep live large off the public largesse. At this year's grazing fee rate, a sheep owner pays only forty-two cents per animal for a month at an all-you-can-eat buffet on our public lands.

When we emerge from the tent, the sheep are nowhere to be seen and peace has settled into our valley. From the meadow, we climb up through dense willows. One of the sheepdogs, snowy white and tall as a pony, stands near the trail, regarding me with suspicion as I pass. I come around a bend to see Emmet frozen in the trail, holding a small stick in his hand. Two more dogs stand between us, barking. There's no sight or sound of sheep, just their enormous caretakers. I grip my poles and hurry forward, ready to defend my son from these gigantic hounds. One of the dogs turns to face me, still barking. "Hush!" I yell. "Go away!" To my surprise it moves off into the bushes. I yell at the other dog, "Go away! Go lie down!" It, too, trots off. Emmet drops his stick and we hike together, climbing up, up, up. Looking back down the hill, I see sheep milling among the willow bushes we passed through, explaining the sheepdogs' presence, but not why the sheep are silent now when they made a racket all night.

As we pick our way along the steep, rocky switchbacks that climb to the ridge of Cony Summit, I try to remember what it was like to hike here in the snow twenty years ago. After we'd settled in for the night outside Lake City with our stash from Jerry, snow continued to fall, piling up to a depth of six inches. The sun came out in the morning and shone bright and blinding off the fleecy white, but a bitter wind blew all day. Again today the sun shines brightly. The ground is free of snow, but the trail is little more than bare talus and the wind is fierce, whipping across Ruby Creek Saddle, pushing me to the trail's edge. It's cold, too, though not nearly as cold as it was that October day when we trudged through icy wind and slippery snow.

After lunch we reach the high point of the Colorado Trail, 13,271 feet, just below Cony Summit. We take a family photo with the sign and I ask, "Anyone want to climb the peak?"

"I do!" Emmet shouts. He drops his pack and runs up the rocky but gentle slope. The rest of us flop down on the side of the trail. Emmet reaches the cairn and disappears, his tan clothes and blue hat camouflaged against tan stones and blue sky. After a while, I zoom my camera on the summit and watch him move back and forth between the cairn and other parts of the mountain top, bending over and standing up. I can't figure out what he's doing.

When he comes running down, I ask, "Did you make it to the top?"

"Yes. And I made the mountain two feet taller." That explains all the back and forth. He was stacking rocks to increase the height of the peak, defying nature's everlasting project of eroding mountains to plains.

From Cony Summit, we drop into a valley that must once have been gorgeous, with mountain peaks fringing the rim of undulating green slopes. But now it's pocked with old mines, scarred with tailings piles, ribboned with jeep trails, and littered with the rusting machinery of mining's past—the remains of the town of Carson, which boomed in 1892 and fizzled out soon after, leaving behind a mess. Trail builders have made switchbacks that meander down the steep slope, but I forego the trail in favor of skidding down the jeep track. I can't possibly worsen the erosion. Curry and the boys inspect one of the mines on the valley floor, poking into a dilapidated log cabin, climbing on a rusty hunk of metal, and clambering over tailings. I try to put the hazards of old mines—open shafts, hazardous gases, cyanide, heavy metals—out of my mind and pretend I don't see them as I hike past. Where the trail leaves the jeep road behind, I sit and eat a granola bar. When the others catch up and pass me by, I follow them up the trail and back into resplendent wilderness. The trail passes through an area of lumpy gray rocks covered in rust-red and lime-green lichens, interspersed with scrubby vegetation, then rises through a cool green valley, mountain gentian growing in deep purple-blue clumps along the trail. Smoky gray peaks rise steeply on the other side of the creek, and patches of spruce—both living and dead—dot the lower slopes. Near the pass at the top of the valley, I find Curry and the boys sitting on the side of the trail, looking down at the creek.

"There are four moose down there," Zephyr says.

Four sets of antlers and ears barely rise above the willows as the animals nose among the bushes. One sports velvety nubs on his forehead, but the other three balance huge racks. I wonder if the antlers we saw on the moose near Breckenridge a month ago have reached this size. Antler is among the fastest growing tissues and moose antlers can grow an inch and gain a pound per day during the five-month growing season. Eventually, one of the moose makes his way to an open patch of grass and we see him in his full glory—long, knobby legs, ponderous big head, swinging bell.

We continue up the trail, passing an army of hoodoos, then cross a broad, flat saddle before dropping down to the lakes where we plan to camp. At the bottom of the descent, we set up camp near a pool of clear water with a peaked hill rising behind it. The small lake's outlet forms Pole Creek, which feeds the headwaters of the Rio Grande.

In the tent that night, Emmet says, "When we get home, I'm going to walk to Canada, spend the night with some Canadian people, and walk home."

I don't know if he's making a joke or has no idea how far Canada is from our house—we live anywhere from 143 miles to 306 miles from the Canadian border, depending on which way you go—but I love that he feels confident enough from having hiked 380 miles that he could do anything.

Once the sun drops behind the hills, the temperature drops, and we wake in the morning to frost on the ground and a skim of ice in our water bottles. At this point on the trail twenty years ago, the sun had returned to warm us after the icy climb to Cony Summit, but I had reached my mental nadir. The rain, my illness, and the snow had taken a toll on my psyche. I was worn out, exhausted. I wanted a bed, a shower, a flush toilet, fresh fruits and vegetables, central heating, a house I didn't have to dismantle and rebuild every day. I wanted to go home. In two days we'd reach our next resupply at Silverton and seven more would get us to Durango, but even that seemed like too much. I knew I would regret quitting one week shy of completion, but I didn't want to make myself miserable any longer. In my journal I made a list of reasons to finish the hike and reasons to go home. "Neither my reasons to stay nor my reasons to go are compelling enough to do either," I concluded.

Again I'm ready to be done. Though I am tired of the repetitiveness of camp chores, I'm *not* tired of hiking, wildlife, or scenery. I'm not worn out, though my body aches. Rather I feel full—full of mountains and wildflowers, beautiful vistas and dramatic landscapes, big skies and extreme weather. My soul had been depleted by years of unhappiness from an abusive workplace and the often thankless tasks of parenting and homemaking. These weeks of traveling through my heart's home have replenished me, and I sense this feeling of fullness will follow me home to Maine and stay with me for some time to come.

We set off from camp and climb up a green valley. Fractured blocks of pink stone rise above us to the right. Tiny streams cascade through meadows dotted with wildflowers. Milo's far ahead of me as usual, and, as he ascends toward the saddle, I see a big animal with antlers and a white rear trot across his path. Our first elk! When I reach the saddle I find Milo sprawling on the grass with his brothers.

"What kind of animal has big antlers and a white butt?" he asks.

"Elk," I tell him, though I feel I have somehow failed in his education that he doesn't know this.

"Cool. I saw one on the way up the hill."

I sit beside the boys in an expanse of malachite green stretching and smooth and flat in all directions. Here Curry and I had our most spectacular wildlife sighting on our first Colorado Trail hike. As we approached the meadow, we counted eighty-seven elk crossing our path. They walked in single file, threading a narrow track through the three inches of snow that remained on the ground. We stood in awe, imagining we were witnessing one of the great animal migrations from pre-European times.

The boys hike on, but I rest a bit longer, savoring the memory of the elk. It's so peaceful here. It's not silent—a steady wind blows and grasshoppers and crickets chirp and whir—but it feels deeply still, another sacred place. When I hike on, the trail takes me along rolling hills, velvety green with smooth, sandy-looking tops. Sharp stony gray peaks rise in the distance, patches of snow dotting their ridgetops. Around a bend, the trail enters a valley where the hills are topped in blue-green stone, with sand piles in the valley of the same hue.

Later in the day Jean and Rick pass by. Even having taken an extra day in Creede, they've caught up with us. The trail climbs a steep slope where gem-like pebbles sprinkle the ground—quartz crystals, pyramids of shiny pink rock, geodes. I pick up a few pieces and slip them in my pocket. At the top of the slope, I find Curry and the boys resting in a meadow with views upon views of mountains. We pull out lunch food while they tell me about more elk they saw after they left me on the green saddle and show me the crystals they collected. Several groups of day hikers pass. One woman gives us sheep's wool for blisters. A couple gives us energy bars and pieces of fool's gold they found at a mine and call us their "favorite hiking family."

The trail continues on, high above tree line, with views of mountains and valleys, slopes of green sand, hoodoos marching up hillsides. It crosses another valley, scarred with jeep roads and old mines, the air echoing with the drone of four-wheelers, then wraps around a steep hillside, high above the road to Stony Pass, where ATVs rumble up and down the road. A fat, billowy cloud drifts across the blue sky and obscures the sun briefly. I feel wet droplets on my face and look down to see a half dozen snowflakes melting on my jacket, a reminder that winter's on its way, even though patches of snow left over from last winter still cling to the ridges. Summers here in the San Juans are short and winters are harsh. Not far from here a party of prospectors got lost in deep snow during the winter of 1874, and at least two of the men resorted to killing and eating their comrades. Among the cannibals was the infamous Alfred Packer, who escaped arrest for nine years before finally standing trial. An earlier case of suspected cannibalism in this area occurred in 1849 when members of a survey expedition led by John Charles Frémont became trapped by heavy snows in the La Garita Mountains.

The cloud scuds across the sky, revealing the sun, the snow squall passing as quickly as it came. We're safe, for now, from becoming trapped in the mountains and eating each other. The trail resumes across the road, passing an abandoned mine and entering the Weminuche Wilderness. It winds around humped hillsides of green-blue sand speckled with clumps of grass and pink and yellow paintbrush. As I pass a pond, two miles shy of where we intended to camp, some campers with a pack llama call out to me, "Are you with a group? They're over there." I hike around a knoll and find Curry and the boys unloading their packs. I'd hoped to hike farther today, to put us in position to get to Silverton a day early, but my shin hurts and I'm happy to stop. During the night, as I toss and turn on my crinkly sleeping mat, all I can think about is how badly I want a hot meal and a real bed.

In the morning, we wake to a clear, cloudless sky, ice again skimming the water in our bottles. Already, in mid-August, winter is creeping in here above twelve thousand feet. After we slurp oatmeal and pack gear, I propose the idea that gnawed at my mind all night, couching it as a request.

"If we hike seventeen miles today, can we get pizza and a hotel in Silverton?"

"Yes!" Curry replies with enthusiasm.

"Yes!" the boys agree.

We scramble to get on the trail, and I insist on hiking at the front of the pack. If there are elk around here, I want to be the one to see them. I'm greedy to repeat the moment when a huge herd crossed our path.

We travel over undulating meadows, with sharp gray peaks in the distance and patches of snow clinging to ridges. There's not a cloud in the sky. A sign marks the point where the Continental Divide Trail and the Colorado Trail part ways. The two have shared tread for the last 314 miles, but from here the divide heads south and we continue west, climbing up meadows and around hillsides. After we cross a snowfield, I give up on my elk hunt and let the boys go ahead. At the top of a hill, I come upon the iconic Colorado Trail view: a spectacle of turquoise pools nestled in a velvety green meadow, steep walls of broken gray stone rising on both sides, the blue peaks of the Grenadier Mountains in the distance. We weave back and forth down the steep hillside to Elk Creek. I lose track of the number of switchbacks after twenty-four. Wildflowers paint the slope pink, red, yellow, blue. A tiny butterfly with blue-green wings that match the blue-green dirt sits on the trail. A red admiral drifts from blossom to blossom. A tiny brown velvety butterfly flitters across my path. Orange-brown butterflies chase each other drunkenly across the hill. I smile at these constant friends who have helped me along when I've struggled and are here even now, when I feel good.

When we cross the headwaters of Elk Creek, below the splintery remains of an old mining cabin, the soil changes from blue-green to bright red, and we amble down the gorge along Elk Creek between walls of strange, beautiful stone. The trail clings to the right-hand cliff as it makes its steep and rocky way, at times tracing a ridge of layered rock that's been uplifted and turned on its side, as if we're walking along the edge of a wafer cookie, some layers sharp and hard, others soft and eroded away. Big chunks of smooth orangey pink feldspar alternate with stripes of white quartz and a seam of crumbly black. The trail goes down, down, down. Small waterfalls pour over the opposite wall, cascades that were frozen on that snow-covered north face when we hiked here in early October twenty years ago. A side stream flowing orange-brown and slimy fouls Elk Creek's clear water. This "yellow boy" coating the rocks of the stream and fanning into the creek is a telltale sign of acid mine drainage. When iron pyrite is brought to the surface along with gold and silver ore, it reacts with air and water to form sulfuric acid and sulfates, oxides, and hydroxides of iron. Rain and runoff carry these compounds, along with dissolved heavy metal salts, to nearby streams. The insoluble ferric hydroxide precipitates out of the water, turning the rocks of the streambed yellow-orange and rendering the water lifeless.

Elk Creek drops down its steep channel while the trail continues on a level path, the two growing farther and farther apart. The trail descends below tree line, into what I described twenty years ago as "a forest of ancient giants, enchanted, with moss carpeting the floor and lichens draped over the branches." Today it's a ghost forest of dead spruce, the enchantment broken. In and out of trees and across talus slopes, the trail continues down through stands of big Douglas fir (blessedly alive) and into an aspen woodland. We stop for lunch on the edge of a meadow with an enormous pile of boulders at its center, eating quickly and swatting at biting flies. From the meadow, we enter another gorge along Elk Creek and stop to collect water from its clear rushing flow while the boys heave rocks into the stream.

In the valley, we make our last contact with Colorado's railroads. The Denver and Rio Grande, having won the railroad war, ran narrow gauge track along the Animas River to Silverton and created the town of Durango, bypassing and killing off the existing town of Animas, which did not want to play by the railroad's rules. A National Historic Landmark, this portion of the old train route has been renamed the Durango and

Silverton Narrow Gauge Railroad, and tourist trains run between the two towns, giving visitors a miner's-eye view of Animas Canyon. Some hikers, to avoid the climb to Molas Pass, catch the train here for a ride into town or hike along the tracks.

"Do you want to follow the tracks into town?" Curry asks me.

"No," I say, "as long as we don't have to climb that." I point to the sheer cliff rising on the opposite side of the river.

Across the tracks and through lush riparian shrubs, we come to a bridge that spans the Animas River. The river runs fast, its water a clear aqua blue. It looks clean and pure, but the blue tint likely comes from copper salts washed in from mines, and a little over a year ago the river ran an opaque school-bus yellow. Contractors working with the U.S. Environmental Protection Agency on remediating the mess left behind by mines six miles upstream from Silverton inadvertently breached a wall of mine waste that held back three million gallons of water and sludge at the Gold King Mine. Orange water came out as a trickle, then a stream. Then a surge of water contaminated with iron, manganese, zinc, copper, cadmium, and arsenic flowed into Cement Creek and on into the Animas and, eventually, the San Juan River.

Mining began in Silverton's mining district much as it did in Colorado's other boom towns. Prospectors found rich ores in the Sunnyside Vein on the north shore of Lake Emma in 1873. The Sunnyside Mine produced gold, silver, lead, zinc, and copper and became one of Colorado's largest, with more than sixty miles of underground tunnels. The Gold King Mine, on Sunnyside's western boundary, was one of the area's largest producers in the early 1900s, shutting down in 1924. Like many mining towns, Silverton's boom peaked early, with more than half of the town's four thousand residents employed in the industry in 1907, and slowly petered out. But the Sunnyside operated until 1953 and came back for a revival from 1959 to 1991.

A century of mining left more than four hundred sources of water pollution among the thousands of prospects, shafts, tunnels, and tailings piles in the upper Animas basin. Two tributaries of the Animas, Mineral Creek and Cement Creek, are highly acidic, with high levels of dissolved iron and heavy metals and almost no microorganisms. Water quality in the Animas deteriorates below the point where these two streams feed into the river. The Gold King blowout last summer wasn't the first spill from Silverton's mines into neighboring streams and the Animas; a major spill occurred in 1975 and another in 1978. For decades, Silverton fought Superfund designation, fearing it would place a stigma on a town struggling to remake itself after its identifying industry faded away. Unlike Leadville, which got designation and the money for cleanup, Silverton avoided both the stigma and the funding and tried to make do with a consortium of local stakeholders. This worked, for a while, until the Sunnyside Mine shut down, along with its water treatment plant. Plugs placed in the Sunnyside to stem the flow of water and acid drainage led water to flow into the nearby Gold King and Red and Bonita Mines, eventually leading to last summer's blowout. So far, researchers have found minimal impacts to fish and aquatic life due to the spill, but the jury is out on long-term effects. Meanwhile, the town of Silverton and the San Juan County commissioners requested that the mining district be placed on the Superfund priority list.

Beyond the river, we begin to wind up dozens of switchbacks. We are climbing that sheer cliff I'd hoped to avoid. In my head, I sing every cheerful and long kids' song I can think of: "I've Been Workin' on the Railroad," "Darlin' Clementine," "There's a Hole in the Bucket, Dear Liza," "She'll Be Comin' Round the Mountain." Curry hikes behind me, driving me up the mountain. Zephyr and Milo have hiked out of sight. Emmet is a switchback ahead of us. Each time he passes by, one level up, he wolf-whistles. After a while, his whistles come from two switchbacks up. And then he gets so far ahead I don't hear his whistles at all. At the sharp corners of the switchbacks, views open up of the river below and of the sharp-pointed mountains beyond. I want to stop and take pictures, but Curry's on my heels, and I feel the urgency of getting to the highway and town before nightfall, so I keep climbing.

We emerge abruptly at the top of the cliff into a big meadow. The trail takes a long, roundabout way, sweeping back and forth across the meadow before it pops us out on the highway at Molas Pass. We stick out our thumbs, but the cars fly past. Eventually, a blue van with a pink sun painted on the side pulls over. A guy with long, tangled brown hair stuffed under a baseball cap hops out.

"I've been working on my van. If you don't mind the smell of gas, I can give you a ride."

He opens the side door and rearranges an inflatable raft, climbing ropes, a guitar. The boys and I squeeze onto a futon couch covered in a Mexican blanket and Curry climbs into the passenger seat. The driver, Michael, speaks in a slow, deliberate manner, looking at Curry while he talks, the van drifting toward the drop-off at the edge of the road. I close my eyes, certain, as I am every time we get into a car after days of hiking, that we're going to fly off the road and die. Michael drops us off at a pizzeria, where we find Nightmare and Pinecone Mama and other thru-hikers sitting on the patio and downing slices of pizza, except for Nightmare, who's eating refried beans out of a silicone bowl.

He holds up the bowl. "Look what I found in the free box at the hostel."

Inside, the restaurant is small, crowded, and noisy. An electronic menu displays a revolving slideshow of options. I tell Curry what I want and return to the patio, escaping the sensory overload. We fill up on hot pizza, cold drinks, and, for me, a gloriously crisp salad as the moon rises over the hills at the edge of town. After dinner, we head across the street to our hotel room above an old-timey saloon and fall into soft beds.

With only one week left to go, Durango is no longer a crazy goal. We're actually going to pull it off, hiking five hundred miles through the wilderness with three kids. I snuggle into the blankets and smile, as if I'd never had a single doubt.

12

TERMINUS

So I have found what I set out to find. I set out on my journey in pure love. . . . There was the whole plateau, glittering white, within reach a sky of dazzling blue. I drank and drank. I have not yet done drinking that draught.

—NAN SHEPHERD

DAYS 37–42: AUGUST 15–20, 2016
Molas Pass to Junction Creek

In the morning we find breakfast at a cafe on the wide main street of town, then pick up our resupply box at the post office and buy moleskin and new socks for Milo, who has developed blisters across the balls of both feet. Back at the hotel, Emmet settles in to watch *Tom and Jerry* cartoons while Curry takes our clothes to the laundromat and Milo, Zephyr, and I sort snacks and organize meals. When Curry returns, we dress in clothes still warm from the dryer and head downtown for lunch and a trip to the candy store that we've heard gives a piece of fudge to every Colorado Trail thru-hiker. We help ourselves to huge slices of delicious fudge and the boys wander the two small rooms of the store, trying to decide what additional sugary delight they'll bring on the trail. On our way to the grocery store, we see Nightmare and Pinecone Mama outside the hostel.

FIG. 13. White admiral (*Limenitis arthemis*)

"We thought you guys were heading up early this morning," I holler across the lawn.

Nightmare laughs and holds up a beer.

After we finish shopping, we loiter on the deck outside the grocery store, packing and repacking our new supplies, eyeing the gray clouds that loom over Molas Pass, reluctant to return to the highway to hitch, reluctant to hike in the rain. Finally we can put it off no longer. We head to the gas station near the highway and throw out our thumbs, holding up signs we made out of pieces of our resupply box: *Molas Pass. CT Hikers.*

Vehicle after vehicle drives by. Jeeps don't stop. Station wagons with bike racks don't stop. Cars with Texas or Missouri license plates definitely don't stop. Big diesel pickups driven by men with straw hats and chin-strap beards don't stop. Old people don't stop. Young people don't stop. I have about lost all faith in humanity when an old blue pickup with a cap and a paddle board strapped to the top pulls over down the road from us. A woman with long black hair hops out of the driver's seat.

"Are you Colorado Trail thru-hikers? I don't have much time; I'm late getting my son to his lesson in Durango, but I had to stop. I hiked the AT in 2000. I know how hard it is to get a ride. My name's Kris. Hop in."

She opens the back of the truck, pushes a kayak to the side, and we scramble in and watch the world fly by out the back windows of the truck.

"How many of your friends can say they hitchhiked around Colorado this summer?" I say to the kids as we slide around the bed of the truck.

"How many would want to?" Emmet says.

Kris drops us off at the pass, wishes us well, and speeds off. A large map at the trailhead shows the remainder of the trail—only seventy miles to go. As we set off up the trail, Emmet and Zephyr drag their feet. They had too much sugar in town. Too much TV in town. Too much town in town. We have two camping options. The first, Little Molas Lake, is down a side trail about a mile from the pass. The second is near a stream about five miles in. When we reach the turnoff to the lake, Curry says we should keep going. But Emmet wants to go to the lake. He lies down in the middle of the trail in protest. I coax him onto his feet and hike slowly with him and Zephyr. We have all afternoon to go five miles and, as long as it doesn't rain, no need to hurry.

As we pass landmarks, I remember seeing them in reverse on our last day on the trail twenty years ago—the tree where an owl perched, the forest of stumps leftover from the 1879 Lime Creek fire, the red-green-and-gray-striped humps of Grand Turk and Sultan Mountains. After a day and night in Silverton, Curry and I had set out on a cool but clear day to complete the final seventy miles of our journey. Eleven miles from the trailhead, we pitched our tent in a meadow between Rolling Mountain and a pair of peaks called the Twin Sisters and retired, full of excitement for the final leg of our journey. Hours later, I awoke, muffled under a great weight. Thinking Curry had rolled on top of me, I shoved at him, but it wasn't Curry smothering me; it was the tent. Blue nylon, bowed under heavy, wet snow, hovered inches above my face, and the space between the ground and the fly, where fresh air was supposed to enter, was completely buried. I shook Curry.

"Wake up. Snow!"

Curry came to and unzipped the vestibule to let in much-needed, but frigid, oxygen, and we pounded the walls of the tent until the roof sprang back into its normal, rounded shape and the fly came loose from the snowpack. All night, we beat at the tent, shaking it free of snow, and opened the vestibule to let in blasts of cold air. When morning finally came, we ate a breakfast of granola bars and crackers, got dressed, and packed our gear inside the tent. We hadn't yet looked out to see what the world had in store for us.

"It only snowed eight inches. No big deal," Curry said, whistling "The Sun Will Come Out Tomorrow."

But when we unzipped the tent, we faced a world of white: white sky above, white snow blanketing the ground, white fog in the air, white flakes falling. The only way to tell up from down was the tug of gravity holding our boots to the earth and pulling ever more flakes out of the sky.

We looked in the direction of the mist-shrouded peaks we would have to pass through over the next few days. Fifty-nine miles to Durango. We looked in the direction we had come. Eleven miles back to Molas Pass.

At least a foot of snow had fallen in the night, with more coming down. This was not an early-season snowfall, a temporary blip, like at Sargents Mesa and Spring Creek Pass. This was the real deal. Winter had set into the mountains, and it would not go away until June. If we went forward, we might wander off the almost invisible trail and get lost or fall down a steep slope. Our tent might again become buried, with us breathless and frozen inside. We had to go back, down a trail we'd already hiked, toward a road only eleven miles away.

The decision to turn back was inevitable, but once we made it, I collapsed into the snow, sobbing. The day before I had contemplated quitting. I was exhausted, sore, and not experiencing the spiritual awakening I imagined. I wanted to get off the trail, out from under my pack, off of my aching feet. But not this way. I didn't want to be driven off by forces outside my control. Now that it was impossible, I wanted to complete what I'd set out to do, hike the remaining sixty miles, finish what we'd worked so hard for over the last eight weeks.

But we had no choice. We rolled up the wet tent and set off, back the way we came. A few yards beyond camp, a crack of thunder shook the air, so loud and unexpected I screamed. The Twin Sisters letting us know, in case we hadn't gotten the message, that we were unwelcome there.

We waded through wet, heavy snow, trying to distinguish the faint dip of the trail from the smooth expanse of snow that stretched across the meadow. Drifts obscured even that faint dip in places, the snow thigh-deep. When we wandered off trail, we became entangled in willow bushes lurking beneath, and we'd wallow and flounder, trying to find our way back to solid ground. My hands and feet were wet and cold. I slipped and fell. I cried, "We're going to die," while Curry urged me on, assured me we'd be okay. In this way we crept toward the highway, over the rolling meadows, into the trees and out again, along steep slopes, the fog thinning as we reached the ghost forest, the stumps silent witnesses to our struggle.

The snow let up and the hum of cars on Highway 550 below assured us we'd make it. The farther downhill we went, the less snow we had to shuffle through, the less fog there was to obscure our view. As we entered the last grove of trees before the pass, a great horned owl watched our progress down the trail. A good omen, perhaps, or a final warning to stay away?

Tonight our campsite will be much lower in elevation than that ill-fated site of twenty years ago, and we'll arrive nearly a month and a half earlier in the season. We should be safe from blizzards, but dark clouds circling the sky have threatened rain all afternoon. When we reach a meadow tucked between two groves of spruce trees, we find our tent already set up and Nightmare and Pinecone Mama's green tarp pitched nearby. Somehow they beat us here, beer and all.

Zephyr and Emmet, who were too tired to hike five miles, run in circles around the meadow, jumping off rocks and turning cartwheels. While I mix cold noodles, Emmet and Nightmare enter into a snack-trading scheme, comparing serving sizes and calories of toaster pastries and energy bars. After dinner, we crawl into bed and I read a chapter of *The Adventures of Tom Sawyer* to the boys. I feel self-conscious reading out loud with neighbors nearby. What if the noise bothers them? What if they're offended by the terms used in the book for slaves and Native Americans, about which the boys and I had a discussion prior to reading?

After I finish the chapter, Nightmare calls out, "What was that?"

"*Tom Sawyer.*"

"Thank you for reading to us."

In the morning, I take some of our extra water to our neighbors, still lounging under their tarp.

"Do you read to them every night?" Pinecone Mama asks.

"Yes."

"I'm studying education. That's one of the best things you can do."

"I felt like you were reading to me," Nightmare says. "No one's ever read to me before."

"That's the saddest thing ever," I say.

Pinecone Mama laughs. They're so young, closer in age to my children than to me. I feel a motherly urge to watch over them. I want them to stay with us for the rest of the hike, so I can read to Nightmare at bedtime. But today they're sleeping in and we're heading out early, determined to make it over the pass and past the Twin Sisters before they can rain their wrath down on us a third time.

Three years after our abrupt departure from the Colorado Trail, Curry and I returned to finish the last leg on our honeymoon. We again set off up the trail from Molas Pass late on a September morning. As we hiked, Curry's steps grew slower and slower and his face turned greenish gray. By the time we reached our campsite—almost the exact spot where we'd camped three years before—he was suffering from acute mountain sickness and a thunderstorm was brewing. We'd gotten a new tent for our wedding and had committed the cardinal camping sin of not learning to set it up prior to our trip. The wind ripped the instruction sheet out of my hands as we tried to thread color-coded poles through sleeves while lighting and thunder crashed around us. Once we got it set up, we crawled inside and I coaxed Curry to drink water and eat hot soup while rain lashed our nylon roof.

This morning is clear and sunny, but still I tell Emmet and Zephyr, "As the Twin Brothers, you have to use your force to hold the Twin Sisters in check, so they don't try to drive us off this mountain again."

I have low energy—post-town lethargy. We start out the morning with fairly level walking, contouring along and gradually ascending a green hillside rising up to red sandstone bluffs. Sheep graze high on the hill, tiny white dots on the green. The exposed soil of the trail is a rich, rosy hue. Like the Fountain Formation, whose red rocks we hiked among in Roxborough State Park, this Cutler Formation rock is formed of sand from the Ancestral Rocky Mountains, washed away grain by grain, oxidized red, and laid down as sediment by ancient rivers. In the folds of the hillside, the rock is exposed and waterfalls trickle down the slick red surface. Huge conglomerate boulders have tumbled down from cliffs high above us, littering the hillside with hunks of gray and brown stone made up of many smaller, varied rocks glommed together, like enormous chunks of fruitcake. Paintbrush and sunflowers bloom along the trail, among crepe-papery corn lilies, and the trail winds among groves of living spruce. I hope we've left behind dead and dying trees for the rest of this trip. Mountain bikes wheel by, heading toward the pass. A man on horseback leading several pack mules loaded with supplies passes.

"That's how I want to hike the Colorado Trail next time," Emmet says.

We stop to eat lunch near a small lake, but Emmet, in the exact opposite mood he was in yesterday afternoon, protests the stop, saying, "The more we do now, the less we have to do later."

As we near Rolling Mountain Pass, thunder rumbles in the distance. I slip the rain cover on my pack and put up my umbrella. A group of mountain bikers passes on their way down.

"We decided it would be safer to go back," one of them says.

"Yeah, it can get pretty nasty up there," I reply.

The Curse of the Twin Sisters. But today they let us pass with no more than a few drops of rain. Through the afternoon, we travel over high, rolling meadows with steep, reddish rocky peaks all around. Milo hikes behind me for part of the afternoon, so my pace can slow his and allow him to baby his blisters and a sore ankle. Usually I don't like being herded, but I've hardly hiked with Milo these last few weeks, so I don't mind him dogging my heels.

Over the pass, we descend through Cascade Creek drainage, where spectacular waterfalls pound down tan and gray rock fractured and splintered into horizontal plates. Curry and the boys climb up for a better look, while I enjoy the view from the trail. After entering a dense forest of living spruce, we set up camp in a clearing with a small stagnant pond in the middle of it. Emmet and I hike back down the trail a short distance and scramble down a steep slope to where water seeping down the hillside converges into a finger-sized trickle. We hold the mouths of the water bladders in the trickle and wait for them to fill, one after the other, then take them back to camp to treat while we wait for dinner to reconstitute. Curry collects tiny wild onions, cuts them paper-thin, and mixes the slices into our beans and rice. Dark blue-black clouds spread across the sky, and we hurry through our chores, trying to beat the rain, but the weather holds off and we enjoy a leisurely evening in camp. After we crawl into the tent, we hear footsteps outside. Zephyr pokes out his head and reports that deer are mingling nearby.

In the morning, Zephyr and Emmet don't want to get going and Milo's blisters are hurting him. The three of them hike in the slow lane with me. We cross a meadow of tall waving grass and even taller corn lilies. Conical peaks like cartoon mountains rise around us. In the distance, a huge rock shaped like an ancient Egyptian cat statue rises from the top of a mountain.

"Look at that rock," I say. "It looks like a sitting cat."

"Nah," Milo replies. "It's an orc hiding behind its shield."

"Nope. Definitely a cat."

"I don't like hiking above tree line," Milo says as we move on.

"Why not?" I love being above the trees, with endless views, twisted krummholz, and tiny wildflowers, where the sky is vast and the weather changes moment to moment.

"There's nothing there," Milo says. "I prefer trees."

"It feels more secure in the trees," Emmet adds.

These boys have lived their whole lives surrounded by trees. Our house in Maine is set in a small clearing between hemlock and pine, maple and beech, a tall red oak outside our front door. The landscapes of our childhood imprint on us. My mom tells me my grandmother, who came from Nebraska where flat land stretches from horizon to horizon, hated it in the trees and even found mountains oppressive. I grew up in the suburbs, so I suppose I should feel most at home among green lawns and chain-link fences, but it's big sky, wide-open views, and bare bones of the earth that I long for—mountains and deserts. In *The Blue Jay's Dance*, Louise Erdrich describes being "horizon sick," pining for North Dakota while living in New Hampshire. "I am suspicious of Eastern land," she writes, "the undramatic loveliness, the small scale, the lack of sky to watch, the way weather sneaks up without enough warning." In Maine I am sky sick. Desperate for a big, open dome of blue or white or thundering gray above me, reaching to the hem of the earth. I don't want to feel secure. Above the trees, my lungs open, my heart soars. I can see. I can breathe. I am free.

The trail reenters the forest and joins a dirt road. Emmet, Zephyr, and Milo squelch through mud puddles, and we come upon a small band of mule deer in a clearing. They watch us watching them for a while then drop their heads and nibble at the grass as we hike on. The trail leaves the road and emerges from the trees along the edge of a hump of land that drops steeply to our left. We follow the hump to a meadow, where we stop to collect water from a clear snowmelt stream below a mountain of loose boulders. The Shy Couple, with whom we leapfrogged in the Mount Massive Wilderness area, passes by. In the mysterious way of trail life, we haven't seen them for weeks, and now here they are. The trail continues to weave in and out of trees and boulder fields. Clumps of gray clouds alternate with patches of blue, threatening rain. After lunch, we follow a long ridge up to Blackhawk Pass, where the earth has again turned red. Emmet reaches the pass ahead of Milo and me.

"Are we going to climb Blackhawk Mountain?" he calls down.

"I don't think so. Does the trail go that way?"

"A trail goes up it. I'm going to climb part of it." He drops his pack and runs to the top of a small hump of land, then comes back.

"It was a false summit," he says when we reach the pass. "Is Blackhawk a fourteener?"

I check the data book. "It's 12,681 feet."

"That's pretty respectable."

Curry and Zephyr catch up to us on the pass and hustle us down beneath looming gray-blue clouds. We fill up on water at Straight Creek, the last source for twenty miles, and each of us takes a bladder in addition to our two bottles. Emmet puts his bladder in the mesh side pocket of his backpack, but the pocket is large and loose and the bladder slumps and slides back and forth, banging him in the arm with each step. After walking this way for a half mile or so, Emmet loses it. He screams and pummels his pack with his elbows. I thought he was impervious to discomfort, but the swinging water bladder has pushed him over the edge. I strap the bladder to the top of his pack, and he resumes hiking, his usual easygoing attitude restored.

All afternoon we follow the Animas-Dolores Divide, a snaking ridge of land that is flat on top and drops steeply off on both sides. Where the crest bends to the west, opening up to spectacular views of the Needles

Mountains and Weminuche Wilderness, we find the Shy Couple. They've set up camp and are taking pictures of each other doing handstands at the edge of the drop-off. We take a campsite next to theirs, and I copy them, taking pictures of the boys in funny poses in front of the view.

While we wait for dinner to reconstitute, Milo and the twins argue over who has to start school sooner. I'd checked the high school calendar to verify that Milo's first day is August 31, two weeks from today, but I hadn't checked the elementary school calendar, because they *always* start after Labor Day. Since we have a rare bit of cell service here, I open the school's web page and discover that the twins are due back August 29, eight days earlier than I thought. That gives us just over a week to get home after we finish the trail. My chest tightens and my skin buzzes as I feel time speeding up. These weeks on the trail have let us step off the rushing tramway of life and slow to the pace of walking. With nowhere to go except the next campsite and nothing to do but walk, I've been able to concentrate on the here and now, not the next thing and the next one after that. Although life in rural Maine is not exactly a rat race, we rush around far more than I'd like, and though I strive to keep things simple, even a single regular activity per child makes me feel like I'm running the Red Queen's race. Meanwhile, life is passing me by, or maybe I'm speeding past life, in too much of a hurry to find the Jack-in-the-pulpit in bloom or pick wild strawberries. Shedding that hectic pace and living at two miles per hour, focusing on the here and now, neither in a hurry to get to the next thing nor pining for what has passed, has been the trail's greatest gift, and I can already feel it slipping away.

In the morning, we continue along the winding snake of the Animas-Dolores Divide, with the spruce-forested top of the ridge on our right and on our left a steep drop-off and views of blue-hazed, tree-covered mountains, unmarred by road, structure, or any sign of humanity.

Throughout the morning, my body goes through all the uncomfortable sensations—tired, chilled, sore, hungry—as if to recap the trip. It gets stuck on hungry, and I eat more snacks than usual. Still I'm not sated. Though I've craved certain foods and known when my body needs fuel,

I haven't felt truly stomach hungry on this hike until this moment, and no amount of snacking satisfies. Zephyr hikes with me, and we both get hungrier and hungrier as the morning goes on, but we find no sign of the others. Zephyr is getting furious with low-blood-sugar-fueled rage, and I'm feeling a little put out as well.

"If we don't find them by one o'clock," I say, "we'll have our own lunch, okay?"

We finally catch up with the others at five minutes past one. After we eat, a thunderstorm rolls in, drumming us with hail. We put up our umbrellas and hike through it for a while, climbing higher and higher, until we reach the last grove of trees before we have to cross exposed hillsides. We stop to shelter in the copse of spruce to wait it out.

When the hail slows I say, "I guess we better get moving; it seems to be letting up." But before we can move, a new volley of hail pours down.

"At least I haven't heard thunder in a while," I say after a while. Moments later, thunder shakes the mountainside.

"Can't you say you haven't seen s'mores in a while?" Emmet asks.

"It's been ages since I've had a grilled cheese sandwich with a big pile of chips. And a pickle. With a cup of hot chocolate," I say, but no magic food appears. "I guess my powers only work with weather. I haven't seen the sun in a while." The sky doesn't take this hint, either.

When the hail really does stop, we continue on, alternately through forest and along steep, bare, rocky slopes. Milo hikes behind me again. We stop and rest in a clearing in the woods to wait for Emmet and Zephyr, who fell behind after a bathroom break. When they catch up, a guy with a bushy beard walks by, heading in the other direction.

"Sunshine ahead," he says. He wears a white Gilligan hat and a green canvas army surplus backpack with a brown plastic tarp tied to the top with twine. Poking out from beneath the tarp is a blue-striped cotton hammock. Over one shoulder, he carries a black camcorder bag.

"I think he started the trail in 1950," Emmet says as soon as the guy is out of sight.

When we catch up with Curry, Emmet and Zephyr troop ahead with him, and Milo walks behind me as we climb the backbone of Indian

Trail Ridge. With Milo on my heels, I move faster than I normally would and forego many photo opportunities. The land drops away on both sides of the narrow causeway to deep, green valleys. Small lakes in the valley bottoms reflect the pewter gray of the sky. Jagged peaks rise up beyond, red and gray dusted with green. Farther in the distance, more mountains stretch hazy and blue to the edge of the sky. Pikas peek out of their talus homes. The grass is turning gold and many flowers have faded, but the paintbrush flowers bloom in every shade of pink—rose, blush, magenta, fuchsia, coral.

We climb up sharply, heading toward a rocky knob—the high point mentioned in the data book, I hope. I lift one foot after the other, repeating my mantra: *I have arrived. I have arrived.* Among the jumbled rocks of the trail, I notice the knobby track of a mountain bike tire.

"What a stupid place to ride a bike," I say.

"What a stupid place to do anything," Milo replies. Though he's been cheerful and easygoing most of this hike, he never misses a chance to make a wisecrack to remind me that this was not how he would have chosen to spend his summer.

I hike in silence, focusing on breathing, listening to Milo talk, grunting replies. After what feels like hours of climbing, we crest the knob of land we've been aiming for only to find it's a false summit. We have to travel downhill a bit and then climb toward a higher, steeper, knobbier pile of rocks. Dark clouds amass around the jagged ridges of Sharkstooth Peak to our west. We need to get over the high point and down to lower ground before the clouds break free of the peak and come our way. I propel my legs forward with all the strength I have, and we reach the top, the actual high point, and see our destination below, Taylor Lake, a turquoise gem set in red earth. The gold pyramid of our tent is already pitched among the willow bushes on the other side of the lake, and Emmet and Zephyr are working their way down the switchbacks. We catch up to them partway down and the four of us make our way to the lake together.

This togetherness was one of my hopes and dreams for the hike, and though we're not often all together at the same time, each time I've hiked with one kid or another has brought me closer to him. I've heard more about their hopes, dreams, and ideas than they share at home. Just being together, whether snuggled in the tent reading, sharing camp chores, or slurping cold meals, has made us closer as a family. The kids have also created bonds with each other, through working, hiking, and goofing around together, that would have been impossible to achieve at home. An added bonus has been watching each kid grow into his own strength—Milo's astounding ability to cover the miles fast and without complaint, Zephyr's sharp eyes that spot wildlife no one else notices, Emmet's generosity that's inspired him to give trail magic to other hikers and his surprising bursts of energy that send him scaling mountains when the rest of us are too tired to move.

The lake, shaped like a dog bone, according to Emmet, sits in a basin surrounded by steep treeless peaks, each topped in reddish stone ridges. Tall willow bushes ring the lake and a few skinny spruce trees poke up here and there on the hillsides. At the bottom of the slope a small stream crosses the trail. Emmet and Zephyr drop their packs and crouch on the ground, mounding red sand in the streambed to block the flow. The stream blows out the dam and they build it again. Milo and I leave them to their hydroengineering project and circle the lake in search of our campsite nestled in the willows on the other side.

On our honeymoon, rain followed us from the Twin Sisters through two more days of hiking and two more nights of camping. Curry was ready to cut our losses and quit the trail, but the skies cleared on the third day, and on the fourth we hiked Indian Trail Ridge. The vistas of mountains as far as the eye could see sent me back in time ten thousand years. We had left behind the dirt bikes that had roared over the trail the previous day, and a handful of cows grazing the ridge were confined to the lower reaches of the rocky slopes, leaving the wildflowers and grasses thick and full. Fuchsia paintbrush covered the hillside, and a few late-season columbines peered from behind blocks of stone. But once we dropped off the ridge on the descent to Taylor Lake, we ran into crowds of people hiking up, hiking down, and surrounding the lake, which we walked past into a packed parking lot. A blank kiosk, empty trail register box, out-of-order outhouse, and vehicles parked all over the grass lent further evidence of overuse and neglect. Beyond the lake, two guys were kickboxing on top of the pass. Taylor Lake may be the one place along the trail where usage is both lower and better managed now than it was twenty years ago. The broken outhouse is gone and a new kiosk marks the trailhead. Most of the campers around the lake are backpackers and few cars are in the parking area. We retire into the tent to slurp cold noodles as cold rain blows down off the ridge. A lone coyote serenades us to sleep from his perch on the hillside above the lake.

The sun rises in a clear, frosty sky. As we eat breakfast, a buck treads through the meadow near our campsite, his antlered head high and alert. We hike away from Taylor Lake through willow bushes and grassy meadows dotted with small spruce trees, toward Kennebec Pass, our last pass of the trip. It's a fitting final climb, since the Kennebec River is the defining geographical feature in our region of Maine. I imagine some homesick logger from Maine naming the pass. We pause on the saddle and view an undulating ridge of green grass barred with buff and red stone and clusters of bluish-green spruce. Our last crossing from one valley to another. Our last view of a mountain range to come. A golden eagle glides over our heads as we stand on this doorway to the end of the trail and a return to normal life.

We hike down through a gorge of red sandstone, yellow sunflowers, and cascading waterfalls. The trail skirts a steep talus slope and I fight off vertigo one last time. Beyond the slope, tall corn lilies and larkspur crowd the trail. Huge spruce shade our path. We wind downhill into aspen groves and step over little streams. The slope drops steeply down from the right edge of the trail and climbs straight up from the left, trees growing thick on both slopes. A group of mountain bikers comes around the corner, but there's nowhere for me to go to get out of the way. I press myself against the steep uphill side, and they are forced to walk their bikes past. When Curry and I hiked through this portion of trail on our honeymoon, we rounded a corner and met not mountain bikers but a cow. Curry, taking on the role of protective male, moved between me and the animal and looked around for a throwing rock, while I scrambled up the steep bank. The cow, as startled as we were at the sudden meeting, bolted. But since her head was pointed in our direction, she ran straight at us. Curry joined me on my hillside perch and we clung to tree branches as Bessie thundered past, buttering the trail with excrement. Today I stay mindful of both cows and mountain bikers as I hike on.

The trail winds down into a canyon of red and brown sandstone, dense with cool green vegetation. A grouse waddles off the trail into the shrubbery. At the bottom of the canyon, we collect water from Junction Creek before crossing on a bridge then climb uphill, out of the gorge and into a dry forested area high up the slope. Zephyr and I hike together, well behind everyone else as we travel near the top of the ridge, winding around the tops of gullies. We come upon a ponderosa pine, the first we've seen in a while. Then another. And another. We stop to smell the bark. Butterscotch. We're back in the foothills. Mountain-ash trees along the trail droop with clusters of orange-red berries. The mountain-ash were fruiting when we hiked here last time, as well, and the trail was littered with piles of bear scat made up entirely of orange berries. Though fresh, the cheerful piles of undigested fruit did not frighten me the way a tree trunk shredded by claws that we saw a few days earlier had. Despite our friends' and families' fears, those were the only signs of bear we saw all along the trail, on either hike.

When Zephyr and I reach the place we'd planned to camp, there's no sign of the others. The data book indicates campsites at this point, but the high, flattish area above the trail is dense with trees. Still, I'm annoyed they didn't wait to discuss options. I'm tired. My shoulders and back ache, and my right foot is killing me. I want to rest. To stop and camp. We don't have far to go tomorrow, so there's no need to go too far today. When we catch up with Curry a mile later, he's talking to another hiker.

Spoiling for a fight, I interrupt their conversation. "Why didn't you stop back there, where we were supposed to camp?"

"I didn't see any campsites."

"You could at least have waited."

He ignores my complaint and introduces me to the hiker, Proper Cheddar, a retired British civil servant. Proper Cheddar has a clean-shaven face and is wearing a spotless pale-blue woolen sweater and brilliant white shorts and hat. He looks like he's spent the last six weeks staying in bed and breakfasts, not sleeping on the ground in the blue tent he's set up in a tiny clearing near the trail. He tells us that last summer he hiked from Denver to Durango and back again. This year he's rehiked the whole trail, including both Collegiate routes and a partial detour on the Continental Divide Trail in the Weminuche Wilderness.

"Are you going to hike it again next year?" I ask him.

"No, I don't think so. I'm slowing down too much." I laugh. He must hike at least twenty to thirty miles a day to cover so much ground in so little time. Slow is relative.

We continue down the trail, searching for a place to set up our tent. Two young women heading the other way ask us about the campsite in the data book.

"It should be about a mile-and-a-half that way, but we didn't see it," I say. "Where you headed?"

"Denver." They say it with a hopeful kind of determination.

"Good luck. It's starting to get cold up there."

Every day this week we've met northbound hikers just starting out. When Curry and I hiked the trail the first time, we started on August 12, a week earlier than these two, and hit snow on September 15. If they hike the trail in six weeks, as we have this time, they'll finish September 23, possibly avoiding snow, since their last week will be in the foothills, but not cold, as our icy water bottles over the last week can attest.

Half a mile down the trail, we find a flat spot just big enough for our tent, with one corner almost touching the trail. We dive inside as another rain shower passes over. I think of the two young women, caught in the rain as they hike toward their first campsite. I hope they make it to Denver.

"What's the first thing you want to do when we finish the trail tomorrow?" Curry asks the boys.

Emmet says, "Get in the car and drive to a candy shop and get a lollipop this big—" he holds his hands about six inches apart "—and lick it."

Zephyr says, "Eat a hot dog and fries."

Milo says, "Breathe a sigh of relief."

August 20. My birthday. Today I turn forty-three. I really am going to finish the "CT by 43." We get up early, eager for town and food and the future. I mix bowls of granola and powdered milk—a treat for our last day of hiking. Never again will we eat cold oatmeal. Curry declares we should all hike together, so that we arrive at the trailhead at the same moment, and that I should lead. I take this as a peace offering after a fractious few weeks and take my place at the head of the pack. Milo, Emmet, and Zephyr jockey for second in line. The trail makes a winding, circuitous path through aspen groves, spruce trees, ponderosa pine woods, and Gambel oak forests. I stop to sit and rest at frequent intervals. I want to soak in this last day, take my time, enjoy being in the wild. This is, I understand now, the secret to happiness: living an unhurried life. Back home I can remind myself of this when life threatens to overwhelm.

We stop at Gudy's Rest, a hunk of rock that juts over a steep hillside, offering a view of the forested canyon, with the hazy blue mountains of the Colorado Plateau in the distance. Milo and I sit on a log bench. Emmet and Zephyr perch on the edge of the cantilevered rock, their feet dangling over the canyon below. I feel immensely at peace, looking out over the forested hills, the warm scent of ponderosa pine in the air, a deep sense of satisfaction that we did it. I brought my family to Colorado and we hiked nearly five hundred miles, and though we had some challenges, we did it better than I had any reason to expect. Now is the moment to take in the enormity of our accomplishment, enjoy the last few moments on the trail, and let the trail's lessons sink in. Sitting quietly at Gudy's Rest, is exactly how I want to live my life: with my kids, outside in nature, and slowly. I can, I think, take this moment, that lesson home with me.

But Curry is restless. Antsy. He wants to rush to the trailhead, to the food that waits in Durango. It is fitting, almost, that right to the last moment, our goals and priorities don't align. But this time I don't back down.

"Just sit still and try to enjoy the view," I say. He pulls out the tent to dry it in the sun, needing to do *something*.

From Gudy's Rest, we hike back down into the gorge where Junction

Creek flows. Near the water, the vegetation is once again green and lush. Tall grasses, wildflowers, and bushes bowing out into the trail brush our legs as we pass. Poison ivy lurks in red sandstone grottoes along the creek. Black slugs longer than a finger creep along the trail. Though the canyon's not an exact match to Roxborough—cooler and shadier, the soil grading from rust to ivory, the air moist from the creek—it's close enough, a fitting bookend. I pause to take a photo of a white admiral butterfly on an oak leaf. Its tattered wings have faded from black to chocolate brown. It looks how I feel—worn out but exultant. We have each accomplished our mission—she spent the summer pollinating flowers and laying eggs; I spent it hiking with my family. I say a silent thank you to this butterfly and the others that guided me along the trail. The butterflies helped me to relive that first Colorado Trail hike as a stronger, more confident person. Yet I also learned that the way my younger self hiked the trail was just fine, that she was a lot stronger than she thought she was.

At the bridge, we meet two families—four parents with two little kids and two babies riding in backpacks. The kids whine that they are tired of walking. One of the moms passes out snacks and juice boxes.

"Where you guys coming from?" one of the dads asks.

"Denver." It's definitely real now. We're three miles from Durango.

"Wow! That's amazing! All the way from Denver? With kids!"

It feels like we are passing on a gift, letting harried parents know that there is, indeed, life after kids. That great adventures are still possible.

On our honeymoon hike of the last portion of trail, when we arrived at what we thought was the trailhead, we found a parking lot with no marker indicating that we'd reached the southern terminus of the Colorado Trail. Confused and disappointed, we stopped to check our map, and a day hiker asked if we were lost.

"Is this the end of the Colorado Trail?"

"No. This is Junction Creek Campground. You have one more mile to go, down that trail. Did you just finish the whole trail?"

"Yes and no. We just finished the last seventy miles. We hiked the other four hundred miles three years ago and got snowed out."

The long explanation took some gloss off our accomplishment. The false trailhead—like a false summit—was a letdown. When we reached the actual trailhead, we hugged and high-fived and had our picture taken with the sign. But still it felt anticlimactic, to finish the trail three years after we started it, three years after winter drove us out of the mountains. Today I'm worried we'll experience the same disappointment. That we'll arrive at a false trailhead. Anxiety about this possibility, the logistical details we need to manage over the next week, and what my life will look like in the months and years to come buzzes through my veins.

As we near the end of the trail, Curry mounts his phone on his hiking pole and presses "record." The five of us walk side-by-side. I'm still skeptical that this is the real end of the trail. Then I see the kiosk and my parents, cameras in hand. We're really here. We really did it. We take pictures with the map of the Colorado Trail behind us, and when I smile, my face doesn't hurt at all. Then we step off the trial into the parking lot, where our car awaits. Five hundred miles behind us, the rest of our lives ahead.

FIG. 14. Five-nerved sunflower (*Helianthella quinquenervis*)

EPILOGUE

Returning to daily life after a trip to the mountains, I have often felt as
though I were a stranger re-entering my country after years abroad, not
yet adjusted to my return, and bearing experiences beyond speech.
— ROBERT MACFARLANE

JUNE 2021
Whitefield, Maine

From the trail, we headed straight for a restaurant in Durango. Curry
and the boys got their longed-for feast, and I got a free beer for my birthday. Still, I felt anxious, unsettled, like I'd left something undone. We
walked around town for a little while, found Emmet his giant lollipop,
then escaped to the relative peace of Mesa Verde National Park, an hour
to the southwest. There we eased into civilization over two days—still
sleeping in a tent, but with pillows and showers and a pancake breakfast
at the visitors' center. Then we beelined for Maine, arriving home at
two o'clock Sunday morning. Emmet and Zephyr started sixth grade the
next day. Two days later Milo began his sophomore year of high school.

When people outside the family asked them how they enjoyed the
hike, the boys responded positively, but at home they complained that
it was the *worst summer of their lives*. When Curry and I planned a short
backpacking trip that fall, they threatened mutiny and we abandoned

the plan. Yet, despite their complaints, the confidence they built over five hundred miles of hiking survived the transition to off-trail life. Milo took up two sports he hadn't tried before, cross-country running and tennis, and he joined the drama club. Emmet and Zephyr, who had always been inseparable, began the process of individuation in earnest, seeking out different friends and activities. Meanwhile, I unpacked from the trip, cleaned the house, and tried to resume normal life while feeling like an astronaut who returns to Earth after a trip to the moon: *Now what?*

Nearly five years have passed since we began our hike. After a couple of years of unsuccessfully trying my hand at freelance writing, when the expenses of a family of five became too much for one income and one of the kids needed braces, I went back to work, finding a job that's not particularly inspiring but gives me the summers off and provides dental insurance. I've tried to maintain the slow pace of the trail, but time continues to gallop forward. Emmet and Zephyr just completed their sophomore year in high school and Milo his sophomore year in college. The twins are now the tallest members of the family and almost unrecognizable from the little boys we took on the trail. The passage of time is even more poignant with the passing of family. Grandma Meyer died not long after we got home from our hike and my aunt Georgine died last year.

The summer after our hike, we visited Colorado again, for my parents' fiftieth anniversary. While in Denver, we hiked the official first six miles of the Colorado Trail through Waterton Canyon. With a smooth, gradual road underfoot and outhouses and picnic tables situated every couple of miles, it was a style of hiking I could get used to. At the end of the road I finally came face-to-face with the Strontia Springs Dam. Beyond the last picnic shelter in the canyon, just shy of the spot where we joined the Colorado Trail a year earlier, we followed the road around a righthand curve to a gate. On the other side of the gate, the dam rose, smooth and gray and unbelievably large. Water surged out of a sluiceway near the base, thundering into the canyon in a white torrent. We had, I felt, come full circle. Back to the beginning of the trail, back to the source of life.

We haven't gone on another family backpacking trip in the last five years, but Milo chose backpacking for his outdoor orientation trip at college and Curry and the boys are planning to hike a section of the Appalachian Trail in July. These days the boys won't even go on a day hike with me unless it's Mother's Day or my birthday, when they have no choice, and they all hike too fast for me anyhow. Next time I go backpacking, I'll probably go alone or with a group of women who share my hiking style, pace, and expectations. Regardless of who my hiking companions are, I'll bring a stove. No one in this family wants to suffer through cold oatmeal again.

I only hope that wildlands will remain to hike through. A few months after we completed our hike, Donald Trump was elected president. Along with other abhorrent policies, his administration initiated a wholesale rollback of decades of environmental progress, in four years overturning or weakening more than one hundred policies and regulations intended to protect public lands, wildlife, clean air, and clean water and reduce greenhouse gas emissions. Meanwhile, climate change rages on. In the past year, extreme weather events rattled nearly every corner of the country and Colorado experienced the three largest wildfires in the state's history; more than 625,000 acres of the state burned, and the fire season pushed into December. The future of wild places hangs in the balance.

Last year also brought the COVID-19 pandemic. Milo came home from college in early March, and my job and the twins' school shut down not long after. A summer spent backpacking and sharing a tiny tent was good preparation for months of lockdown. We were used to being together in close quarters without contact with other people, we knew how to make do with minimal supplies and no chance of running to the store, and we understood the healing power of time in nature. People everywhere sought solace in the outdoors, and, despite the pandemic, the Colorado Trail saw a record number of hikers, with more than 585 people registering as completers by the end of the year.

As for me, am I happier than I was five years ago, before we hiked the trail? Surprisingly, despite once again working a boring job, despite being stuck in Maine for the foreseeable future, despite enduring over a year of pandemic and concomitant social and political upheavals, I *am* happy. I've taken the lessons of the trail to heart and tried to live an unhurried life. I've excised the word "busy" from my vocabulary, and when life threatens to overwhelm, I go outside to watch birds, draw flowers, or paddle my kayak in slow strokes around a nearby pond. I try to appreciate the here and now and approach obstacles like mountain ranges, one step at a time.

A few months after we returned from the Colorado Trail, when the boys were still either not speaking about the hike or complaining when it came up, I picked up a package of the large, dry crackers we ate for lunch on the trail and served them for dinner alongside soup. I hadn't intended for them to trigger memories of the hike—I'd bought them because they were on sale—but once we started breaking apart and crunching them, the kids started reminiscing.

"Can you believe we ate these every day?" Milo said.

"Can you believe this was the best food we had?" Curry replied.

"You know, if it weren't for the dirty and disgusting parts of the trail, I'd probably do it again," Milo said.

"I would do it again if we could ride horses," Emmet said.

"I'd do it again if it was in Norway and I could ride a sleigh pulled by six huskies," Zephyr added.

"Remember how we ate cold oatmeal for breakfast every morning?" Milo said. "And it was disgusting? But you had to eat it or you'd get light-headed and have to sit down with your head between your knees an hour later?"

"Remember the wildflowers?" I said.

"I didn't really pay attention to those," Milo said.

"You didn't see all those wildflowers?"

"I saw them, but that's not really what I was interested in. I remember the mountains."

This set off a series of remember-whens: *Remember how we pooped in a hole forty-two times? Remember the herd of bighorn sheep? Remember swimming in the ice-cold lakes?*

"You know," Milo said, "hiking the trail is a lot better in retrospect than it was when it was happening."

"A lot of things in life are like that," I told him, adding in my head, *including parenting.* The trick—which I'm still working on learning nearly five years later—is to appreciate life while it's happening, to realize that *I have arrived.*

FIG. 15. Fairy trumpets or scarlet gilia (*Ipomopsis aggregata*)

ACKNOWLEDGMENTS

First I want to acknowledge the privilege that allowed me and my family to take this extraordinary trip. While the reduction in income from my quitting my job led to inconveniences over subsequent years, these were on the order of paying out-of-pocket for dental appointments, curtailing dining out, and checking the bank account before buying sneakers for the kids. We were never in danger of losing our home or going hungry. I also recognize that camping is an appealing activity only to those whose day-to-day living is far removed from sleeping on the ground and doing without plumbing. As a white woman, though far outnumbered on the trail by white men, I never had to endure the suspicion and hostility often experienced by people of color who venture into this country's wild places.

Hiking a long hike and writing a long book both require an extensive support team. In the hiking department, I'd like to thank first and foremost my parents, Kurt and Julene Lani, for taking me into the mountains from the time I was a baby and for not freaking out too much when I decided to hike five hundred miles into those mountains at twenty-two or when I took their grandchildren over the same miles twenty years later. My parents were our number-one trail angels, taking us to the beginning of trail in 1996, picking us up at the end in 2016, and managing our resupply packages, including several in-person deliveries complete with hot meals, on both hikes. Thanks to my aunts, Sharon Moore and the late Georgine Meyer, who delivered our Twin Lakes resupply and let us take over their hotel room for a day. Thanks also to Valerie Lani and Josh Hillis for letting us stay with them before hiking, accompanying us along the first couple miles, delivering our car back to town, and celebrating the finish with us at Mesa Verde. Thanks to Juliana Lani and Morgan Thompson for the trail-eve junk-food feast and for housing our car for six weeks. Thanks also to my other siblings, Kurt, Elyse, and Eric, for their moral support. Much gratitude to our long-distance trail angels, Yvette Munier and Jennifer Mora, for keeping us supplied with sweets from Maine. Finally, thanks to all the people we met along the trail who shared water, snacks, or words of encouragement. I also owe a dept of gratitude to the late Gudy Gaskill, the Colorado Trail Foundation, and all of the volunteers who have built and maintained the trail over the years.

Writing this book has been an incredibly long journey, from the moment the idea came into my head to when I wrote the final word. Many thanks to the writing teachers I've had over the years, especially Cheryl Drake Harris, Kate Hopper, and my mentors at Stonecoast, Suzanne Strempek Shea, Sarah Braunstein, and Aaron Hamburger. Immense gratitude and an IOU for dinner out goes to writer friends who reviewed early drafts: Libby Maxey, Mary Heather Noble, and Amanda Jaros. Your comments and suggestions were invaluable. Thanks to the websites that published bits and pieces of this book essay form: *Role Reboot* ("How I Went from Domestic to Wild"), *Mothers Always Write* ("Five Hundred Miles"), and *TrailGroove* ("Thru-Hiking en Famille"). Thanks also to Maine's interlibrary loan system, which kept me supplied with research material, and to the staff at Gardiner Public Library, who processed the dozens of books I requested. Special thanks to my uncle Stefan Quido Lani, who wrote a thrilling family history and answered my questions about my grandparents and life in Leadville. Thanks also to the Hewnoaks artist colony for a glorious week in a fairy cottage, where I revised the first draft.

For bringing this book from my laptop into your hands, I thank team at Bison Books, especially Haley Mendlik, Anne McPeak, and Clark Whitehorn, whose enthusiasm for this book and the Colorado Trail is matched only by my own.

Enduring love and gratitude to Curry, Milo, Zephyr, and Emmet, who reluctantly joined me on this crazy trip, hiked like champs, and put up with me while I went through the throes of book writing.

Finally, I wish to acknowledge the people of the Ute tribe and culture, through whose ancestral lands the Colorado Trail travels. My ability to hike the trail was predicated on their removal by the United States Government and the State and Territorial Governments of Colorado. Nothing I write can make amends for this historical and cultural violence.

APPENDIX

EQUIPMENT LIST

To keep down the costs of outfitting a family of five, I made some of our gear and bought most of the rest from factory outlets and discount stores.

Andrea

ITEMS WORN	BRAND	POUNDS	OUNCES
Tank top	Eddie Bauer		3
Skirt	Purple Rain		4
Socks	Smartwool		1
Underwear	Champion		1
Bra	Champion		3
Shoes*	Altra	1	2
Hat*	Columbia		2
Gaiters	Dirty Girl		1
Trekking poles	LEKI	1	0
Total		**3**	**1**

ITEMS CARRIED	BRAND	POUNDS	OUNCES
Pack	Gossamer Gear	1	1
Pack cover	DIY		3
Fanny pack	Gossamer Gear		1
Sleeping quilt & stuff sack	DIY	2	2
Sleeping mat	Therm-a-Rest NeoAir Xlite		11
Rain coat	White Sierra		9
Wind pants	DIY		5
Down jacket	Patagonia		11
Sun shirt	Patagonia		6
Turtleneck*	LL Bean		3
Long johns	Jockey		3
Socks (2)	Champion		2
Underwear (2)	Champion		2
Beanie	DIY		1
Neck gaiter	Eddie Bauer		1
Gloves	Grand Sierra		1
Bandanna			0.5
Towel	Lightload		0.5
Umbrella	euroSCHRIM		7
"Cook" set (5 plastic containers, 5 bamboo spoons, scrubbie, soap, stuff sack)			10
Water treatment set (UV wand, case, prefilter, spare batteries)	SteriPen Adventurer		10

Water bottles (2), half-jug	Nalgene (1), energy drink (1)		12
Water bladders, 2.5 liter (5)	Platypus		7
Stuff sacks (4)	DIY		4
Carabiner			0.5
Personal kit (journal, pen, colored pencils, field guides, book, knife, head lamp, hair brush, lip balm, toothbrush, toothpaste gummies, sun block, hand sanitizer, nail clippers)		2	0
Camera, case & charger	Panasonic Lumix		12
Phone, charger			10
Data book			3
Emergency kit			7
First aid kit			8
Shovel			1
Total		14	**10.5**

Curry

ITEMS WORN	BRAND	POUNDS	OUNCES
T-shirt	Eddie Bauer		5
Shorts	Columbia		6
Socks	Champion		1
Shoes	Altra	1	5
Hat	Columbia		2
Gaiters	Dirty Girl		1
Trekking poles	LEKI	1	0
Total		**3**	**4**

ITEMS CARRIED			
Pack	Gossamer Gear	1	1
Pack cover	DIY		3
Fanny pack	Gossamer Gear		1
Tent	GoLite	6	0
Groundsheet			10
Sleeping quilt	DIY	2	2
Sleeping mat	Therm-a-Rest RidgeRest		13
Rain coat	White Sierra		10
Rain pants	Patagonia		9
Fleece	Eddie Bauer		10
Sun shirt	Eddie Bauer		7
Thermal top	Kenyon		7
Long johns	Kenyon		7
Socks (2)	Champion		2

Underwear*	ExOfficio		2
Beanie	DIY		1
Neck gaiter	Eddie Bauer		1
Gloves	Grand Sierra		1
Bandanna			0.5
Towel	Lightload		0.5
Umbrella	euroSCHRIM		7
Water bottles (2)	Nalgene (1), energy drink (1)		8
Stuff sacks (4)	DIY		4
Bear cord			2
Carabiner			0.5
Lip balm, head lamp, hand sanitizer			4
Phone, batteries, charger, tripod		1	11
Maps & compass			4
Shovel			1
Total		18	1.5

Milo

ITEMS WORN	BRAND	POUNDS	OUNCES
T-shirt	Russel		5
Zip-off pants	Columbia		7
Socks*	Champion		1
Underwear	Champion		1.5
Shoes	Asics	1	4
Hat	Eddie Bauer		3
Gaiters	Dirty Girl		1
Total		2	**6.5**

ITEMS CARRIED	BRAND	POUNDS	OUNCES
Pack	Equinox	1	8
Pack cover	DIY		3
Sleep quilt	DIY	2	2
Sleeping mat	Therm-a-Rest RidgeRest		13
Raincoat	LL Bean		9
Rain pants	LL Bean		5
Puffy jacket	Patagonia		13
Sun shirt	Eddie Bauer		6
Thermal top*	Kenyon Polarskins		6
Long johns	Kenyon Polarskins		6
Socks	Champion		2
Underwear (2)	Champion		3
Beanie	DIY		1
Neck gaiter	Eddie Bauer		1

Gloves	Grand Sierra		1
Bandanna			0.5
Towel	Lightload		0.5
Umbrella	euroSCHRIM		7
Water bottles (2)	energy drink		4
Stuff sacks (2)	DIY		1
Personal kit (journal, pencil, knife, lip balm, cards, toothbrush, head lamp, book, ukulele*)		2	0
iPod, headphones, charger			10
Total		**11**	**6**

Emmet & Zephyr

ITEMS WORN	BRAND	POUNDS	OUNCES
T-shirt	Champion		3
Zip-off pants	Columbia		6.5
Socks	Smartwool		1
Underwear	Champion		1
Shoes (Zephyr)	New Balance	1	2
Shoes (Emmet)	Columbia	1	12
Hat (Zephyr)	Eddie Bauer		3
Hat (Emmet)	Columbia		2
Gaiters	Dirty Girl		1
Total, Zephyr		**2**	**1.5**
Total, Emmet		**2**	**10.5**

ITEMS CARRIED	BRAND	POUNDS	OUNCES
Pack	Gossamer Gear	1	0
Pack cover	DIY		3
Sleeping quilt	DIY	2	2
Sleeping mat	Therm-a-Rest RidgeRest		13
Stuff sacks (2)	DIY		1
Raincoat	LL Bean		10
Rain pants	LL Bean		5
Puffy jacket	Patagonia		14
Sun shirt	REI		5
Thermal top	Kenyon Polarskins		5
Long johns	Kenyon Polarskins		5

Socks (2)	Smartwool		1
Underwear (2)	Champion		3
Beanie	DIY		1
Neck gaiter	Eddie Bauer		1
Gloves	Grand Sierra		1
Bandanna			0.5
Towel	Lightload		0.5
Umbrella	euroSCHRIM		7
Water bottles (2)	energy drink		4
Personal kit (journal, pencil, knife, lip balm, head lamp, toothbrush, book)			10
Camera	Canon PowerShot		13
iPod & charger (Zephyr)			9
Total, Zephyr		10	0
Total, Emmet		9	7

*Indicates an item that was either added, sent home, or replaced.

RECOMMENDED READING

Bird, Isabella L. *A Lady's Life in the Rocky Mountains*. Norman: University of Oklahoma Press, 1960.

Blair, Rob, and George Bracksieck, eds. *The Eastern San Juan Mountains: Their Geology, Ecology, and Human History*. Boulder: University Press of Colorado, 2011.

———, eds. *The Western San Juan Mountains: Their Geology, Ecology, and Human History*. Boulder: University Press of Colorado, 1996.

Colorado Trail Foundation. *The Colorado Trail: The Official Guidebook of the Colorado Trail Foundation*. 9th ed. Golden: Colorado Mountain Club Press, 2016.

Fielder, John, and M. John Fayhee. *Along the Colorado Trail*. Englewood CO: Westcliffe Publishers, 1992

Hall, Gordon Langley. *The Two Lives of Baby Doe*. Philadelphia: Macrae Smith, 1962.

Hanh, Thich Nhat. *How to Walk*. Berkeley CA: Parallax Press, 2015.

Jenkins, McKay. *The Last Ridge: The Epic Story of America's First Mountain Soldiers and the Assault on Hitler's Europe*. New York: Random House, 2004.

Klucas, Gillian. *Leadville: The Struggle to Revive an American Town*. Washington DC: Island Press, 2004.

Limerick, Patricia Nelson, with Jason L. Hanson. *A Ditch in Time: The City, the West, and Water*. Golden CO: Fulcrum Publishing, 2012.

Matthews, Vincent, ed. *Messages in Stone: Colorado's Colorful Geology*. 2nd ed. Denver: Colorado Geological Survey, 2009.

Nash, Roderick Frazier. *Wilderness and the American Mind*. 5th ed. New Haven CT: Yale University Press, 2014.

Nikiforuk, Andrew. *Empire of the Beetle: How Human Folly and a Tiny Bug Are Killing North America's Great Forests*. Vancouver: Greystone Books, 2011.

Pyne, Stephen J. *America's Fires: A Historical Context for Policy and Practice*. Durham NC: Forest History Society, 2010.

Reed, Jack, and Gene Ellis. *Rocks Above the Clouds: A Hiker's and Climber's Guide to Colorado Mountain Geology*. Golden: Colorado Mountain Club Press, 2009.

Ross, Cindy. *Scraping Heaven: A Family's Journey Along the Continental Divide Trail*. Camden ME: Ragged Mountain Press, 2002.

Ubbelohde, Carl, Maxine Benson, and Duane Smith. *A Colorado History*. 10th ed. Portland OR: Westwinds Press, 2015.

Wilkinson, Charles F. *Crossing the Next Meridian: Land, Water, and the Future of the West*. Washington DC: Island Press, 1992.

Zwinger, Ann. *Beyond the Aspen Grove*. New York: Random House, 1970.

Zwinger, Ann, and Beatrice Willard. *Land Above the Trees: A Guide to American Alpine Tundra*. Boulder CO: Johnson Books, 1996.

Lightning Source UK Ltd.
Milton Keynes UK
UKHW012358260122
397769UK00001B/26